Stanley Leathes

Old Testament prophecy

Its witness as a record of divine foreknowledge

Stanley Leathes

Old Testament prophecy
Its witness as a record of divine foreknowledge

ISBN/EAN: 9783337221881

Printed in Europe, USA, Canada, Australia, Japan

Cover: Foto ©Lupo / pixelio.de

More available books at **www.hansebooks.com**

OLD TESTAMENT PROPHECY.

OLD TESTAMENT PROPHECY

ITS WITNESS AS A RECORD OF DIVINE FOREKNOWLEDGE

The Warburton Lectures for 1876—1880

WITH NOTES ON THE GENUINENESS OF THE BOOK OF
DANIEL AND THE PROPHECY OF THE
SEVENTY WEEKS

BY THE
REV. STANLEY LEATHES, D.D.

RECTOR OF CLIFFE-AT-HOO,
PREBENDARY OF ST. PAUL'S CATHEDRAL,
PROFESSOR OF HEBREW, KING'S COLLEGE, LONDON.

London:
HODDER AND STOUGHTON,
27, PATERNOSTER ROW.

MDCCCLXXX.

AND I BELIEVE IN THE HOLY GHOST,

THE LORD AND GIVER OF LIFE,

WHO PROCEEDETH FROM THE FATHER AND THE SON,

WHO WITH THE FATHER AND THE SON TOGETHER IS WORSHIPPED AND
GLORIFIED,

WHO SPAKE BY THE PROPHETS.

PREFACE.

THE Lectures which form the bulk of the present volume were delivered in the chapel at Lincoln's Inn upon the foundation of Bishop Warburton, whose will directs that the lecturers endeavour " to prove " the truth of revealed religion in general, and of the " Christian in particular, from the completion of those " prophecies in the Old and New Testaments which " relate to the Christian Church, especially to the " apostasy of Papal Rome." Strictly speaking, however, I have confined myself to the confirmation of the Christian faith arising from the fulfilment of Old Testament prophecy in the person of Christ and the foundation of His Church, and have altogether left untouched the subjects of New Testament prophecy and the apostasy of Papal Rome, not because of any lesser interest seeming to attach to them, but because my own argument admitted of fuller and more complete development independently of and without them.

The present Lectures, therefore, deal with the

evidential value of certain typical portions of Old Testament prophecy as shown by their fulfilment in Christ and His Gospel ; a sufficiently important subject, it will be allowed, in the existing condition of religious thought. My object, however, has not been so much to treat of the entire mass of Old Testament prophecy as to illustrate the special relation of a few salient and typical samples of it to Christian evidence. If their value can be established, it would seem that a solid ground is discovered for our estimate of prophecy as a whole ; or at all events we cannot set it aside as a whole if parts of it are characterised by features so remarkable. For that these are the only parts so characterised is not for a moment to be supposed. They are merely treated as specimens of the rest.

Objections are raised against the Christian revelation mainly upon two grounds, the critical and the physical. Doubtless the real difficulty rests upon the physical ground. Indeed as a rule the critical objections to the Divine authority of Holy Scripture resolve themselves into the historical improbability and psychological impossibility of a supernatural communication that can be trusted by any one besides the immediate subjects of it, which is, strictly speaking, a physical objection.

Now there can be no question that the New Testament is written in apparent ignorance and in entire disregard of any such theoretical difficulty as this. There can be no question that the several writers of the New Testament advance and maintain the position that Old Testament prophecy generally is and was fulfilled in Jesus Christ. As, however, the tone of our own thought is vastly changed from theirs, the problem arises how to reconcile the statements of the New Testament writers with our more advanced knowledge of psychological facts and the laws of nature; and if this cannot be done, then their statements must simply be set aside, and the supposed prophecies of the Old Testament be explained away, or explained in any way they can.

Undoubtedly the most elaborate and considerable attempt that has been made in this direction by any modern writer is that of Professor Kuenen, in his "Prophets and Prophecy in Israel,"* and it would ill become any one to handle the subject of Prophecy who had not patiently and conscientiously weighed his theory. To those who are acquainted with his writings it is superfluous to say that he is a strong and determined anti-supernaturalist. There are doubtless many things that we all have to learn from

* The Prophets and Prophecy in Israel. An Historical and Critical Inquiry, by Dr. A. Kuenen, Professor of Theology in the University of Leyden. Translated from the Dutch by the Rev. Adam Milroy, M.A., with an Introduction by J. Muir, Esq., D.C.L. London: Longmans, 1877.

Professor Kuenen; and he has, we are willing to admit, thrown much light upon some of the more forgotten features of prophecy; but his writings are the more valuable because he leaves us no vestige of 'supernaturalism' to deal with. According to him, Old Testament prophecy is a purely natural and psychological phenomenon, unique and historical indeed, but simply natural as the accidental form in which one of the 'principal religions' of the world developed and expressed itself. It has no claim to be regarded as a direct and supernatural message from God. All its manifestations can be explained on psychological principles, and must historically be so explained; so that we have, according to Professor Kuenen, no longer any ground to look upon prophecy, and if not prophecy the Old Testament itself, as in any special sense the word of God.*

It is a mistake, therefore, to suppose that there is anything in the elder volume of Scripture of the nature of real prediction, or that prediction is in any

---

* "Thus then the crown which a later generation had placed upon "the brows of the Israelitish prophets, is, in our time, removed: but "stripped of that supernatural halo with which they glittered, they "reveal all the more clearly their own personal greatness. But—we "have then no longer in their prophecies the word of God himself, "which we, in common with the Christian Church of all ages, thought "that we possessed in them? Do not lament that! Each of their "words that finds an echo in your heart and your conscience—and "their number is great—is to you a word of God."—P. 593. What then, may we be allowed to ask, if it finds no echo?

sense an evidence of prophecy or of the supernatural. Prediction was a form that prophecy assumed, but merely an accidental form. It varied with various prophets; sometimes in the writings of the same prophet; was in many cases notoriously falsified by subsequent events; and even where not, was always to be referred to the prudential foresight of the prophets if, as was not seldom the case, owing to the credulity of the actors, it was not itself an efficient and effectual means of working out its own fulfilment.* Now the beauty of this theory is its thoroughness. There is no mistake about it. We see and know exactly where it lands us. The Professor is determined to deliver us from subjection to the authority of the prophets. They have no longer any claim to our allegiance as the messengers of God. We may respect their earnestness, we may gratefully acknowledge the result they have bequeathed to us in ' ethical monotheism ';† but as for looking up to them as depositaries of a superhuman and Divine truth, that is impossible and absurd. They were essentially human, and nothing more than human.‡

* * Pages 298, 308, etc.   † Page 589, etc.

‡ " It [Hebrew prophecy] does not disown its human origin ; that
" is borne witness to, both by its gradual ripening and by many imper-
" fections which cleave to it.   Every attempt to derive it directly and
" immediately from God must therefore fail.   But yet if we view it as
" one of the many revelations of man's spiritual life—and surely that
" life, as a whole, points back to God and testifies of Him—then we
" cannot estimate it highly enough, and we are right in calling it
" unique."—Kuenen, p. 591.

It is manifestly impossible, nor have I attempted, to traverse the whole of Kuenen's long argument in these Lectures. I have only dealt with that argument in detail in places where it contravened my own, —and I venture to hope, especially with regard to his treatment of Daniel, not without success. It is far more important to find, if possible, a solvent for his *principles*. These are either true or false : if true, then there is an end to Hebrew prophecy as a Divine gift, and to so much of the Gospel as is involved in the Divine authority of *that* gift; if false, then the sooner it is directly met and effectually disposed of the better. The writings of Kuenen have essayed to do for the Old Testament what the author of ' Supernatural Religion ' has endeavoured to do for the New. But in both cases the true answer lies in a nutshell. It is not a matter of detail, but a matter of principle. The Bishop of Durham has conclusively disposed of the detail so far as relates to the early Christian literature: others have more directly assailed the principle. With regard, however, to the Old Testament, the case is somewhat different. There is not the same evidence within our reach, and the answer must be to a certain extent dependent upon the results of the inquiry with regard to the New. If we have here sufficient evidence to warrant us in accepting the presence of the supernatural, then, so far as the supernatural in the New Testament involves the existence of the supernatural in the Old, the presence of it in the one carries with it the presence of it also in the other. For example, is it or is it not a fact that Christ literally rose from the dead? If it is a fact that He did, then it is simply playing with words to represent that act as a natural and not a supernatural act. Again, is there or is there not evidence that Christ led His disciples to believe that He would rise again from the dead? If He did, then is Christ a supernatural person, not only unique in all history, but separated from every other character that can be named by an impassable barrier. And if this is so, then do what we will there is in the Christian religion a core and kernel of the supernatural which we cannot destroy without destroying that religion. But then, also, not only is it one of the 'principal religions' of the world, but it also has a just claim to be regarded as *the* 'principal religion,' the *only* religion that comes to us with Divine commendation and authority, with the sanction of the 'supernatural.' It is this that we believe the Christian religion to be.

But then, further, if there is this indestructible element of 'supernaturalism' in the origin of the Christian religion, then it becomes only a matter of degree where that element is to be found. If Christ is really a supernatural person, there is nothing improbable in His doing supernatural acts. If He really promised that He would rise again, then it becomes impossible to deny to Him the gift of prediction; then it becomes more probable that He may have exercised that gift on other occasions also, and in other ways; then it is not even improbable that He may have bestowed that gift likewise upon others; and then, finally, if we can trust our records of His words and actions, which is a matter of probable evidence, it is certain that if He appealed to the witness of prophecy in the Old Testament, He did so as to the testimony of a supernatural witness. And thus the existence of a supernatural element in the predictive prophecy of the Old Testament is assured to us on the authority of Christ. There may be other considerations tending to confirm this conclusion; but the conclusion is one not depending entirely upon the evidence inherent in the Old Testament, but partly dependent also upon our previous estimate of Christ.

I am quite aware that this reasoning, however logical and sound, is eminently ' unscientific,' and on that ground will at once by many be rejected, but I believe that after all the *first* question we have to decide is that proposed by our Master Himself, *What think ye of Christ?* and therefore I decline to make my answer to this question depend upon my critical investigation of the scriptures of the Old Testament, and the conclusion to which the conclusions of others may lead me.

For not only are those conclusions self-contradictory, and therefore self-destructive, but I cannot disguise from myself the fact that if my method is vitiated by a foregone conclusion of belief in Christ, the method of the critics is no less vitiated by the arbitrariness of their principles. I am not able to discern any standard of judgment to which they are willing to submit their own judgment, but their principles appear to me to be so arbitrary that I cannot but suspect a certain vitiation in the argument also on their side if only it should arise from the pious and wholesome dread of ‘ supernaturalism.’

But surely it is not more natural to suppose that the phenomenon of Hebrew prophecy sprung, as it were, full-blown into existence in such men as Joel, Amos, and Hosea, out of the soil and environment of Canaanitish idolatrous soothsaying,* and this at the commencement of the eighth century before Christ, for the determination of which epoch there seems nothing to guide us but the alleged inaccurate and untrustworthy post-captivity records of Kings and Chronicles, than it is to assign to it the kind of genesis that the Scriptures themselves imply. Given a truly Divine and providential creation of the Israelitish nation by the discipline of the Exodus and the authoritative giving of the Law,—given, in short, the theocracy as an actual fact existing till the time

* Kuenen, pp. 552-3, 573.

of Samuel,—and it is at least consistent and in some sense natural that prophecy should thrive under. his auspices, and eventually produce the kind of fruits we perceive in the canonical prophets. But understand by the giving of the Law itself only a mythical exaggeration of some attempts of Moses at imposing a legal code upon the people without any extraneous and higher sanction, and one is at a loss to conceive how naturally—for supernaturally is out of the question—it was probable or possible that a class of men like the earliest of the prophets should have sprung into existence as by a kind of reaction against the soothsaying habits and tendencies of the surrounding Canaanites. Is this, we may well ask, in itself and *per se* a more natural process than the other would be, admitting only provisionally the presence and operation of 'supernatural' elements? If we assign the origin of Hebrew prophecy entirely and alone to the subjective conviction of the prophets,[*] can we conceive of the result being an Isaiah or a Micah, a Joel or an Amos? And if so, does that subjective conviction itself present no problems difficult of solution when every support or impulse of a supernatural kind is wholly withdrawn?

Nor let it be said that in thus using the word ' supernatural ' we are dealing with a vague terminology that requires definition. I apprehend that it

[*] Kuenen, p. 363.

is as clear as daylight what Professor Kuenen means
when he attacks what he calls 'supernaturalism.'
He denies that we have any veritable communication
from God that we can absolutely trust; and certainly
this is not to be found in prophecy. It is, of course,
obvious that our contention is the exact opposite.
But which is right? It seems to us also far more
important that we should believe that God has
actually spoken than that we should be able to determine with minute and literal accuracy what He has
said. And it is certain that the testimony of the
Bible is that God has spoken in very deed and in
truth, but at the same time the Bible would have us
believe in the Speaker rather than in the thing He
has spoken. This is surely a legitimate inference
from the duplicate version of the law, and from
numerous other instances that might be named.
And it is only by our believing in the Speaker that
we can enter into life.* *The letter killeth, but the
spirit giveth life.*† Now the 'scientific exegesis' of
which Kuenen is the exponent deals only with the
thing spoken, not at all with the Speaker, except so
far as   denying the connection between the two.
It aims at showing that we cannot trust the words
because they are inconsistent, contradictory, erroneous, and the like, and argues that therefore they
cannot be the words of God. Nor are they the
words of God in such sense as that they have in and

---

* John v. 40, 24.   † 2 Cor. iii. 6.

by *themselves* the promise of eternal life. *The entrance of Thy word giveth light and understanding unto the simple,** but only because it is *Thy* word, for it is *Thou,* and Thou only, who *hast the words of eternal life.*† The question I have throughout maintained is that the evidence of prophecy is such that we can absolutely trust the authority by which the prophets spake. There may be much doubt in many ways attaching to their words; there may be room for very much more as to their meaning and the like; but if they were what they pretended to be, and what we believe they were, then is their mission a mission from God, and their message one which, if received as it is intended to be received, will lead us home to God. Nor will it be possible for any one who has so received it to be led astray by the most destructive of the operations of 'scientific exegesis,' for he will believe, not in prophecy, but in the Author of prophecy; not in the prophets, but in Him who sent them. This will seem, no doubt, very transcendental and very mystical to the anti-supernaturalists, but it may to a certain extent define the position of those who accept prophecy as one of the 'supernatural' agencies by which it has pleased God to work for the education of mankind, and in the process of making known His will to man. I may illustrate my meaning in this endeavour to defend 'supernaturalism' by showing

* Psalm cxix. 130.   † John vi. 68.

why it seems to me to be indispensable How can the Church at large, for instance, or how can any individual Christian believe in the forgiveness of sins unless there has been an actual communication to that effect from the Most High Himself? It is not enough for Christ to have proclaimed the doctrine, for if Christ was not a supernatural person He may not—nay, cannot—have been in any special communion with His Father, and therefore in trusting His word we trust to something which is unauthorised unless He had authority to speak it. But if He had authority to speak it, then we can trust it to the end, and trust it infinitely; and the administration and application of it becomes merely a matter of degree, of time and place and circumstance. We have a Divine basis, a ' supernatural ' foundation underlying all, and on that we can rest; but take away this, and even the forgiveness of sins itself becomes nothing more than a vague, shadowy, and unreliable hope, or mere hallucination. This is only an illustration to show that unless ultimately we have access to the ' supernatural,' we have not access to God; and what is thus true of the Gospel itself is in its degree true likewise of prophecy, which was the preparation for the Gospel.

It is, of course, obvious that in thus pointing out the need for ' supernaturalism ' we do not prove the existence of any ground for believing in it. That

must, after all, be a matter of evidence. Kuenen
and others deny that this evidence exists: they
should say rather that what is evidence to others is
no evidence to them. The real question is whether
the defect lies in themselves or in the evidence. But
here it may opportunely be remarked that if the
theory admitted of absolute demonstration, it would
offer no scope for the exercise of faith, for it would
be impossible to doubt; whereas the ultimate pro-
cesses of the spirit depend solely on the exercise of
faith, *for he that cometh to God must believe that He
is, and that He is a rewarder of them that diligently
seek Him;** and neither of these points selected by
the apostle admits of demonstrative proof. The
evidence of both is, after all, no more than the
balance of probability, and this becomes stronger
and stronger in proportion to the faith that appre-
hends it.

According to Kuenen, the ' moral earnestness '
of the prophets and their intense conviction† was
the sole basis of their communications. There was
nothing in fact and object answering to it. And
who is to *prove* that there was? But ' moral
earnestness ' is not a thing that can generate itself.
It must have an origin. A man may have an intense
conviction and yet be hopelessly in error. The
strength of his conviction is no proof of its correct-

* Heb. xi. 6.   † Pages 354, 363, 584, etc.

ness. But is there reason to suppose that the conviction of Hebrew prophecy was an error? Did the 'moral earnestness' of the prophets, instead of bringing them nearer to the truth, only lead them still further astray; and do their writings when regarded as a whole warrant us in the conclusion that as regards the authority with which they spake it was in no sense Divine? Kuenen thinks that he shows this by discrediting their predictions. I will take another course, and ask whether such passages as Isaiah xxxv. and lxi., for example, setting aside their predictive element altogether, do or do not contain evidence of a principle at work in them which is not of man, neither by man, which is not of the earth earthy, but is more than human, and is, strictly speaking and in fact, Divine. Unquestionably these passages are valueless unless they are true. We cannot *know* them to be true unless we can trust them as Divine; but in whatever sense they are really Divine, they must have been miraculously, 'supernaturally' given to the prophet, so that they rest not on *his* authority, but on the authority with which he uttered them. If he had any such authority, it is conceivable that that authority may have given him likewise predictions to utter such as I cannot but recognise in the promise of the unlimited expansion of the Jewish Church by the admission of the Gentiles, and in the portrait of the mysterious sufferer of the fifty-third chapter; and

in proportion as his words really were Divine, it is
conceivable that they would be felt ages afterwards
to have a fulness of meaning which there is no
reason to believe that he himself could fathom.
Now this, which is the settled conviction of the
whole Christian Church, it is impossible to disprove
or shake by the carping criticism of a ‘scientific
exegesis’ which would limit the meaning of isolated
passages to some narrow and transient occasion by
the application of the ‘historical method’ :—

> Vex not thou the poet's mind
> With thy shallow wit :
> Vex not thou the poet's mind :
> Thou canst not fathom it,

is no less applicable to prophetical than it is to
poetical critics.

To take one instance of the application of this
‘scientific exegesis’ which is of a crucial nature,
because it is advanced with triumphant confidence.*
St. Matthew applies to our Lord the words of Hosea,
out of Egypt have I called my Son.† Now it is
admitted freely and at once that Hosea was speaking
of the historic Exodus, and of that only. But is that
any proof whatever that when the evangelist appro-
priates his words he does not thereby legitimately
give them a fulness of meaning which till he so used
them they neither had nor could have had ? "Unless

* Kuenen, pp. 452, 475.   † Hosea xi. 1.

"typology," says Kuenen, "is to degenerate into mere
"caprice, the requirement must be rigorously main-
"tained that an *actual* agreement between type and
"anti-type be shown, and that everything which is
"accidental and unessential be excluded. This con-
"dition is not here fulfilled. As regards Israel, Egypt
"is the land of servitude; as regards the child Jesus,
"it was a temporary refuge; the calling out of Egypt
"is thus also an entirely different thing with the
"evangelist from what it was with Hosea." Then be
it so. But what if the 'servitude' on which the
critic fastens was itself an 'unessential accident'
which, so far as it represented bondage under *sin*,
was exactly that feature which the Redeemer, in
whom was no sin, could not exemplify? Whereas it
surely was highly significant that He, in common
with all His people, should have so much contact and
acquaintance and personal connection with the land
of bondage, as in His own history to illustrate that
act which characterises all those who are His, and
condescend in this degree and in this sense to comply
with the Father's 'call,' and, like Israel of old, to
come up out of 'Egypt'? And what if the evangelist
trusted to the intelligence of his readers to trace out
the points of likeness and unlikeness in the case of
Israel and of Christ, and to apply the words of the
prophet only as they would apply? Surely if exegesis
is thus to put shackles and fetters on the 'hands and
feet' of the living word, we had better cease to be

exegetes, for we shall assuredly cut ourselves off from the school of the apostles, if not from the school of Him who said, *Thinkest thou that I cannot now pray to my Father, and He shall presently give me more than twelve legions of angels? But how then shall the scriptures be fulfilled, that thus it must be ?* *

It would require a large volume to follow up the criticisms of a like nature which this writer so freely gives; but as in one place he has made mention of another work of mine, I must be pardoned if I offer a word in reply. In page 449, n. 1, referring to the Bampton Lectures for 1874, he says, " Those who " know the real state of the question do not need to be " informed expressly that the lecturer, while declaring " that he leaves undetermined the traditional ideas " about the age and meaning of the documents, yet " takes these for granted throughout, so that no single " adherent of the historico-critical interpretation can " assent to his argument." Now here I must observe that I take these traditional ideas for granted no more than nor even so much as Professor Kuenen takes his ideas for granted, as he does throughout his book ; but, on the contrary, I have framed my argument from first to last in entire independence of these ideas, which however I personally thoroughly believe

* Matt. xxvi. 53, 54. The principle which, according to Kuenen (p. 448), " is assented to by all the writers (of the New Testament) " without distinction," is obviously one for which 'the Master' Himself is responsible, if we can trust our authorities.

to be in the main sound. I no more than Kuenen renounce my own belief in the matter, but whereas his argument falls to pieces if his premises are not granted,—for example, as to the age of Daniel and the latter portion of Isaiah,—mine, on the contrary, is constructed in absolute independence of these questions, with what result I leave to others to determine. If I have not given greater scope to the interpretation of passages, it is solely because I believe my conclusions are in the main untouched by any of the proposed modifications of meaning. Till it can be shown, for example, that the twenty-second Psalm says no syllable more than is likely to have been historically true of David,* I shall not cease to believe that it applies with greater accuracy to Christ than it does to David, and that therefore it was *intended*—not perhaps by David, but by the Holy Ghost—to do so.

The controversy is a long one, and we are not likely to see the end of it in our own days. The only consolation is that there is an historical fact which must for ever give the lie to the conclusions at which Kuenen arrives. If the *whole* truth is as he would have us believe, then the foundation of the Christian Church rests upon a misapprehension—nay, more, that Church itself is a mistake. There is, strictly speaking, no Christ; there never was, and never

* The position *generally* of Kuenen, see p. 492, and others.

could have been. The idea was a misconception
from the first, and not only the Church ought historically never to have existed, but exegetically the New
Testament ought never to have been written.*   But
it is surely too late in the day to argue thus, for
not only is the Church of Christ a fact, but the
marvellous way in which she has adopted and
entered into the treasures of the Jewish Church,—
as, for example, by the constant and universal use
of the Psalter, which on critical principles is wholly
indefensible,—is itself a standing witness to a power
of spiritual insight which testifies to its own Divine
origin, and shows that the anticipations of the
prophets have been something more than fulfilled,
and that prophecy may well claim to be regarded
as a record of Divine foreknowledge, an indication
of the Divine purpose.   And as for anything further,
the Church may rest secure in her belief of the
promise, *Behold, I have created the smith that
bloweth the coals in the fire, and that bringeth
forth an instrument for his work; and I have created
the waster to destroy.   No weapon that is formed
against thee shall prosper; and every tongue that
shall rise against thee in judgment thou shalt condemn.   This is the heritage of the servants of the
Lord, and their righteousness is of me, saith the
Lord.*†

* See *e.g.* Kuenen, pp. 469, 473, 487, etc.
† Isaiah liv. 16, 17.

CONTENTS.

INTRODUCTORY.

Acts x. 43.—*To Him give all the prophets witness, that through His name whosoever believeth in Him shall receive remission of sins.*

LECTURE I.

INTRODUCTORY.

THERE is no reasonable doubt that words such
as these formed part of the address delivered
by Peter when Cornelius the centurion was received
into fellowship with the Christian Church.   They
are found in the earliest and the only historical
document which professes to record the events of
the time, and they are sufficiently confirmed by
many similar statements in the two epistles ascribed
to Peter.* It is indeed true that the Acts of the
Apostles has not escaped unchallenged as an authentic history, nor either of the epistles of St. Peter
as a genuine work of that apostle.   But if the
challenge in any case has been from time to time
thrown down, there have never been wanting many
who were eager to take it up, and have been able
to defend with something more than success the
several points attacked.   And even if it could be
proved to demonstration, which it manifestly cannot,
that no such position was assumed by St. Peter on

* See, _e.g._, 1 Peter i. 2, 9, 10, 11, 19, 21 ; ii. 6, 7, 10, 24, 25 ;
2 Peter i. 1, 2, 19,; ii. 20 ; iii. 18, etc.

the occasion referred to, it would still remain none the less certain that this was the position assumed and maintained habitually by the earliest teachers and propagators of that body of doctrine and belief which we commonly term and understand by Christianity.

The writers of the several books of the New Testament, whether of those whose genuineness has never been called in question, or of those whose claim to it has indeed been disputed, though without adequate or at all events conclusive reasons, are alike unanimous in their appeal to prophecy as that which had received a new and unexpected light in the recent and notorious events which they proclaimed, and as something which vouched for the importance of those events. It is a phenomenon in these writings which has yet to be explained, how it was that the prophetic language of the Old Testament lent itself with such marked facility to the purposes of their authors, and how they of all men were the only persons to avail themselves of it, if, as it might be alleged, that language was inherently devoid of any significance, and did not become unexpectedly significant and luminous when applied by them.

This is unquestionably the problem to the solution of which those should address themselves who would disparage and depreciate the value of prophecy as a substantive element in the evidences of the Christian faith, and a known factor in the historic foundations of Christianity.

The apostles and first Christian preachers may have been right or wrong in their use and application of prophecy, but that it was an engine which they used, and that it became in their hands an engine of unexampled and enormous power, is one of the facts of literature and of history which criticism and investigation will never be able to disprove. We must not only show, for example, that the words cited were not used by Peter at the baptism of Cornelius, that the baptism of Cornelius was itself a mythical incident of no historic value; but also, that the Gentiles were not gathered into the Church of Christ, in no small degree *because* they saw in Him the fulfilment of Old Testament prophecy, and that those who were most conspicuously instrumental in their conversion had uniformly and consistently taught them that the Scriptures were fulfilled in Jesus.

And before we can make good *this* position, we must not only disprove the genuineness of the various books of the New Testament, but must also deny to it the right to be, as it obviously is, an accurate transcript of the thought, belief, and sentiment of the first two or three generations of Christian disciples. But that it is this there cannot be a shadow of doubt.

If, however, the fulfilment of prophecy was a powerful engine in the original founding of the Christian Church, and the first promulgation of Christianity, we may not unreasonably ask whether its evidential functions are ever likely to cease altogether, or its evidential value to fail. If it ever was true that all the prophets gave testimony unto Jesus, can this ever cease to be a truth? And in whatever sense it was at any time true, will it not rather in that sense be true at all times? If there is any witness to Jesus in prophecy, is not that a witness which must be intrinsically permanent and unchanging? Our method of apprehending this testimony may indeed change as we change ourselves, but if the testimony is true, it can never lose its value. The particular value of this or that part may vary in relation to our special circumstances, but that circumstances will arise to bring out more or less this or that particular aspect of the truth, if truth it be, we cannot doubt. The testimony can only cease to be of value upon its being found to be untrue.* We may not assume it to be untrue in order that we may deny its value, any more than we may assume it to be true in order to affirm or enhance its value. That value must entirely and alone depend upon the evidence of its truth.

It is remarkable, however, that the early preachers

---

* It is of course perfectly obvious that prophecy will assume a totally different aspect according as we regard it from the standpoint of history or the standpoint of fulfilment, (see Kuenen, p. 12, who quotes Kueper,) but the phenomenon which has to be explained is that what was enacted on so large a scale on the platform of history, became, ages afterwards, when collusion and adaptation were out of the question, *capable of being regarded from the standpoint of fulfil-ment.* It is not Homer, and not Æschylus, that is susceptible of anything like the same treatment that Joel and Isaiah, for example, are; and are we not, therefore, entitled to ask whence this intrinsic difference which is a fact?

of Christianity seem generally to have contented themselves with affirming the existence of the prophetic testimony, rather than furnishing a demonstration of its truth. When Philip preached Jesus to the Ethiopian eunuch * as the fulfilment of Isaiah's prophecy, he took no pains to defend himself against the multiplicity of previous questions which might then have been raised, and which have actually since been raised by modern criticism. When St. Paul, in his letter to Corinth, reaffirmed the gospel he had already preached there, that *Jesus Christ was raised from the dead the third day, according to the Scriptures,*† he was at no pains to record the process by which he proved this, nor the particular scriptures upon which he relied in support of his assertion. His silence on this head has bequeathed no little vexation and difficulty to us, when we attempt to fill up the outline he has so faintly and yet so confidently sketched. When St. Peter opened the gates of the kingdom to the first Gentile converts, and declared unhesitatingly that the ancient prophets were unanimous in the witness they bore to Jesus, he does not seem to have been careful to make good that statement by any method of citation or illustration that we can appreciate; or, however this may have been, the historian to whom we are indebted for the narrative has not thought it worth while to record the instances adduced, or the incidents appealed to, for our benefit, though most undoubtedly we should have highly valued any such record. What

* Acts viii. 35.   † 1 Cor. xv. 1—3.

are the natural inferences from these facts? Are we to suppose that the apostles and evangelists were unconscious of or indifferent to the various questions which are of such deep interest to ourselves? Are we to suppose that they who received their testimony were, as we should judge, incompetent to estimate the value of it, and incapable of doing so? Are we to imagine that the privilege of doubt is one which belongs exclusively to ourselves, or that the tendency to question is not characteristic of other minds besides our own? Or may we not rather infer that the agency which was adequate to producing results which we know to have been so mighty and so general, was itself not only effectual, but efficient: that it was followed by the results recorded, and evidenced in a variety of ways, because it was actually capable of producing them?

That the element of doubt was not lacking in the early Church is evident from the case of those at Corinth who questioned the resurrection. That which must ever remain an insuperable difficulty to the natural reason had aroused in them the spirit of unbelief. And yet it was to people such as these that St. Paul did not scruple to declare that *Christ was raised from the dead the third day, according to the Scriptures.* Those therefore who could be critical on the subject-matter of his teaching were surely so far competent to test the arguments which he advanced to support so much of that teaching as they seem themselves to have accepted. For that it was not the personal resurrection of the Lord

Jesus, but rather the general resurrection of the dead that they denied, is clear.

True as it is, however, that we do not know in detail the nature of St. Paul's appeal to Scripture, we know perfectly well what it must have been, for we have in our hands the very Scriptures to which it was made. We have, therefore, before us the entire area that the discussion occupied. There were certain limits within which it must have ranged, and what they were we know; and, strange to say, so far as we can at all trust our records, we know that the resurrection of Christ the third day was part, not only of St. Paul's teaching, but of His own. The first three evangelists are unanimous upon this point.* Somehow, therefore, it was supposed that the conditions of Scripture demanded a resurrection the third day. And yet, to the critical judgment of our own time, how very uncertain and insecure such reasoning must seem! This is one of the points in which the argument from Scripture or from prophecy will vary in its strength according to circumstances. And it would assuredly be very unwise in us to place such an argument very prominently before those to whom we desired to commend the doctrine of the resurrection. But it is no less evident that it had its place in the earliest Christian teaching, and was not without its logical weight upon the minds of men.

The conclusion, then, at which we arrive from

* Matt. xvi. 21, xx. 19; Mark viii. 31, ix. 31, x. 34; Luke ix. 22, xviii. 33, xxiv. 6—8.

these considerations, is that there is no question but that we have the highest possible authority for finding in the Scriptures of the Old Testament the essential foundations of the Christian Church, and the intrinsic and inherent principles of Christian teaching,—that is to say, we have indicated in the original and earliest documents of the *New* Testament the existence of a vast and practically inexhaustible field in the scriptures and prophecies of the *Old* Testament which may again and again be worked to almost any extent, and may yield results in confirmation of the truth of Christ. The lines of the arguments originally used are drawn in the barest possible way, and many of them may be such as appear to us nowadays anything but conclusive; but if it is in any sense true that the Holy Ghost spake by the prophets, we cannot but believe that prophecy itself is one of those treasuries out of which He, as a faithful and wise steward, will never fail to bring forth things new and old.

It must, however, not be forgotten that the office of prophecy is not to convert, but to convince ; not to lay the foundation, but to confirm those in whom it has already been laid ; for we are told on sufficiently high authority that *prophecy serveth not for them that believe not, but for them which believe.** Let us not seek, therefore, to make prophecy, or the study of prophecy, do a work for which perhaps it was not designed. Let us not endeavour to make it sustain or support the whole superstructure of the Christian

* 1 Cor. xiv. 22.

fabric. That it is one of the converging evidences
of the Christian faith we are only too thankful to
remember. Let it not be supposed that it is the
only one, and let us not reason as if it were. Christianity is an historic religion, and its central weight
reposes upon a small group of facts,—those, for instance, which are gathered together in the Apostles'
Creed. If the main facts of the Christian creed are
not accepted, it is utterly useless to appeal to prophecy. If we do not accept the verdict of history,
we shall certainly reject the testimony of that which
claims to have anticipated * history. When Peter
preached to Cornelius, he began with the notorious
facts of the life of Jesus : *That word ye know
which was published throughout all Judæa,†—*
these, therefore, were already, at all events to a
certain extent, accepted,—they were at least not
put aside as impossible, improbable, or untrue: it
was when they had been fully recounted that the
apostle continued with his declaration, *to Him give
all the prophets witness.* This was his goal, and not

---

* In applying this term to prophecy and the prophets, it may be
as well to say that there are two ways in which it may be used. The
prophets may have anticipated history by *fore*seeing and *fore*telling
that which was to happen ; we are not anxious in every case to show
they did this, though we believe in many it is impossible to deny it :
and prophecy may have anticipated history by containing in germ
that which afterwards was developed in full, even as the seed contains the plant, and the bud the flower. It was part of the revelation
of Christianity to make manifest and expand the latent meaning of
prophecy. We sin equally against fact when we forget or deny that
the meaning was *latent.*

† Acts x. 17.

his starting-point,—his conclusion, and not his premises. And so when Paul could point the unbelievers
at Corinth to the living testimony of the more than
two hundred and fifty brethren * who had seen the
Lord Jesus after His resurrection, it would appear
that there was little more that needed to be said
to establish the fact of His resurrection, which indeed they may be presumed to have accepted by
consenting to be baptised into Christ. But if he
had so far won his way with the Corinthian converts
as to get them to acknowledge and accept this superhuman, supernatural fact, the steps would be comparatively easy by which he would be able to bring
them to believe that it was in accordance with the
Scriptures that Christ was raised from the dead the
third day. Conviction is a very complex operation.
It may often be very difficult to say exactly by what
process it is wrought in our minds, or what was the
exact order of time in which this or that of the
several independent lines effectually reached us. It
is the combined effect of all which eventually brings
about conviction. That the mere acceptance of
certain facts is insufficient of itself to produce Christian conviction, however indispensable it may be as
a preliminary element, is clear from St. Paul's own
history. There is no evidence that he denied at any
time the facts of our Lord's life and death. Indeed,
they must have been too notorious for that to have
been possible. But such an acceptance of the facts
was perfectly consistent in his case with determined

* 1 Cor. xv. 6.

anti-Christian zeal. Another element was wanting, and that with him was to see how these facts bore upon his own life and being. And this could only be shown by a direct spiritual agency, which, in the language of the New Testament, is ascribed to the Holy Spirit of God.

And we are taught to believe that none of these elements are wanting now. If the facts of Christ's life, death, and resurrection ever were facts, they are facts still. Christ, in the language of St. Paul, not only was, but *hath been raised from the dead.* No interval of time can ever destroy the importance of these facts, or weaken the power of their moral influence. No *transmission* of historic testimony can ever invalidate it, if it was once valid. That it was once valid there is every reason to believe from the tokens of the effects produced by it which survive to this day, and are still in our own hands. But if so, it is not one whit less valid now than it was then because a long line of centuries has separated us from those who first accepted it: any more than if it is valid now it will in the slightest degree be less valid for those to whom it shall be submitted after a thousand years to come. *For the word of the Lord endureth for ever; and this is the word which by the Gospel is preached unto us.**

And, lastly, there is yet another consideration to be borne in mind, and that is the moral condition of heart which the apostolic appeal to prophecy assumes, and the nature of the testimony it is

* 1 Peter i. 25. τὸ ῥῆμα.

declared to give. It professes to reveal Christ as the one antidote for sin, *that through His name, whosoever believeth in Him shall receive remission of sins.* There is a moral purpose, therefore, in prophecy. It is not that we are to expect to find in the prophetic page certain points and passages marked out and delineated as in the map of a country in which we are about to travel; but much rather certain principles and truths in germ, certain apparent indications of a conceived design awaiting accomplishment, which shall prepare us for the fuller enunciation of those truths, and shall themselves receive an accession of light as the progress of events rolls on. It may be that walking in twilight or early dawn through an unfamiliar region, while the mist was yet in the valley and the mountain-tops lay hidden, we could form but a poor idea of the road or the country traversed; but when the mists had cleared away before the risen sun, and we had scaled some one of the heights before concealed, we could trace out the various windings of our path and understand the bearing of the several places we had touched in relation to each other and the landscape around; and so, when standing in the full sunshine of the Gospel light on the high vantage-ground attained for us by Christ, we can see, as His revelation streams back upon the past, that many a fact and incident before dark has become golden and glorious, and many a promise and prophecy before narrow or unintelligible has become vested with marvellous significance, and received a capacity for almost infinite expansion. But more especially will this be so if His office is recognised as that of the one Mediator, and He Himself accepted as the one remedy for sin. Then, and then only, can we see His glory; then, and then only, can we know His worth, or rightly apprehend His place in history. For those who have no sense of the burden of sin will naturally care nothing for its remedy; those who on metaphysical or philosophical grounds deny its existence will obviously find no room in their system for the advent of One whose very object in coming was to make an end to sin, nor will they be ready to believe in His claim to having done so.* But those who know

---

* Many efforts, honest and well-meant, are made in the present day to commend a belief in Christ to the minds of men otherwise indifferent or prejudiced, and to that end concessions are granted which will dispense with miracles, prophecy, and the supernatural generally; but in so doing it seems to be not seldom forgotten that Christ Himself unquestionably asserted the impossibility of His truth being accepted by any mere movement or resolution of the unaided human will. He taught even His apostles, and if it applied to them, it must all the more forcibly apply to others, *Except ye be converted, and become as little children, ye shall not enter into the kingdom of heaven* (St. Matt. xviii. 3); and said, *No man knoweth the Son but the Father, neither knoweth any man the Father save the Son, and he to whomsoever the Son will reveal Him* (xi. 27); while Nicodemus, who no doubt thought that he was very candid and generous in his admissions in favour of Christ, was met with the answer, *Except a man be born again, he cannot see the kingdom of God* (St. John iii. 3); and the disputatious and murmuring disciples were expressly warned, *No man can come to me except the Father which hath sent me draw him* (vi. 44). This is an aspect of the truth that we can by no means afford to disregard, and it may serve to modify much of our modern apologetics and advocacy of Christian truth.

full well the plague of their own hearts, and have found by constant and bitter experience their personal inability to cope with indwelling sin, and yet more to efface the stained memories of the past, will, at all events, be so far prepared to welcome the apostolic declaration concerning Christ, *To Him give all the prophets witness, that through His name whosoever believeth in Him shall receive remission of sins.*

Acts iii. 25, 26.—*Ye are the children of the prophets, and of the covenant which God made with our fathers, saying unto Abraham, And in thy seed shall all the kindreds of the earth be blessed. Unto you first God, having raised up His Son Jesus, sent Him to bless you, in turning away every one of you from his iniquities.*

LECTURE II.

THE PROMISE TO ABRAHAM.

IT will be my object and endeavour in these Lectures to show the reality of Old Testament prophecy as an abiding witness to the Divine foreknowledge; to examine the records that contain it, so far and in such a way as to discover its essential characteristics, and to determine the points in which it differs from other phenomena of a similar kind, enshrined in the literature of other nations, with a view to ascertaining what ground there is for dwelling on the completion of Old Testament prophecy as one of the evidences that Christianity is a revealed religion.

It has already been shown that a large portion of what is historically known to have been the foundation of the Christian Church was laid in Jewish prophecy. Seeing, therefore, that there is a definite historic result which is directly traceable to this cause, it would seem as though it were somewhat too late in the day to maintain that the result was one which ought never to have been produced,—that because there was a flaw in the premises, the conclusion must necessarily be wrong; because the conclusions of history are not matters of argument, but matters of fact, and therefore cannot be wrong. Our methods of dealing with the facts may indeed be liable to serious error, but the facts themselves, so far as they are facts, are beyond the reach of any such possibility, and may therefore be safely trusted.

Now it is a matter of demonstrable fact that the supposed fulfilment of Old Testament prophecy was one of the principal engines, or agencies, in the first conversion of mankind to Christianity, and one of which the influence has lasted to the present time. Unless, therefore, it can be shown that the historic facts themselves in relation to Christ were distorted in order that they might be made to correspond with the alleged prophecies, or unless it can be shown that the alleged prophecies were not written till after the occurrence of the presumed events, it is useless to deny the very great importance of this known historic fact, to which the mere existence of the New Testament, as a whole, bears unanimous and incontrovertible testimony.

And it will be apparent that this ground is not only, as we believe, substantially unassailable, but that it is also virtually unassailed.   For the position that is commonly assumed by the impugners of prophecy is this, that 'to regard the New Testament explanation' of Hebrew prophecies 'as binding,' involves a dogmatic assumption ' at variance with' the true critical method;* that the true way of studying prophecy

* Kuenen, "The Prophets and Prophecy in Israel." English edition. Introduction by Dr. Muir, p. xi.

is to ascertain what the prophets meant; and that if
it can be shown, as it obviously very soon can be,
that the New Testament meaning was one which
never entered into their minds, then it must forthwith
be rejected. Whereas to reason in this way is only
to cast dust in men's eyes, because it is no part of the
argument from prophecy to assert that New Testament historical events entered into the area of the
Old Testament prophets' vision, nor is that the
teaching of the Nicene Creed, which declares that the
Holy Ghost ' spake by the prophets.' What we
affirm is that the broad, general, and patent correspondence between Hebrew prophecy and New Testament history being such as was manifestly not brought
about by the apostles and evangelists of the New
Testament, on the one hand, and such as the prophets
themselves were clearly altogether unconscious of
producing, on the other, is nevertheless a phenomenon
which points us no less distinctly to the operation of a
will rather than to the forces of blind chance than
do the manifold and undeniable tokens of design in
nature. There are those, one is aware, who steadfastly refuse to acknowledge any evidence of design
in nature, but it may fairly be presumed that the
verdict of the great majority of mankind will always
and ultimately be opposed to theirs; and so we may
also conclude that when the phenomena of prophecy
are fairly and fully considered, and duly weighed, the
tongue of the balance will unmistakably point to
the acknowledgment of an all-wise and foreseeing
Providence as the original and ultimate cause of

correspondences so minute, so consistent, and so wonderful.

And if this, which is really the point of greatest moment on the other side that we have to consider, does not vitally touch the heart of our own position, still less does another which has frequently been advanced of late, and that is the comparative date of the alleged prophecies, and of the compositions in which they are found.

The critical study of the volume of revelation, both old and new, has of recent years received an enormous impetus, and it is one we may be sure in which the cause of truth has everything to gain and nothing whatever to lose. Nor only so, but it is also one without which we cannot reasonably hope to arrive at anything that can claim to be true. By all means treat the Bible exactly like any other book; let it have a fair field and no favour; let us only be careful that we show it no *disfavour*; let us guard our hearts against any the most secret wish to find it false; let us be rightly and wisely jealous of any lurking prejudice against as well as for it; and then we may be quite sure that our decision, like that of the Psalmist, will eventually be, *Thy word is tried to the uttermost, and Thy servant loveth it.**

But then it must not be overlooked that a very large portion of that which has successfully usurped the name of criticism is, after all, and notoriously, most uncritical; and that this is peculiarly the case, and must of necessity be so, in such matters as the

* Psalm cxix. 140.

date of ancient literary compositions. When critics do not agree among themselves within many centuries with reference to the date of certain productions, what are we to think of the confidence with which, on one side or the other, such productions are assigned to any definite period? What are we to think of the reasonable prospect of certainty held out by a science in which the conclusions of its ablest professors are so contradictory and so vacillating? Are we to wait patiently till some agreement is arrived at, and to hold our judgment in suspense till such time as the critics are at one? But time presses, and what are we to do meanwhile? It may be that certain issues are involved which are of vital import,—at all events, if we are really in earnest about the decision of questions which depend on them.

But, in point of fact, two considerations meet us here. There is not even a remote prospect of agreement, because the essential principles of such criticism are entirely subjective, and because of the great dearth of objective fact which unfortunately exists, by which alone it might be corrected. But, on the other hand, the determination of any such questions is not an essential pre-requisite in our case. The validity of our position is virtually and entirely independent of it. For, place the date of the Old Testament, as a whole, as late as you please, it cannot be placed late enough not to be long anterior to the New. Of the existence of prophecy, therefore, as a substantive fact, for ages before Christ came, there not only is no reasonable doubt, but, as far as I am aware, no man in his senses and possessed of competent knowledge has ever denied it. The question, therefore, of the genuineness and integrity of the book of Daniel, for example, of the existence of one or two or three Zechariahs, or the deeply interesting and eagerly debated question of the existence of a second Isaiah, is not one, in any case, upon which the claims of prophecy to our careful attention must stand or fall. For however these and the like questions are ultimately decided, if they ever are decided, which we may well venture to doubt, they in no degree affect the validity of our position, which is that under all circumstances the compositions in question existed long before the appeal to them was made by the writers of the New Testament. Indeed, the very fact that they were so appealed to must be allowed to go not a little way with unbiassed minds towards the decision of such critical questions, because, in a consolidated and highly conservative condition of society like that of the ancient Jews, it must be something more than doubtful whether writings like those of the received prophets could have won their way to the position they manifestly held under many generations; and consequently their universal acceptance in the time of Christ is itself a piece of positive and external evidence in their favour which can only be set aside by strong and distinct internal evidence to the contrary.

To vaunt, therefore, the uncertainty attaching to individual prophecies in respect of authorship and date, as though it were an item calculated to depreciate the value of prophecy generally, is not less unwise than it is disingenuous, inasmuch as any such uncertainty in no way affects the real point at issue, which is whether or not the prophecies alleged were in existence for ages before they were appealed to, and whether or not there is any evidence that they were uttered after the events occurred which were claimed to have fulfilled them.

· Let it not, however, be supposed that, in maintaining the essential independence of such questions of date and authorship as we have mentioned, and the real point at issue in the argument from prophecy, it is therefore a matter of indifference how such questions are decided; for the light in which we regard the volume of Scripture will be largely affected by their decision, just as it will undoubtedly in no slight degree influence our judgment in deciding them. If Isaiah is destined to be again torn limb from limb and sawn asunder in the school of modern criticism, the operation is one which no true friend of the prophet can be expected to regard with equanimity, even though the ultimate interests of truth may survive the effects of it. We may therefore be rightly jealous of the license rather than liberty which men allow themselves in their treatment of these matters, even though we may feel ever so strongly that our own central position is secure against their conclusions, however adverse.

But let me proceed to illustrate specifically these general observations. There is this characteristic of Old Testament prophecy, that it is by no means exclusively contained in the writings of the prophets. The book of Genesis is one of the most remarkable records of the Old Testament, not to say the world at large and of universal ancient literature. It is hopeless to advance any opinion as to its date which will not at once be disputed in some quarter or another. It is more than probable that the tradition which assigns its composition to the fifteenth century before Christ will never be generally abandoned, however scornfully some may reject the idea.* But let us suppose, for the sake of argument, that it is many centuries later. Even then, the narrative portion of that book is not only replete with prophecies, but the history of it is itself a prophecy. We have, then, in that book the record of a promise purporting to be given to the patriarchs, and many times repeated. It is utterly futile to inquire *how* this promise was given. It is sufficient to observe that it was recorded, and the record of it is the phenomenon for which we have to account. The promise was virtually twofold: relating to the

---

* I may say, in passing, that to my mind Joel ii. 3 alone is conclusive evidence of the existence at that time of Gen. ii. 8, 9,—that is to say, in the ninth century before Christ, Genesis was in existence. A few natural inferences will soon show us that it must have existed long before. If received in the divided kingdom, it must have been in existence previous to the division ; and as *all* the history subsequent to it implies its existence, we can find no natural resting-place till we come near to the one which tradition has provided. There may not be much science or criticism in such reasoning, but there seems at all events to be common sense. Cf. Isa. li. 3; and cf. also Joel ii. 13, with Exod. xxxiv. 6.

possession of Canaan, and to the prospect of being
made the centre of universal blessing. *Unto thy
seed will I give this land; . . . . and in thee and
in thy seed shall all the families of the earth be
blessed.** Here then, in this book, which upon
the very lowest computation must be assigned to
many centuries before Christ, we have hazarded on
the part of the writer, no matter who he was, a
definite and distinct twofold promise or prophecy,
many times repeated, and renewed on three several
occasions to three successive generations. The problem, therefore, that we have to solve is the existence
of this promise or prophecy as a literary fact. It
does not matter now when it was given; it is no
concern of ours how it was given; for our present
purpose it is even a matter of subordinate interest
whether it was ever given at all. The only point for
which we have inevitably to account is that for some
indefinite period before Christ—shall we say a thousand years?—there existed, and was highly prized in
the Jewish nation, the record of this promise. And
be it observed it is no such easy matter to account
for this phenomenon, whenever it first appeared,
because the historic condition of the whole Jewish
nation, and the character of the whole Jewish literature, is bound up with it. If we turn to the national
poetry, it is full of it. If we examine the historical
writings, they imply the existence of it. If we
inquire of the prophets, they abound with allusions
to it. There is no analogous instance in all human

* Gen. xii. 7, 3, xxii. 18, xxvi. 4, xxviii. 14.

literature of a national history and a national literature being thus permeated, transfused, and inspired with one idea. The influence of the original promise supposed to have been given to Abraham upon the history and literature of Israel may be illustrated, but very faintly, by the influence of the Norman conquest upon our own national history and literature. Eight centuries have elapsed since that event, and our language, our literature, our history, our laws, our social life, still bear witness to its abiding influence. But take the Hebrew history at any one point you please, and it will be impossible to account for the phenomena presented on the supposition that this promise, or something answering to it, was then unknown, or had no existence. If we begin with the century before Christ,—though the interval was then more than twice that which has elapsed since the occupation of this country by the Normans,—we find the effect of the supposed promise distinct and deep; and if we go back in succession to the era of the Maccabees,* to the return from Babylon, to the

* It is important to trace the unbroken chain of evidence pointing continuously to the existence and knowledge of the history: see, *e.g.*, to begin with the latest, 1 Macc. ii. 52, Mal. i. 2, 3, ii. 4, 5, (Num. xxv. 12, Deut. xxxiii. 8, 9,) Haggai ii. 11—13, (Lev. x. 10, 11, Deut. xxxiii. 10,) Nehem. ix. 7, seq., Isaiah xli. 8, etc., 1 Sam. xiv. 3, xv. 2, (Exod. xvii. 8—14, Num. xxiv. 20, Deut. xxv. 17—19,) etc., Ruth iv. 11, 12, Judges xi. 16, etc., Exod· xii. 40, iii. 15, etc. It is impossible to suppose that this continuous chain of evidence is the result of design on the part of one writer or of many. Take the history at any one period, and there is a witness in it to the history of an earlier period. For example, it is impossible to imagine that the promise to Abraham was invented to account for

divided monarchy, to the undivided monarchy, to the period of the judges, to the exodus from the thraldom in Egypt, we shall find it equally difficult to account for the phenomena which confront us on the hypothesis that the supposed promise to Abraham was unknown to the nation before the time of Moses, or was the invention of Moses, or was the self-originated idea springing up in the minds of the people—how, we cannot tell.

Nor is it otherwise when we examine the literature. The sense of being the chosen people of the Lord, in virtue of a promise or covenant made with their fathers, is implied or expressed everywhere. *Abraham was one, and he inherited the land,* writes Ezekiel.* *Look unto Abraham your father: for I called him alone and blessed him, and increased him,* says Isaiah.† *He remembered His holy promise, and Abraham His servant,* sings the Psalmist;‡ and so on perpetually, in one form or another, throughout the entire literature. We have, therefore, distinct and independent evidence, at all events in the eighth century before Christ, to go no further, that this ancient promise was a kind of pole-star in the national life : the nation's existence, and their thoughts, revolved round it. So that to do away with the belief in that promise would be to do away with the separate and known existence of Israel as a nation.

the exodus and the conquest of Canaan ; and that being so, as the conquest witnesses to the exodus, so does the exodus witness to the antecedent history connected with the promise.

* Ezekiel xxxiii. 24.　　† Isaiah li. 2, xxix. 22.　　‡ Psalm cv. 42.

Here, then, we have something like solid ground to stand upon, a concrete and substantial fact to deal with, which criticism may strive in vain to dissolve or to dislodge : that for centuries before Christ there was in existence the record of this promise to Abraham ; and that, for aught we know, or are ever likely to discover, the oldest form of it is that which is found still in our existing book of Genesis. It matters nothing, comparatively speaking, from whom we derive the record, or what was its original authority : it is enough for us that this promise is fastened like a nail in the fabric of the world's literature and history, and that the national history and literature of Israel, and the national existence of the Jews, depends on it. Take away that one fact, and we are met at every step by historic incidents and by literary productions for which we can find no rational solution or satisfactory explanation.

But perhaps not the least remarkable circumstance is yet behind. It was observed that the promise to the patriarchs was twofold, one part of it referring to the possession of Canaan, and the other to the prospect of becoming the centre of universal blessing.* It is a very significant fact that, common as are the allusions in the Old Testament to the former part of this promise, there is no distinct allusion to the terms of the second, from one end of it to the other. It is not till we come to the New Testament that we find Peter appealing as he does to the promise given to Abraham, and applying it to Christ, and Paul, in

* See Note at the end of this Lecture.

the Epistle to the Galatians, saying, *and to thy seed, which is Christ.* Here, then, the question of the original date of the promise is of no concern whatever. At all events, it had been in the Hebrew rolls of Genesis for ages before Peter and Paul appealed to it. Neither is it a matter of the smallest concern what was the personal intention of the author in recording it. We freely admit that there is no evidence whatever to show that he, whoever he was, anticipated the purpose to which his words would afterwards be applied. There is ample evidence to show that the Jewish nation, as a whole, were more occupied and engrossed with the former part of the promise than the latter. They cared more for the land flowing with milk and honey than for the prospect of being the centres of blessing to the world. But there is also unimpeachable evidence to show that after the death and alleged resurrection of Jesus of Nazareth, when the fulness of the times was come, Peter and Paul, who were both Jews, and were deeply attached to the hope of the promise made of old unto the fathers, not only saw in Jesus one who invested the ancient promise with a meaning it had never had before, but were also mainly instrumental in laying the foundations of a society, on the belief of this fulfilment of the promise, which has lasted for well-nigh as many centuries after Christ as the hope enshrined in the words of the promise had survived before Him.

Manifestly, it is open to us now, as it has been in all ages, to say that there is no relation between the promise and its alleged fulfilment; but at least we cannot say that the promise was a prophecy after the event, nor can we deny that in the providence of God materials had been provided in the earliest Hebrew literature which in process of time, and long after their value was thought to have ceased, were found to be capable of being worked up into the very foundation of the goodly edifice of the Christian creed and the Christian Church. Nor if we believe that *God, having raised up His Son Jesus, hath sent Him to bless us in turning away every one of* us *from his iniquities*, shall we be very likely to stumble at the declaration of Peter to the men of his own time and race, *Ye are the children of the prophets, and of the covenant God made with our fathers, saying unto Abraham, And in thy seed shall all the kindreds of the earth be blessed.*

NOTE TO LECTURE II.

Kuenen's remarks on this promise are as follows :—

"There is one promise which interpreters usually separate by a very sharp line of demarcation from those made by God in regard to Israel's settlement in Canaan." Does he really suppose, we must venture to ask, that any promise was made by God in regard to Israel's settlement in Canaan? If so, then more than half the difficulty vanishes: but if not, it is surely mere word jugglery to mislead the reader by suggesting that there is a special difficulty existing in the case of the second promise which is not found in the first. We believe that Canaan was promised to Abraham, as well as that he saw the day of Christ (John viii. 56); but if neither was the case, why speak as though it were harmless to believe that Canaan was promised to Abraham, so long as we acknowledge the critical error of interpreting the second promise of Christ? The *promise* that Abraham should be a standard of blessing was intrinsically and *per se* as supernatural as the assurance that mankind should be blessed in his seed in the traditional sense." "It is a promise which is from time to time repeated, and which, according to the usual translations of Genesis, and a well-known citation in the New Testament, purports that all the families of the earth (or all the nations of the world) *shall be blessed* in the patriarch to whom Jahveh speaks, or in his seed, or also in him and in his seed. In these words theologians find the idea that the blessings bestowed on Abraham and his posterity should at some time be extended to the other families and nations: in other words, that they should obtain a share in the spiritual blessings which originally were enjoyed by the chosen of Jahveh alone. But the independent expositor is utterly unable to grant that such is the meaning of the passages in Genesis which have been referred to. If the author had wished to say 'the nations of the earth *shall be blessed*,' he would have used a different form of the verb. (The pual form which is altogether unequivocal, and is far from being uncommon in the Old Testament: Judges v. 24, 2 Sam. vii. 29, Psalm cxii. 2, cxxviii. 4, Prov. xx. 21, xxii. 9; and in the participle, Num. xxii. 6, Deut. xxxiii. 13, 1 Chron. xvii. 27. Job i. 21, Psalm xxxvii. 22, cxiii. 2.)   The words must be translated ' the families of the earth (or the nations of the earth) *shall bless themselves* (or one another) *with Abraham*'—that is, shall wish for themselves, or for one another, the blessing which Jahveh bestowed upon him ; (in this way the Niphal and Hithpael forms receive their proper power : compare, for the latter, Deut. xxix. 18, Isa. lxv. 16, Jer. iv. 2, Psalm lxxii. 17 : and also the usual meaning of the phrase is retained, of which meaning Gen. xlviii. 20 gives unequivocal evidence. ' To bless in' or ' with any one' signifies to wish for oneself or for others the blessing which the person in question enjoys.)   He shall be so prosperous, his posterity shall be so numerous and fortunate, that nothing better or higher can be imagined than the enjoyment of what he or his race possesses. (For this reason Abraham is called, Gen. xii. 2, a blessing, *i.e.*, a person whose name serves as a formula of blessing. Compare the use of ' curse' in Numb. v. 21, 27, Jer. xxiv. 9, xxv. 18, xlii. 18.)   This is undoubtedly a comprehensive promise.   It stands, according to the writer himself, in close connection with Abraham's fidelity to Jahveh, which, as it became more conspicuous, had also a claim to larger recompense.   (Compare Gen. xviii. 19, xxii. 16, xxvi. 5.)   But it is not of another kind than the promises regarding the descendants of the patriarchs, and their settlement in Canaan, with which we first became acquainted.   Whoever finds in it, not something more, but something of an altogether different nature, forces upon the writer of Genesis ideas which are in truth foreign to him," pp. 378—380.

Now, as already said, everything turns upon whether or not a *promise* was really given, and given by God : if so, then it is absolutely certain that the words are grammatically capable of the New Testament meaning, whether or not that meaning was the one *primarily* intended.   If no promise was given by God, then of course it matters not what meaning we give to the words, though as to the *possibility* of the New Testament meaning we still have no doubt.   There is no reason to distinguish between the meaning of the niphal and pual, as is here done.   The pual is manifestly the passive of the piel, and the piel is used in an ' unequivocal' sense in Gen. xlviii. 20 : but if so, then the pual ought unquestionably to bear the meaning which Kuenen assigns exclusively to the niphal, whereas it is undoubtedly used in the other sense as well.   And it is no less certain that if the pual had been used in

the passages of Genesis, it would, according to analogy, have borne
the meaning that Kuenen now assigns to the niphal and hithpael.
It is futile therefore to attempt to discover in the language and
grammar of the places in Genesis grounds of objection to the New
Testament meaning.   The niphal is naturally the passive of the kal,
and the common meaning of the passive participle of the kal is
unambiguous : analogy, therefore, would make the meaning of the
niphal equally clear.   It is moreover well known that the meaning
of the hithpael is oftentimes a simple passive (see, *e.g.*, Prov. xxxi. 30,
Lam. ii. 12, iv. 1, Mic. vi. 16, Ezek. xix. 12, etc.)   On the other
hand, suppose the whole narrative a fiction, and that no promise was
made ; yet even then the fact remains that in this very early fictitious
story about Abraham, words were found, and language was used,
and thoughts were expressed, which ages afterwards were seen and
felt to be susceptible of a meaning which was exemplified and realised
in Christ to a degree which had never before been expected.   Was
this a matter of chance, or was it not rather an indication of the
Divine will ?   Let it not, however, be thought that we regard the
historic truth of the narrative as an open question.

And later Kuenen observes : " The promise to Abraham : ' With
thee (making use of thy name) shall all the peoples of the earth
bless themselves' (or each other), is understood differently by the
Greek translator, who renders it thus : ' In thee shall all the
peoples of the earth be blessed.'   The apostle Paul adopted this
interpretation from him, and thus naturalised it in the Christian
world," p. 456.

At all events, the Greek translator was not biassed in favour of
Christianity, nor is it certain that he did not rightly understand
the Hebrew.

Lastly, after treating of this and other passages, his conclusion is
expressed as follows, p. 496 : " When it has become evident to us
that the New Testament citations cannot be maintained before the
tribunal of scientific exegesis, our final verdict upon the common
view need no longer be delayed.   That view is altogether untenable.   The *real* expectation regarding Israel's future glory lies
before us in the Old Testament : no one, therefore, thinks of
denying it ; we are able to follow its origin and history in all its
details ; the one prophecy supports and explains the other.   The
traditional Messianic prophecy is undoubtedly a beautiful whole.
As an expression of the belief of Christendom in the unity and

regular development of God's plan of redemption, it preserves its value for us also, and for all subsequent ages. But it forms no part of the historical reality. One stone after another must be removed from it and placed elsewhere. When, finally, the support which the earliest Christian literature seemed to offer has fallen away, the whole edifice collapses."

Messianic prophecy has surely no "value for us," unless it not only represents Christian belief about "God's plan of redemption," but the actual method of that plan. If it does this, then the more we study "the historical reality" of the prophecies, the better we shall understand them and the plan which they discover: and we shall learn to correct our own mistakes and misapprehensions, and to believe that truth is independent of, and will survive, both. As it is, prophecy is a fact; and Christian truth, which rests not on prophecy, but on "historical reality," is a fact likewise; and it was the reality of Christian fact which enabled the disciples to make the use of prophecy they did, and not their use of prophecy which made the reality of the facts. And therefore as no error or omission in their use of prophecy can invalidate the facts, so neither can it render the prophecies less capable of application to the facts, or account for the marvel that they are so. The Christian edifice reposes in its grandeur and stability, not on the apostolic interpretation of prophecy, but upon the reality of its own facts, and upon the realities of ancient prophecies viewed in relation to them. It is one thing to study the prophecies historically, and another to reject them as prophecies if it cannot be shown that the prophets saw the history as we see it, which no one surely can suppose they did.

ACTS III. 24 —*Yea, and all the prophets from Samuel and those that follow after, as many as have spoken, have likewise foretold of these days.*

LECTURE III.

THE INFLUENCE OF THE PROMISE.

THERE is no question that the first proclamation of the Gospel was based on the supposition that Jesus Christ was the person who had been spoken of in the writings of the Old Testament as about to come. There is, and can be, no question that the entire bulk of these writings was in existence sufficiently early for them to have derived no sort of modification or colouring from the use which was thus made of them. The schism between the Jewish and the Christian Churches which followed almost immediately upon the foundation of the latter, had at all events this effect, that the more jealous watch was kept by the Jews on the text of their national writings, lest it should be corrupted or distorted by the Christians to their own purposes. Indeed, it is only in one or two very unimportant instances that even the insinuation of such a charge can be made. There is but one Hebrew Bible, and that is the common property of the Christian and the Jew. Every one, therefore, is capable of judging whether, and to what extent, the main position of the early Christians is capable of being established in relation to the Jews. And the experience of eighteen centuries has shown us that it can only be affected by the adoption of arguments that are equally fatal to both. Once admit the Divine authority of the Old Testament scriptures, and it can hardly be questioned that those of the New Testament are Divine too. In the present day it is rather the Divine authority of either and of both that requires to be shown.

We have seen that it is very difficult to eliminate the original promise to Abraham, so far as it concerned the possession of Canaan, from its actual place in the literature, because of certain effects which may be traced throughout the history that can only be assigned to it. We cannot imagine, for instance, such passages as that of the 105th Psalm, no matter when it was written, *The covenant that He made with Abraham, and the oath that He sware unto Isaac; and confirmed the same unto Jacob for a law, and to Israel for an everlasting testimony: saying, Unto thee will I give the land of Canaan, the lot of your inheritance,** were earlier than the corresponding passage in Genesis, and did not rather refer to it. Indeed, we may even question whether it is possible to account for the history of the occupation of Canaan as we have it, except on the supposition that the record of the promise to Abraham was in existence when that was written. But probably no one would think of asserting that the history of the occupation was written designedly with the view of illustrating the record of that pro-

* Psalm cv. 9—11.

mise, any more than the record of the promise was
written subsequently to that of the occupation for
the purpose of explaining or accounting for it.

Treat the history how we will, as exaggerated
or fictitious, we must yet deal with the features of
the literature as they present themselves, and it is
impossible not to see that the record of the promise
to Abraham was the foundation of a large portion of
the recorded history just as it enters into every part
of the existing literature. The antiquity, therefore,
of the promise to Abraham is a fact that we may
fairly consider established, while the relation in
which it stands to the subsequent history is significant and remarkable.

But we have now to consider the second part of
that promise which relates, not to the possession of
Canaan, but to the blessing which was to come upon
the world in Abraham and his seed. It is this which
has no immediate relation to the other, and yet
cannot be separated from it. And the early existence
of this part of the promise as one of the substantive
features of the literature is the fact to be carefully
noted, for it is this part of the promise of which the
early Christian writers so freely availed themselves.
What, then, is the evidence to be adduced in support of the existence of this promise, and what are
the traces of its influence on the nation and the
literature ?—because it is this which will throw light
upon the application the apostles made of it, and
will show the extent to which they were justified
in so applying it.

Looking at the book of Genesis merely as a literary production, we may perhaps fairly question whether the reader was not intended to discern some connection between the words spoken to Eve in Paradise about the *seed* of the woman bruising the serpent's head,* and the promise to Abraham that in

* "The punishment pronounced on the serpent is executed upon the real serpents, which, in fact, 'go upon their belly and eat the dust of the earth all the days of their life.' Finally, the conflict which is so picturesquely represented to us in the curse on the serpent is nothing else than the perpetual battle between man and his dangerous creeping enemy, which is, indeed, fought in such a way that man aims his attack at the head of the serpent, while it tries to strike the man in the heel. Gen. iii. 15, when thus interpreted, has no connection with our subject, and must lose the name of 'Protevangelium,' or 'Paradise-promise,' which it owes to the traditional but positively incorrect view."—*Kuenen*, p. 377.

It must be borne in mind that this promise is given in direct connection with the expulsion of man from the garden of delight. To say, therefore, that it is no more than a "picturesque representation of the perpetual battle between man and his dangerous creeping enemy," is surely to make the historian responsible for profound bathos. There seem to be two allusions to this passage in the Old Testament, one in Isaiah lxv. 25, "And dust shall be the serpent's meat," and the other in Micah vii. 17, "They shall lick the dust like the serpent," and the first of these is evidence to the "traditional but positively incorrect view" of, Kuenen will allow, the sixth century before Christ,—I should say the eighth. The word *shuf*, which is rendered in the authorised version *bruise*, but which Kuenen renders *lie in wait for*, or *seek to strike*, occurs but three times in the Old Testament,—here, and Job ix. 17, "He *breaketh* me with a tempest," and in Psalm cxxxix. 11, "The darkness shall *cover* me." In neither of these passages is Kuenen's rendering applicable. St. Paul, in the Epistle to the Romans, xvi. 20, hands on the 'traditional' view, and applies the 'Paradise-promise' with reference to Satan: and St. John, in the Revelation, xx. 2, is the latest witness to it. These writers are, of course, no authorities as 'critics,' but they are historically witnesses to it as a fact; and we must of course

his *seed* should all the families of the earth be
blessed. Setting aside altogether the historic value
of either narrative, it may be questioned, I say,
whether the reader was not intended to discover
this connection in the record. And if so, we must
then look at the promise to Abraham, not only in
the light of all that followed after it, but also in that
of something, likewise, which went before it. And
then the difficulty is increased of accounting for
those various phenomena as so many designed and
intentional features in a merely fictitious narrative.
It is admitted on all hands that the Jewish literature, from first to last, was the work, not of one
writer, but of many; and it is surely too much to
affirm that the delicate and yet strong and tenacious
lines of interconnection to be traced throughout were
the result of the deliberate plan consistently and continuously wrought out by various writers of various
ages, under ever-varying circumstances and conditions. There would be no less difficulty in accounting
for such a result naturally than there would be in
hypothecating the operation of the supernatural.

decide whether, under the circumstances, we are at liberty to brand
their 'view' as 'incorrect.' That it is as old as Isaiah, and has
the support of St. Paul and St. John, seems pretty clear : and after
all due allowance has been made for erroneous and traditional misconceptions, it may perhaps be doubted by some whether Professor
Kuenen has gone to the bottom of the promise given in Paradise, to
which he is desirous of assigning a mere bathos of meaning. That
promise was manifestly one which could only be understood as ages
had revealed its meaning; but when they have done so, it seems
somewhat presumptuous and perverse to insist only upon the barest
possible literal meaning, which, after all, is no meaning at all.

And the more obvious will this appear when we note carefully the way in which the promise of the seed developed itself in successive ages, and compare therewith the definite shape which the supposed fulfilment of it finally assumed under the teaching of the apostles and evangelists. Two remarkable prophecies occur in the other books of Moses, however they are to be explained. One is the prophecy of Balaam that a Star should arise out of Jacob, and a Sceptre out of Israel;* and the other that of the law-giver himself, that a prophet should arise like unto him.† It is of course impossible to say what was in the mind of either speaker when the words were uttered; it is very easy to affirm that that which was in his mind cannot have been the person of the historic Jesus.‡ Strictly speaking, however, such an assertion admits no more of demonstrative proof than the contrary. But all that we wish to insist upon is the actual existence of these prophecies as they stand in the ancient literature of Israel, and the way in which, altogether apart from any will or intention in the mind of the writer, they furnished a possible basis for the subsequent establishment of Messianic hopes upon them.

It is not improbable that the promise of Moses that a prophet should arise in Israel may have been the *natural* cause of the prophetic order having

---

* Numbers xxiv. 17.

† Deuteronomy xviii. 18.

‡ "David is suggested to us because Balaam knows that Israel shall be ruled by a king," etc.—*Kuenen*, p. 367.

arisen.* It may have stimulated the latent energies of the people, and tended to produce that of which it held out the hope. In that case, however, we are compelled to regard it as a promise put on record before the birth of Samuel, the first of the order of prophets. If otherwise, then we must take the prophetic order as we find it, and account for its having arisen independently of any influence to be ascribed to this promise of Moses, which can then only be regarded as a subsequent device intended to cast a halo of romance around an existing body of men whose words and deeds had become historic and illustrious. On either supposition, however, it may strike us as rather strange that nowhere in the prophetic writings is there the slightest indication that any existing prophet regarded himself, or was regarded, as at all answering to the promise in Deuteronomy. Whether the document in which it is found was early or late, genuine or fictitious, there is no trace afterwards of its having been supposed to have been fulfilled in the history of the nation. On the contrary, there is distinct evidence that it was regarded as unfulfilled, for the very last words of the latest prophet ran thus : *Behold, I will send you Elijah the prophet before the coming of the great and dreadful day of the Lord : and he shall turn the heart of the fathers to the children, and the heart of the children to their fathers, lest I come and smite the earth with a curse.*† It is manifest here that the

* This will, of course, depend upon the date assigned to Deuteronomy.
† Malachi iv. 5, 6.

prophet looks back upon Elijah as the greatest of all his order, and yet his very last words give the distinct promise of one to arise who shall be as great as or greater than he.   It is absolutely certain that the prophet Malachi was acquainted with the writings of Moses, as we have them now, and that he was familiar with this very book of Deuteronomy in which the promise of the rise of the great prophet occurs, for he says only just before, *Remember ye the law of Moses my servant, which I commanded unto him in Horeb for all Israel, with the statutes and judgments,** these last words being the familiar phrase of Deuteronomy.† It is absolutely certain, therefore, that he must have known of this promise, and by no means improbable that he referred to it when he spoke of sending Elijah the prophet.   At all events, we who are able to survey the literature as a completed whole have full liberty to draw our own inferences from its manifest features, so long as those inferences are sound. And it is a legitimate inference to draw from these features that in the days of the latest prophet there had arisen no one who was regarded as having filled the

* Malachi iv. 4.

† The *exact* phrase, חקים ומשפטים, occurs only in Malachi iii. 22, and Deuteronomy iv. 5, 8, 14, where it is of the nature of a title to the book ; but the same phrase slightly modified, *e.g.*, with the article or possessive pronoun, is almost peculiar to Deuteronomy, where it occurs some sixteen times, being found elsewhere only in Lev. xxvi. 46, 1 Kings viii. 58, ix. 4, 2 Kings xvii. 37, 1 Chron. xxii. 13, 2 Chron. vii. 17, xix. 10, xxxiii. 8, Neh. i. 7, Psalm cxlvii. 19,— all of which places, except the first, must presuppose Deuteronomy on any theory of its composition.   It is morally certain, therefore, that Malachi by using this phrase intends to imply Deuteronomy.

place of the great prophet like unto Moses spoken of by him ages before.   If we do not point to the Gospel of St. John as manifestly containing further evidence on this head, it is only because we are not willing now to assume the historic value of that gospel, but desire to frame our argument independently of it.

The books of Samuel are historically the most important, after those of the Pentateuch, in the literature of Israel.   Leaving it an entirely open question when they were written, (though it was probably in, or at all events not long after, the age of David,) they bear clear witness to certain literary facts, of which the most significant is this, that they alone of the historical books make use of the term Messiah, which in its regal acceptation they seem to have originated.*   It is a literary fact that the first instance of this use is found in the prayer of Hannah: *He shall give strength unto his king, and*

---

* The term Mashia*h*, Messiah, is applied to the high priest in Lev. iv. 3, 5, 16, and vi. 15 (Heb.) 22 (Eng.)   It occurs ten times in the Psalms, *e.g.*, ii. 2, xviii. 50, xx. 6, xxviii. 8, lxxxiv. 9, lxxxix. 38, 51, cv. 15 (pl.), cxxxii. 10, 17,—the second, third, fourth, and last of these being ascribed to David, the first being probably his, the fifth being attributed to the sons of Korah, the sixth to Ethan the Ezrahite, and the seventh being anonymous.   Elsewhere it is only used in Isa. xlv. 1 (of Cyrus), Lam. iv. 20 (apparently of Zedekiah, as David's representative), Hab. iii. 13, and Dan. ix. 25, 26.   This usage alone is highly significant, as it relates mainly to the person and time of David: indeed, he and Saul are the only kings to whom the term is applied; afterwards, it seems always to have been felt that the true Messiah was an ideal who awaited reality.

The above facts show conclusively that Kuenen's assertion, 'the anointed of Jahveh,' was 'the common honorary appellation of the Israelitish king' (p. 511) is historically false.

exalt the horn of his ANOINTED.* Consistently with the spirit of modern criticism, this prayer has, of course, been denied to Hannah, and declared to be a war-song, but that in no way affects the circumstance that this term Messiah is found eighteen times in the books of Samuel, and is not found in any other historical production.† As, however, it is found in certain psalms ascribed to David, we may reasonably infer that it originated in his time, even if it was not first used at the birth of Samuel. It is not a little remarkable, however, that the earliest recorded use of this phrase is one in which it cannot well have any merely human signification. *The adversaries of the Lord shall be broken to pieces; out of heaven shall He thunder upon them: the Lord shall judge the ends of the earth; He shall give strength unto His king, and exalt the horn of His* ANOINTED, if spoken before there was any king in Israel cannot be understood of either Saul or David. And the very same chapter supplies another instance of a similar use in the words which the man of God addressed to Eli: *I will raise me up a faithful priest, that shall do according to that which is in my heart and in my mind: and I will build him a sure house; and he shall walk before mine* ANOINTED *for ever.* This, as it appears, can only be understood of an ideal anointed whose existence, on the evidence of the literature, was thus declared several years before the

---

* 1 Sam. ii. 10.

† The only exceptions, which, as they contain the duplicate history, are not really exceptions, being 1 Chron. xvi. 22, 2 Chron. vi. 42.

nation had begun to place their hopes upon any earthly anointed king. Nor is anything gained by the gratuitous assertion that all this second chapter of the first book of Samuel must have been written long after Saul and David had severally been called *the anointed of the Lord*, because, place the composition of it when we will, we are still confronted by these two facts : first, that with a very few exceptions—only some five or six throughout the Old Testament—this use of the term is peculiar to the books of Samuel and the Psalms; and, secondly, that it affords in itself conclusive evidence that the nation at the time had learned to look beyond the earthly anointed king to an ideal anointed whom the natural eye could not see. And when we bear in mind that we have documentary evidence that this was so ages before the Gospel was first preached, we can but conclude that there are certain significant features on the surface of the Old Testament literature which criticism may do its best to manipulate and juggle with, but cannot destroy ; and that these features, being what they are, do furnish a substantial basis for the actual Messianic hopes which arose out of them, and for the alleged fulfilment of those hopes which the evangelists afterwards proclaimed.

The promise, then, of blessing in and through *the seed of Abraham* does not stand alone. As we have seen, the subsequent literature contains promises or makes mention of a ruler, a prophet, a priest, a king, and an anointed. In fact, the age of these various productions is a point immaterial to the argument.* It is undeniable that they were in existence ages before the Christian era, and in their present form; but it is also undeniable that this same literature fails to satisfy the promises it has so lavishly made. If we take, for instance, the promise of the priest made to Eli, there is no one in the whole course of the subsequent history to whom we can point with the slightest probability of his having been the person whom the writer had in mind. Indeed, after Aaron and Phinehas, there is, in fact, no high priest whose character has been even faintly sketched in the whole of the Old Testament. And yet the words remain, *I will raise me up a faithful priest;* and they will for ever remain unexplained and unverified except upon the hypothesis which more than fulfils and justifies them.

It is not, however, till we pass to the Prophets and the Psalms that we see the kind of commentary that was written by history on the promise of blessing through the seed of Abraham. There is an unmistakable echo of that promise in the language of the twenty-second Psalm: *All the ends of the world shall remember themselves, and be turned unto the Lord: and all the kindreds of the nations shall worship*

* This is strictly true in as much as the features remain, whatever the age of the several compositions may be: and if these were all late, then the only inference could be that these features and characteristics were imparted to them with an intentional design—namely, that so they might be available for the purposes of such an argument as this: which is simply absurd. It is the impossibility of any such inference that renders it more probable that we may with justice and safety trust the several compositions as genuine: and then, in that case, the argument from these characteristics is simply conclusive.

before thee; for the kingdom is the Lord's, and He is the Governor among the nations. * It is confirmed by the words of the sixty-eighth: *Princes shall come out of Egypt; Ethiopia shall soon stretch out her hands unto God. Sing unto God, O ye kingdoms of the earth; O sing praises unto the Lord;* † and by those of the seventy-second: *He shall have dominion also from sea to sea, and from the river unto the ends of the earth. They that dwell in the wilderness shall bow before Him; and His enemies shall lick the dust. The kings of Tarshish and of the isles shall bring presents: the kings of Sheba and Seba shall offer gifts. Yea, all kings shall fall down before Him: all nations shall serve Him.* ‡ We can hardly imagine the extravagant hyperbole of even Eastern flattery supposing that the significance of such words was exhausted in David or in Solomon; but if not, we can only accept them as a spontaneous and involuntary indication of consciousness on the part of Israel that its mission was to be a blessing to the world. And yet no one can imagine that such words were uttered, on the one hand, as an intentional commentary on the promise to Abraham; or, on the other, that the history of that promise was invented as an incident which should express in a condensed and pregnant historic form the idea that was embodied in this and similar language of the Psalms. But if not, the only course is to look the actual features of the literature fairly in the face, and to estimate them accordingly.

* Psalm xxii. 27, 28.   ‡ Psalm lxxii. 8—11.
† Psalm lxviii. 31, 32.

When we turn to the great prophet of the later monarchy, the witness is even more distinct. The consciousness of the nation has developed and grown deeper, or else what is the meaning of *Behold, these shall come from far : and, lo, these from the north and from the west ; and these from the land of Sinim. Thus saith the Lord God, Behold, I will lift up my hand to the Gentiles, and set up my standard, to the people.** . . . *For thou shalt break forth on the right hand and on the left ; and thy seed shall inherit the Gentiles, and make the desolate cities to be inhabited.† And the Gentiles shall come to thy light, and kings to the brightness of thy rising ; . . . because the abundance of the sea shall be converted unto thee, the forces of the Gentiles shall come unto thee. Therefore thy gates shall be open continually ; they shall not be shut day nor night ; that men may bring unto thee the forces of the Gentiles, and that their kings may be brought.‡ Ye shall eat the riches of the Gentiles, and in their glory shall ye boast yourselves.§ And the Gentiles shall see thy righteousness, and all kings thy glory ; and thou shalt be called by a new name, which the mouth of the Lord shall name.‖ . . . And I will set a sign among them, and I will send those that escape of them unto the nations, to Tarshish, Pul, and Lud, that draw the bow, to Tubal, and Javan, to the isles afar off, that have not heard my fame, neither have seen my glory ; and they shall declare*

---

* Isaiah xlix. 12, 22.
† Isaiah liv. 3.
‡ Isaiah lx. 3, 5, 11.
§ Isaiah lxi. 6.
‖ Isaiah lxii. 2.

*my glory among the Gentiles.** It is impossible to assign any intelligible meaning to language such as this, if it is not the expression of a deep national consciousness that it was the destiny of Israel to be the channel to the world of unimagined and illimitable blessing ; and it is inexplicable if it is not the witness in the later ages of their literature to the truth of that which was spoken to the first father of the race, *In thee shall all families of the earth be blessed.*† But who can venture to say that even on the part of the prophet such language was his own intentional and designed expansion of that original promise ! Manifestly it could not have been if Genesis was a late composition ; and even if it was, then the words of the prophet become no less difficult to account for than the original promise itself.

While, however, we cannot admit that the prophet thus deliberately expanded the promise, we can readily understand that in proportion as the promise was true, and the record of it a fact, it would tend to bring forth this particular result, and consequently we may accept the result itself as evidence confirmatory of the existence of the promise.

It is needless to pursue this matter further through the rest of the prophetic writings. We have proof conclusive that in the time of the first preachers of the Gospel there was a mass of prophetic literature in the Old Testament which plainly showed what had been the hope and expectation of the people for ages ; and though from its very nature that prophetic

* Isaiah lxvi. 19. † Genesis xii. 3.

literature was incapable of suggesting the manner in which it would eventually be fulfilled, and although for this very reason it is impossible that the Gospel record should have been the natural product of the various anticipations embodied in prophecy, the outgrowth of the disciples' fervid imaginations in brooding over them, because of the only too apparent and obvious unlikeness between the Christ of history and the popular conceptions of the Messiah derived from prophecy,—yet we cannot but see that it was not without a definite and sure ground, in Scripture and in fact, that Peter, in view of the recent marvellous events that had taken place before his own eyes and those of his fellow-countrymen, could say, and say with justice, *Yea, and all the prophets from Samuel and those that follow after, as many as have spoken, have likewise foretold of these days.*

Acts xv. 13-18.—*And after they had held their peace, James answered, saying, Men and brethren, hearken unto me: Simeon hath declared how God at the first did visit the Gentiles, to take out of them a people for His name. And to this agree the words of the prophets; as it is written, After this will I return, and will build again the tabernacle of David, which is fallen down; and I will build again the ruins thereof, and I will set it up: that the residue of men might seek after the Lord, and all the Gentiles, upon whom my name is called, saith the Lord, who doeth all these things. Known unto God are all His works from the beginning of the world.*

LECTURE IV.

THIS is reported as being substantially the speech of James, the first president of the Christian Church at Jerusalem, in the council, or conference, which was held there on the matter of circumcision. We may, at all events, accept the words as expressing with sufficient accuracy the tone of thought which prevailed among many Christians at that time. We have, indeed, no reason to believe that the writer of the Acts of the Apostles in any material degree altered or coloured the sentiments expressed by St. James at that important meeting, and we may be quite sure that they were shared by the large majority of the Christians of his day. I mention this merely as a matter of fact, and not as though the opinions in themselves had any force or authority that was binding upon us. But taking them simply in this way, there are certain inferences which we are fairly warranted in deducing from them.

For example, the Septuagint version of the prophet Amos, in the hands of the Jews and Christians of the first century, contained a passage virtually identical with this, notwithstanding several verbal differences. Secondly, whatever differences were apparent between the Greek version and the Hebrew original, as represented in our own authorised version of Amos, they were not of such a character as to awaken jealousy in the minds of the Judaising part of the apostle's audience. He would naturally have been careful not to offend needlessly the prejudices of those whom he desired to win. Again, there was nothing remarkable in appealing to the *authority* of the prophets, or in supposing that recent events attending the establishment and growth of the Christian Church had actually fulfilled their words. Moreover, the speaker evidently believed that the prophet had been used by God as an agent for making known His will, and declaring purposes which had been formed long before, though but lately matured in act.

Clearly, therefore, St. James, and all who heard him, believed that the people of God possessed in the writings of the prophets documents which had not before been rightly understood, but which were replete with information concerning the future which could not have been derived from ordinary human sources, and were instinct with the energies of a will which was gradually unfolding itself. On all these points there is no possible room for doubt. If, therefore, the traditional views of Scripture and of prophecy which we have received from the teaching of the Christian Church correspond, more or less accurately, with these, it is clearly not so much ourselves and the Church that are responsible for them, as the first believers and apostles of the Lord, and the long tradition which they themselves inherited.

People sometimes talk, in the present day, as if the popular views of the inspiration and authority of Scripture were things of recent growth, which the progress of modern discovery and investigation had shown to need correction, whereas nothing is more certain than that the writers of the New Testament regarded the Scriptures of the old dispensation very much as we have been accustomed to regard the Bible at large;* that they received them as the oracles of God, and as the expression of a Divine will and purpose towards man to be found nowhere else, and communicated in a remarkable and super-human, supernatural way. They may have been wrong, but we cannot suppose they were so without supposing that Peter, James, John, and Paul were wrong in this respect, and were not only wrong themselves, but also that the teaching of Jesus Christ, which they manifestly represented, was wrong too. This is a conclusion which at least

* See, for instance, among other passages, Heb. xiii. 5, 9, where the writer accepts the Living Lord as the actual speaker, and takes a promise given to Joshua as a reasonable and valid ground of personal hope in God. This is Faith, or the principle of absolute trust in a spoken word of God, and not a mere assent to the truth or beauty of the sentiment apart from any direct personal reliance of this kind. See also 2 Tim. iii. 15, and compare 1 Thess. ii. 13, Gal. iii. 22, Rom. xv. 4, Acts xvii. 11, Matt. xxvi. 54, John xx. 9, Luke xxiv. 26, 44. It should always be borne in mind, as Lord Hatherley says, that these last words were spoken by our Lord after His resurrection, when no longer subject to the limitations of mortality. All this shows us that the apostles regarded the words of God, like Luther, as living creatures with hands and feet, —a way, it is to be feared, rapidly passing into discredit in the present day.

requires deliberate thought before we commit ourselves to the acceptance of it.

But let us examine the particular scripture to which the apostle James referred. This was taken from the writings of the prophet Amos. Now, it so happens that Amos is acknowledged to belong to the oldest group of the Jewish prophets whose writings have come down to us. He is allowed to have flourished towards the earlier part of the eighth century before Christ. Consequently, when St. James made this allusion to his works, the book of Amos that we now have must have been in existence for some eight hundred years at least. This is a matter that will not be called in question. Moreover, the epoch at which Amos flourished was that of the greatest joint prosperity of the thrones of Israel and Judah. Jeroboam II. was still on the throne of Israel, and in his long reign of forty-one years he raised his kingdom to the highest position of glory that it ever attained. Under Uzziah the kingdom of Judah was probably more prosperous than it ever had been since the death of Solomon, and his long reign of fifty-two years tended naturally to consolidate it. Amos prophesied during the fifteen or twenty years that the two kings were contemporary,—that is, during the latter part of Jeroboam's reign and the early part of Uzziah's. The time is more precisely identified as being *two years before the earthquake* which took place in the reign of the latter king, of which, however, we know nothing more than the mere fact of its occurrence, and that the recollection of it survived more than two centuries and a half afterwards, in the time of Zechariah.* Probably, therefore, at no one period in the joint history of the two kingdoms was there a season of greater prosperity. This will be seen to be important as we proceed.

It is to be observed, then, that twice over this ancient prophet makes allusion to David, who probably flourished some two hundred and fifty years before his time : once (vi. 5) where he rebukes *them that are at ease in Zion, that chant to the sound of the viol, and invent to themselves instruments of music*, LIKE DAVID, where he refers to a point in the history of that king which is chiefly known to *us* from the writer of the first book of Chronicles;† and, secondly, in the passage here cited by St. James : *In that day will I raise up the* TABERNACLE OF DAVID *that is fallen, and close up the breaches thereof ; and I will raise up his ruins, and I will build it as in the days of old.*‡ It is clear, therefore, that in the time of Amos, 800 years B C., two points were distinctly remembered with regard to David, one being his inventive musical genius, and the other some typical glory attaching to his throne. It is important to bear this in mind, because we are asked by a certain school of critics to believe that our records of David's reign are some three centuries later than the time of Amos. It appears, however, that the memory of his personal character was distinctly retained, as indeed it well might be, under the circumstances in which

* Zech. xiv. 5.　　　† xxiii. 5.　　　‡ ix. 11.

the prophet lived, for the space of two centuries and a half. But what is more particularly to be observed is the prophet's allusion to what he calls the *tabernacle,* or *booth, of David,* which he describes as *fallen* or *falling,* while he promises in the name of the Lord to *raise up his ruins,* and to *build* his *booth,* or *tabernacle, as in the days of old.* Such language must, one would think, have had some meaning when the prophet wrote, though under the prosperous reigns of Jeroboam II. and of Uzziah it is not easy to see how it applied. More intelligible appears to be the allusion to the division of the kingdom of David which is probably implied in the promise to *close up the breaches thereof.* But how, when the throne of Judah was flourishing under Uzziah, and that of Israel under Jeroboam, could the prophet speak with any propriety of raising up the *ruins* of David? It is also worthy of note that the house of David is spoken of as a *booth,* or *tent,* and that this tent is to be *built as in the days of old.* However all these singular features of the language chosen are to be explained, one point is, at all events, very clear— namely, that somewhat more than two centuries after the death of David his throne was regarded in a very marked manner by a prophet of the northern kingdom,* as though some special history attached

---

* Tekoa belonged indeed to Judah, but the sphere of the prophet's mission was mainly Israel and the northern kingdom : i. 1, iii. 1, iv. 1, v. 1, vii. 10, etc. : it would seem, therefore, that any individual preference Amos may have shown for the house of David was not such as to injure the prospect of his success with Israel, which he would have been careful to avoid.

to it; that it was likewise spoken of as being in ruins, or about to fall into ruins, and about also to be raised out of its ruins and rebuilt as in the days of old.

The time, moreover, that is assigned by the prophet to the accomplishment of this promise is that mysterious *day* of which it is said, *Lo, I will command, and I will sift the house of Israel among all nations, like as corn is sifted in a sieve, yet shall not the least grain fall upon the earth.** Obviously, therefore, a time future is spoken of, and the terms of the prophet's language cannot be limited in their application to the area of his own age.

In the following verse, moreover, allusion is also made to the conquests of David over Edom, as though the extent of the dominion promised him was to rival that which it had attained of old. The tabernacle is to be rebuilt in order *that they may possess the remnant of Edom, and all the heathen, which are called by my name, saith the Lord that doeth this.*† It is clear, therefore, that the language of Amos holds out hope of future domination over Edom and the heathen nations; and yet, notwithstanding their heathen condition, the reproach of their uncircumcision is to be rolled away, for the name of the Lord is called upon them. And, lastly, the work, whatever it is, which is thus spoken of, is called the Lord's work; and He appears to challenge it to Himself as though it were beyond the power of human agency to bring it about.

Such, then, are the remarkable features of this

* ix. 9.   † ix. 12.

fragment of the prophet Amos which we find apparent on the surface of it. Into their interpretation we do not now enter; we only draw attention to the manifest facts of language. No interpretation or criticism can be satisfactory which does not fully recognise them in detail.

But apart altogether from the interpretation of the language, certain conclusions are fairly warranted from its ostensible features. For instance, eight hundred years before Christ, whether the books of Samuel were in existence or not, the history of David must have been well known very much as we have it now. At all events, Uzziah, the reigning monarch, was his lineal descendant. He must have known, and his people must have known, by what right he held his throne. If the *breaches* of David's house could be spoken of, it must have been known that for some reason or other the house of Jeroboam was an alien and a rival house. The insinuation appears to be dropped that the throne of Israel *de jure* belonged to David; and this admission is the more significant as coming from a prophet of Israel, or from one whose mission was addressed to Israel. Incidentally, then, the prophet's language is confirmatory of the history as we have it, whether or not the record of that history was then preserved,—as I, for one, cannot doubt it was. But when it is said that *the tabernacle of David* shall be *built as in the days of old*, we seem to have even a verbal reminiscence of David's own words (2 Sam. vii. 27): *For Thou, O Lord of hosts, God of Israel, hast revealed to Thy servant, saying, I* *will build thee an house: therefore hath Thy servant found in his heart to pray this prayer unto Thee.* Nor is it unlikely that in the choice of the peculiar and uncommon word *booth*, or *tabernacle*, an allusion may be designed to the original shepherd-calling of David. And if so, this ancient prophet, Amos, furnishes us with incidental reference to the musical skill of David, to his conquests over Edom, to some special characteristic attaching to his house, to some disaster which had befallen it, and possibly to the original employment of David as keeper of his father's sheep. Of course, I do not for one moment suggest that, supposing the authentic history of his times to have been irrecoverably lost, it would be possible for us to reconstruct it out of such slender materials as these; but I do venture to affirm that there is nothing in the language of the prophet inconsistent with the history as we have it, but much, on the contrary, that does serve to illustrate and confirm it.*

The point, however, most important to note is the choice of David's name at all in this connection. Certainly if we might assume the history to have been in existence, nothing could be more intelligible or natural; but it is just this that we are not allowed to assume. We are asked to believe that the history was written long afterwards, possibly after an

---

* It is, of course, preposterous to imagine that the history either in Samuel or Chronicles was constructed out of the allusions in Amos, or with any reference to them. So far, then, both our sources of information are independent.

interval as long as that which already separated the prophet Amos from David; and then, on this supposition, I ask why in this case any special mention of David at all, or at all events why this particular allusion to his house, its ruin and its restoration?

I claim this prophecy, then, in its verbal phenomena as an independent witness of certain particular characteristics attending David's house. If we turn to the history, it will at once become clear what these were. Permanence and stability were, for some reason or other, supposed to be characteristic of David's throne. The history tells us why this was. A promise had been made to him. The Lord in that same chapter of the second book of Samuel had declared that he would *establish his house and his throne for ever.* Had there been any record of such a promise in the days of Amos, we can easily conceive that the stubborn facts connected with the history of Israel, and the unexampled prosperity of Jeroboam's throne, would greatly stagger him. We can even imagine that a considerable impetus would be given thereby to the natural tendency of his aspirations to long for the prosperity of David. If the memory of any such promise existed, we can understand all this; and according to our records, such a promise was not only remembered, but preserved: but take away the promise and the record of it, and the language of the prophet becomes more enigmatical than ever; in fact, it seems hopeless, not only to extract any sense out of it, but still more to account naturally for its utterances. It must not however be forgotten

that the age of the prophet's writing is not a matter
under dispute. The most reckless critics have in
their benevolence left us this; so that in the first
quarter of the eighth century before Christ we have
an original utterance of a prophet of Israel which
is quite intelligible with the aid of the history, but
hopelessly obscure and perplexing without it.*

But then no one can for a moment suppose that
whenever the history was written, the writer of it
had the slightest intention of *explaining*, by way
of historical comment, such a passage, for example,
as this. Whatever his motives in writing, no such
notion as this can have formed part of them. While
obviously on the supposition of the prophet preceding
the historian, he cannot be held to have prepared
the way designedly for the history that would afterwards be written. Whatever coincidence or correspondence, then, exists between the two is beyond all
dispute or question undesigned. And so we are left
to contemplate the progress of this prophetic utterance down the stream of time for eight centuries
without being able to assign to it any meaning, or
to conceive of any which it can have had when
spoken in the glorious era of Jeroboam II. and
Uzziah. One thing, however, becomes clear,—that
as the course of events rolled on, the language of
the prophet became unexpectedly more and more
intelligible. Before three centuries had passed by,
the house of David had been proved to be little
better than a shepherd's tent or booth. The

* See Note at the end of Lecture IV.

breaches of his house, far from being healed, rapidly
went from worse to worse: ten of the original twelve
tribes were carried captive to Assyria, the miserable
attempt at setting up a rival throne had ended, after
repeated efforts, in ignominious failure; even the
direct line of David's house through Solomon seems
to have failed; the representatives of his family were
carried in disgraceful bondage to Babylon; and what
is known to have been uttered two centuries and
a half before about the *ruins* of his house, received
a complete and startling fulfilment, and we who
now survey the entire prospect of the ages past can
see that for many centuries the tabernacle of David
continued in a condition of apparently hopeless ruin.
But still during all this time the promise remained
recorded, *I will raise up the tabernacle of David
that is fallen, and close up the breaches thereof, and
I will raise up his ruins, and I will build it as in
the days of old.* Of course in the face of all this
evidence it is perfectly open to us to deny the
existence of any prophecy or promise here, nor should
I willingly venture to be so rash as to attempt to
prove it. But one thing is absolutely certain,—that
stopping at the seventh century after Amos, and
setting aside all the subsequent history as of no
bearing on the matter, it does look very much as
if the prophet's language, either rightly or wrongly,
had spoken in the palmy days of his nation's life
of ruin that should overtake the royal house, while
yet a hope was embedded in his words that out of
ruin it should again emerge in its pristine glory. And

most unquestionably no Jew who believed that Amos
had a Divine mission would have been to blame if
he had cherished such a hope.

Nor is it possible for us to evade the conclusion
now suggested on the ground of critical uncertainties
or ambiguities attaching to the language. This is
an objection that has long been anticipated in the
providence of God by the very conspicuous variations
we perceive in the version of the prophet quoted by
St. James.* However much the Hebrew and the

* On these variations, Kuenen observes, p. 243, "The reading of
the Greek translator cannot bear comparison with the Masoretic or
common text of the Old Testament. He has made a mistake with
regard to one letter, and, in consequence of that, has put 'seek after'
instead of 'inherit;' and further, by incorrect vocalisation, he has
changed 'Edom' into 'men.' The erroneousness of his reading is
plain at once from this, that 'the nations over whom Jahveh's name
is proclaimed,' necessarily form a part of 'the residue of men,' and
therefore could not be mentioned separately."

That the Greek reading is intrinsically superior to the Hebrew,
we are not at all concerned to maintain, but that the Greek translator
has made a series of blunders, and that St. James has turned those
blunders to his own account, is a rough-and-ready but possibly also
an unworthy and inadequate solution of the difficulty; and again,
p. 457: "Every reader of the Bible must be struck with the great
difference between an utterance of Amos at the end of his prophetical
book, and the citation of the passage in the speech which, according
to the Acts of the Apostles, was spoken by James at the synod of
Jerusalem. The cause of the variation has already been shown : the
Greek translator, from whom the quotation in the Acts is borrowed,
has, by supplying the wrong vowels, read one word Edom as *adam*
(man), and consequently rendered 'the residue of men,' instead of
'the residue of Edom ;' he has further read a letter incorrectly in
the Hebrew verb which signifies 'to inherit,' so that he thought he
recognised in it the verb meaning 'to seek.' This double mistake
readily explains the whole difference. Its importance is at once
apparent to every one who reads the discourse of James as a whole ;

Greek texts may differ as represented in the authorised version of the Old and New Testaments, the *substantial* meaning of the two is alike; or at all events, if there is room for so much literal divergence, there is room for as much as any criticism is likely to demand. The version of the Septuagint quoted by St. James spoke at least no less clearly than that of the Masorites of the tent or tabernacle of David, of its falling down, of its being in ruins, of its restoration. And at the time when the prophet wrote, both these conditions were as yet unfulfilled, nor was there any human likelihood of their fulfilment.

he wishes to show that the prophets had already announced what had now actually taken place: God has looked upon the heathen, and chosen from among them a people for Himself. *According to the Greek version*, Amos does really reveal the prospect of such a future: but the original cannot be understood in this sense. It speaks merely of the restoration of the Davidic dynasty, and of the extension of its rule over the surrounding peoples, first of all over Edom, and then over the nations over which the name of Jahveh—as that of their conqueror—is proclaimed. All attempts to explain away this difference must, from their very nature, prove a failure. The opinion that the Septuagint may have reproduced a purer text than the Masoretic is not worthy of a serious refutation."

The one fact with which the apostle was concerned was the significant fact that the Greek text, which he did not make, but find, lent itself, even more forcibly than the Hebrew, to the peculiar circumstances of the time. He saw in this an indication of the Divine will, a token of the Divine foreknowledge; and if he really was speaking under the guidance of the Holy Ghost (ver. 28), who shall say he was wrong in doing so? That he was not speaking critically we are willing to admit, but are we sure that he was bound to do so? At all events, our criticism will best display itself in judging his words according to his standard, and not according to one which it is plain he did not follow.

Surely, therefore, I am warranted in pointing, as I would point you now, to these prominent and remarkable words, as containing in themselves and on their surface evidence of their really prophetic character. They are manifestly only taken as one example out of many. But if we can adduce even one example from any given prophet of language which could not arise naturally out of the circumstances of his time, which cannot by any means be interpreted of those circumstances, which centuries after he wrote is known at all events in one particular—that of the ruin which befell the house of David—to have been verified by history, we are so far justified in taking our stand on this example, and insisting upon it as possibly furnishing an instance of actual prophecy, and resolving that we will not surrender it for any easily alleged reasons of the *à priori* impossibility of such prophecy.

But beyond all question we can go further than this. When the apostle James stood up in the council of Jerusalem, his nation had for five centuries watched over and mourned the desolation of the house of David. No tampering with the words of Amos could obscure that fact; but as yet the possibility of application inherent in the rest of his words had not revealed itself to Israel. Indeed, the progress of events had but recently made such possibility a fact, and for aught we know the apostle himself was the first to discern it. It was, however, a matter of discernment, not of invention. The apostle had no desire to rewrite the language of the prophet. He merely availed himself of a version which had been for many generations in esteemed and familiar use. And it so happened,—for this also was a matter of fact, or shall we not rather say of Divine providence,—that the version of the Alexandrine Jews had given a breadth and capacity to the language of the prophet that originally his words did not possess. "The remnant of *Edom* and of all the heathen" had been rendered as though by a slight change in the vowels the words had run "the remnant of *Adam*—the residue of men—and all the heathen." And instead of the family of David possessing the remnant of Edom and the heathen, it was rather the nations of the heathen that were to enter into the possession of the sure mercies of David and the promises that were made to him; and thus in the truest and fullest sense they were to become his possession by participating in the blessings that were promised to his throne. The promise and hope of the prophet, then, had been in the highest sense fulfilled by being expanded far beyond their original limits. But can we call this a failure of the original promise? Is it not much rather its most complete justification? Is a man to be held guilty of violating his word who does for his fellow-man more than he could either ask or think? And shall we say that the word of prophecy has failed when it is discovered to be instinct and replete with a meaning that certainly we cannot understand the mind of the prophet as a human agent to have entertained, but which, if he was indeed the minister and spokesman of the Most High, is altogether and

for that very reason most in accordance with the
theory that the omniscient Spirit of the living God,
*who worketh all things after the counsel of His own
will*, actually and in very deed "spake by the prophets." This, as I have already observed, is in no
case a matter for demonstrative proof. If we could
prove it to demonstration, where would be the room
for the exercise of that moral faculty which we call
faith? No man *believes* in the truth of a mathematical theorem, though none the less he cannot
doubt it, because he *knows* it is true. But if a man
acts in a particular way towards me, and does so by
a long chain of habitual conduct which I, perhaps,
do not discover till I have had to mourn his irre-
parable loss, I then learn by faith to interpret the
significance of innumerable actions which I never
can have the opportunity of testing categorically, but
must be content to accept upon the weight and
reasonableness of probable evidence. Nor is it
otherwise with the dealing of God in Scripture, and
more especially in prophecy. The life and death of
Jesus Christ, if they mean anything at all, have
given a meaning to the Old Testament revelation
which it never had before: they have shown more
than ever that it was in the truest and highest sense
a revelation, the more so because all its significance
and wealth of meaning was not discoverable by those
to whom it was at first entrusted, nor for many ages
after they had passed away. But surely this supple-
mental significance, if I may so call it, is not on that
ground to be rejected. On the contrary, we accept

it the more readily, because, had it not been for the life and death of Jesus, and the revelation of God in Him, we should never have known it. But the degree of our faith in the one revelation will be measured by the reality of our acceptance of the other. If we believe that God so loved us in our sin as to give His Son to die for us, we shall not find it hard to believe that His dealings with David and with Abraham may have been preparatory for that great event; nor that the oracles of the prophets may have been instinct with truth of which *they* were but partly conscious, but which our own freedom through the knowledge of His truth may lead us more abundantly to perceive, and more thankfully to accept. That at least will assuredly be our conclusion if we believe with St. James that *known unto God are all His works from the beginning of the world,* and that in the process of making them known to man He has made use of the ministry of patriarchs, apostles, and prophets.

PROFESSOR KUENEN ON AMOS.

It may be as well that the reader should have the advantage of Professor Kuenen's observations on the prophet Amos, which are as follows :—

" It was in the reign of Jeroboam II., about the year 800 B.C., that Amos, an inhabitant of Tekoa, in Judæa, appeared as a prophet in the kingdom of the ten tribes. By the successful wars and vigorous government of that king, Israel had attained to a high degree of prosperity and wealth; but judged from a moral and religious point of view, the state of the kingdom left much to be desired. The poor were oppressed, and the victims of extortion. The sensual worship of the nature-gods numbered many adherents. There was no lack of noisy festivals and loud songs in honour of Jahveh, but the people did not trouble themselves about his commands, and imposed silence on those who ventured to urge them to obedience to his will.* Is it surprising that Amos, called to be a prophet in these circumstances, raises his voice in severe reproaches, and predicts to the people a mournful future? He directs his attention only in passing to his native country, the kingdom of Judah. He is not blind to the sins which are committed there also, (ch. ii. 4 ; comp. vi. 1, and the mention of Beersheba, v. 5, viii. 14,) and announces that Jahveh will cast a fire upon Judah which shall devour the palaces of Jerusalem (ii. 5); but he seems to expect that such a severe chastisement will be sufficient to bring the inhabitants of the southern kingdom to repentance, and that the extinction of Judah's national existence will not be required for that purpose. In his prophecy of Israel's restoration, he mentions the ' falling tabernacle of David,' ' of which the breaches shall be closed up and the ruins raised when it is built as in the days of old ' (ix. 11), which implies that the dynasty of David, in however sunken a condition, shall continue to exist at the time when the better days dawn. The prospects which the prophet descries for the kingdom of the ten tribes are much more

* These statements can be deduced from the following utterances of Amos, quoted in the order of the chapters : ch. ii. 6—8, 11, 12, iii. 10, iv. 1, v. 7, 10 11, 12. 21—23, vi. 4—6, 12ᵇ, viii. 4—6, 10.

unfavourable. If we were asked, What are the judgments against
that kingdom which he expects? we might answer, What are the
judgments that he does not expect? For as, before he came forward
as a prophet, calamities of all kinds had already smitten 'the house
of Joseph,' without, however, effecting the change for which they
were sent (iv. 6—11), so also, in the future, the apostate nation
shall not be spared one single description of suffering.* But again
and again Amos reverts to the sorest punishment which could be
imagined, the people's *being carried away captive to a foreign country.*
'Israel shall surely go into captivity, forth of his land' (ch. vii. 17 :
compare ch. v. 5, where the same thing is said of Gilgal). In
another passage he says, 'I (Jahveh) will cause you to go into
captivity beyond Damascus' (v. 27); and once more, 'I will shake the
house of Israel to and fro among all nations, like as corn is shaken
to and fro in a sieve' (ix. 9). The promise that Jahveh 'shall
bring back the captivity of his people Israel' (ix. 14) is founded, of
course, on the same conception of the nation's future. The higher
classes, who now indulge in revelry and excess, shall first be smitten
by this judgment (vi. 7). If, however, the question is asked whether
the prophet had formed to himself a clear conception of the realisation
of this threatening which agreed with the subsequent reality, we
must return an answer in the negative. It was, as may be remembered, the Assyrians who, about eighty years after the appearance of
Amos, conquered Samaria, and carried into captivity the flower of
the citizens of the kingdom of Ephraim. Now with regard to the
Assyrians, Amos nowhere names them, but yet alludes to them on one
occasion when he mentions a nation that Jahveh shall raise up, and
which shall afflict Israel from 'Hamath to the brook of the wilderness'
(from the northern to the southern boundary—vi. 14). But it is not
said here that this people is destined by Jahveh to deprive Israel of
its national existence : it is rather mentioned as one of the many
means which he shall employ in order to punish the apostates :
and as regards the time when his threatenings should be realised,
nothing is plainer than that Amos imagined it to be close at hand.
He announces in the same breath that 'the high places of Israel
shall be desolate, and the sanctuaries of Israel shall be laid waste,'
and that Jahveh 'shall rise against the house of Jeroboam with the

* Besides the passages quoted in the notes immediately following, see ch. ii.
13—16, iii. 11—15, iv. 2, 3, v. 1—3, 16, 17, vi. 8—11, vii. 1—6, viii. 3, 9—14,
ix. 5.

sword' (vii. 9).   There may have been a misunderstanding, or even a
malevolent perversion of his words, when it was told to the king
that the prophet had dared to predict that Jeroboam would die a
violent death (vii. 11), still it is plain that in the opinion of Amos
the overthrow of the kingdom coincides with the overthrow of the
reigning dynasty.   This follows, also, from his answer to Amaziah,
the priest of the royal sanctuary at Bethel, who had forbidden him
to prophesy on his territory.   'Thou shalt,' so Amos says to him,
'thou shalt die in an unclean land;' to which he immediately adds,
'and Israel shall surely go into captivity forth of his land' (vii. 17).
This deportation must happen in the time of the generation then
living, if Amaziah is to be one of the victims.   For another reason,
also, we cannot ascribe to Amos any foreknowledge of the future.
He has not yet given up all hope that Israel shall be brought to
repentance, either in consequence of Jahveh's reiterated threatenings, or by suffering the first of the judgments to be executed
upon them.   'Seek the good, and not the evil, that ye may live:
and so Jahveh, the God of hosts, shall be with you, as ye say.   Hate
the evil, and love the good, and establish judgment in the gate: it
may be that Jahveh, the God of hosts, will be gracious unto the
remnant of Joseph.'[*]   If the prophet is in earnest in what he says
here—and how can we have any doubt of his sincerity?—then he can
have had no *certainty* with regard to the future course of Israel's
fortunes, though it be true that, for the most part, he does not
venture to hope, and scarcely doubts any longer that the extreme
inflictions which he from time to time anew depicts are indispensable."—pp. 150—153.

First we ask, how is the call of Amos to be a prophet to be
accounted for under the " circumstances "?   Is there nothing unnatural or " surprising " in it ?   Why did he utter his voice at all,
and from whom did the impulse to do so come?   In all these cases,
just as with the call of Abraham, it is the first impulse that has to be
explained.   Granting the subsequent steps, the process is clear, but
it is just these that we cannot grant till the original impulse is explained.   If there was no Divine law in existence, as Kuenen would
have us believe—nothing but " the ten words "—how was Amos,
or any other prophet, to feel himself called to be a prophet of the

---

[*] Ch. v. 14, 15 ; compare also viii. 11, 12, although the hunger and thirst for
the word of Jahveh described there can scarcely be regarded as the beginning
of repentance, on account of verses 13, 14.

Lord in the midst of surrounding ignorance and idolatry ? Again, as there had yet been no deportation, how was the prophet again and again to revert to it as " the sorest punishment which could be imagined," and *why did that punishment ever overtake the nation?*

To determine whether he had or had not formed to himself a clear conception of how this was to be is unnecessary. We may say, in Kuenen's own words upon another matter (p. 435), " What right have we to prescribe to him how he is to conceive and execute his task ?" or to insist that his foreknowledge shall coincide precisely with our after-knowledge? Here Amos is taken to task because he does not *name* the Assyrians, which is supposed to indicate a flaw in his prophecy; but afterwards, in the case of Micah, it is equally a charge of complaint against him that he does name Babylon (p. 164). Who, then, was right, Amos or Micah? or were they both alike justified by wisdom as the children of wisdom, and therefore right ; and is it Kuenen who is wrong in his method of dealing with them ?

It is entirely gratuitous to affirm that Amos imagined the woes he threatened to be close at hand. The sequence of the climax in vii. 17 is entirely against that supposition, and the analogy of prophecy is equally fatal to it : viii. 9, 11, cf. Jer. xxiii. 5—8, xxx. 8, xxxvi. 37, Zech. xiii. 1, Mal. iv. 1, etc., etc.

LECTURE V.

IN reading these familiar words, most persons probably have been struck with the singular apparent
want of correspondence between the passage referred
to and the incident in which it is declared to have
been fulfilled. What have *the sure mercies of David,*
whatever they may be, got to do with the alleged
resurrection of Jesus Christ? It is evident, however,
that to the mind of Paul, the man of Jewish education, who had been brought up at the feet of
Gamaliel, and to the Jews who heard his address
in the synagogue at Antioch, in Pisidia, on the
Sabbath day, this want of correspondence cannot
have been so patent; for otherwise the fact he was
desirous to establish would not have been confirmed
or illustrated in this way. But there is no reason
to believe that he did not thus appeal to the passage
in question, or that those who heard him would be
disposed to demur to its appropriateness. We may
therefore examine the grounds upon which it rested.

I endeavoured to show in my last Lecture the
evidence that is deducible from the writings of
Amos, one of the oldest of the prophets, to certain

characteristics of the life of David, which are thus established to us independently of any record of them preserved in the books of Samuel, whenever those books may have been written. With a view to estimating the actual character of David's history, in order to understand the cycle of prophecies connected with him, I shall now briefly examine the testimony that is supplied by the writings of Isaiah. He flourished probably some thirty or forty years after Amos, and therefore his testimony is only one degree less valuable than that of Amos, while it can hardly be supposed that anything that was known of David in the time of Amos can have been forgotten in the time of Isaiah.

It is not, indeed, much that we are able to glean from the writings of Isaiah; but what there is can only be regarded as so far confirmatory of results already obtained. From first to last the name of David is mentioned some ten times by the prophet; and all the instances, with the exception of the last, which is the passage here quoted by St. Paul, occur in the earlier portion of his writings. Although, therefore, we cannot consent to the violent dismemberment of his book that some critics insist upon, all must allow that the antiquity of the great bulk of the allusions, occurring as they do in the earlier portion of it, is unquestionable. The first mention of the name of David occurs in the seventh chapter, ver. 2, where we read that *it was told the house of David, saying, Syria is confederate with Ephraim,* in the reign of Ahaz; and afterwards at ver. 13, that

Isaiah said in addressing the royal family, *Hear ye now, O house of David.* This is not otherwise remarkable than as showing that the title by which Ahaz was then recognised as ruling was his descent from David; and further, that his family was the house of David, in contrast to that of the king who was then reigning in Israel.

We pass on to the great prophecy in the ninth chapter, about the child of mystic names, and find it thus written: *Of the increase of his government and peace there shall be no end upon the throne of David, and upon his kingdom to order it, and to establish it with judgment and with justice from henceforth, even for ever.* Now, waiving altogether the interpretation of this passage, it affords, at least, clear proof that the *throne of David* was then regarded as the special subject of expectation, and as intimately connected with the brilliant destiny predicted for this child. And this fact points us, not so much to something yet to come, as to something already past, which caused the throne of David to be then so regarded. Whatever this may have been, it was obviously well known in the eighth century before Christ, when the words were spoken.

The next passage is in xvi. 5, in a prophecy concerning Moab, which runs, *And in mercy shall the throne be established: and he shall sit upon it in truth in the tabernacle of David, judging, and seeking judgment, and hasting righteousness.* As this was no doubt subsequent to the prophecy of Amos, about "the tabernacle of David that is fallen," which we last considered, though the actual words used are not the same, it is more than probable that there is an allusion in it to that prophecy. It again shows that whatever was promised to Moab was promised in connection with one who should sit upon the throne of David. The throne of David, then, was the centre of hope and the basis of prophecy.

In chap. xxii. 9, which is narrative, and not predictive, there is another possible but less probable allusion to the same verse of Amos, and again the words used are different: *Ye have seen also the breaches of the city of David, that they are many.* Here it is not the house or family or throne of David that is spoken of, but the city of David; and this, it will not be denied, is the stronghold of Zion, which was originally taken and fortified by David.

In the twenty-second verse of the same chapter it is said of Eliakim, the son of Hilkiah, that the Lord will *lay upon his shoulder the key of the house of David; that he shall open, and none shall shut; that he shall shut, and none shall open.* He was to exercise the office of treasurer over the house of the reigning heir of David.

The twenty-ninth chapter opens with the words, *Woe to Ariel, to Ariel, the city where David dwelt!* with a probable allusion to the lion's whelp, which was the emblem of David's tribe.* This is confirmatory of the words in the history (2 Sam. v. 9), *So David dwelt in the fort, and called it the city of*

---

* Ariel meaning most probably the " Lion of God," λέων θεοῦ, Aquila and Symmachus.

David.   But it is preposterous to suppose that either passage was written with the view of corroborating or illustrating the other.

The next two passages occur in the famous historical chapters, which are with more probability to be assigned to Isaiah than to any one else. The first is in chap. xxxvii. 35, in the Lord's message to Hezekiah, in reply to Sennacherib : *I will defend this city, to save it for mine own sake, and for my servant David's sake.* As there is no reasonable cause to doubt that these were the very terms of the message sent, it is important to observe that there is some mysterious relation implied in them between the memory of David and the promised protection of the Lord. And even if criticism were disposed to assert that the message was written after the deliverance was wrought, and so contained no promise or prophecy, still the words contain unquestionable evidence of the way in which the memory of David was regarded in the age of Hezekiah. And this is yet further illustrated by the next message of the following chapter, on the occasion of Hezekiah's sickness : *Go and say to Hezekiah, Thus saith the Lord, the God of David thy father, I have heard thy prayer, I have seen thy tears : behold, I will add unto thy days fifteen years.* This may well be accepted as sufficient proof that Hezekiah was regarded as the lineal descendant of David, and that David was supposed to stand in some special relation to the Lord, who is thus called the God of David, as He is called the God of Abraham, Isaac, and Jacob.

It must be borne in mind that this, which at the risk of weariness has now been laid before you, is documentary evidence of the eighth century before Christ, showing the national estimate then formed of the historic position of David after an interval of some three hundred years, or a period about equal to that which separates us from the time of Elizabeth.

We pass on now to an examination of the passage quoted by St. Paul in the text. And for our present purpose it matters not in the slightest degree when it was written, because the antiquity of the passages already referred to will not be doubted. Could it therefore be proved to be of a later age, which it cannot, it would still receive elucidation from those passages, and not they from it. In chap. lv. 3, 4, the prophet says, *Incline your ear, and come unto me: hear, and your soul shall live; and I will make an everlasting covenant with you, even the sure mercies of David. Behold, I have given him for a witness to the people, a leader and commander to the people.* Now, whatever may be meant by the sure mercies of David, it is impossible not to take the expression in connection with the passages already mentioned. There must be involved in them, in accordance with all principles of sound criticism, an allusion to the throne and family of David, the relation in which he was believed to stand to God, and to some future destiny arising from some past promise which was supposed to have been made to him. This is inherent in the very terms used; for *the sure mercies of David* are in the parallelism set over against the *everlasting covenant* which is to be made with those who *incline the ear and come.* David, therefore, was regarded as the heir of some everlasting covenant. His very name is used as symbolic of such a covenant. Surely there can be no stronger proof of a nation's sentiments than a nation's proverbs, and here the national estimate of, or opinion concerning, David has passed into a proverb. That therefore is documentary evidence as to the prevalent opinion of the time; and the convictions on which it rested were as old as the time of Ahaz and Hezekiah. No sooner, however, has the prophet mentioned David, than he says, in allusion to his known history, *Behold, I have given him,* or *I gave him, for a witness to the people,* or *to peoples, a leader and commander to the people,* or *to peoples.* I ask you, then, to observe here that if the prophet is speaking only of something past, his words afford independent confirmation of what we know of David's history from other sources, for this is very much what the historic David really was; but then it is not a little remarkable that neither the prophet nor those whom he addressed could for a moment suppose that *he*, personally, had borne any part in the direction of David's career. It certainly was not Isaiah who *appointed* David *to be a leader or commander of tribes or peoples.** If,

---

* It is especially to be observed that Isaiah, in calling David a *leader*, makes use of the very word in reference to him which was so conspicuous in the books of Samuel, where he is spoken of as the נגיד. Now this is a word first found in these books. Saul is to be anointed as the *nagid* over Israel (ix. 16, x. 1, xiii. 14); afterwards David is recognised as the person who is to take his place (1 Sam. xxv. 30,

therefore, we refer his words only to the past, they contain this remarkable feature, that they altogether identify him with the God who had raised up and chosen David. So that the prophet here is speaking as the very mouthpiece and in the person of God. That is a consideration which must be borne in mind, even if we limit the application of his language only to the past. And it serves to show us something of the special character assumed on the one hand by the prophets, and apparently conceded by those who heard them on the other. For this reason, however, it is far more probable, notwithstanding the "perversity" with which Ewald * is pleased to stigmatise

2 Sam. v. 2, vi. 21, vii. 8). The word is also applied to Solomon (1 Kings i. 35), to Jeroboam (xiv. 7), to Baasha (xvi. 2), and to Hezekiah (2 Kings xx. 5). Its use here by Isaiah, as applied to David, may well-nigh serve as actual proof that he was acquainted with the history as recorded in Samuel.

* "This Prophet (Isa. lv. 3—5) intentionally chooses the word נגיד, rare in antiquity, in the meaning of *a prophetic ruler, i.e.,* one who announces God's will (cf. the *Alterth*, p. 142), as the कवि: becomes the old Persian کی. What perversity it is to refer the words (ver. 4), to the Messiah of the future, ought by this time to be self-evident." (Hist. of Israel, vol. iii., p. 202, n. 3.—E. V.)

Does he suppose, we may ask, there is any connection, philosophical, analogical, or otherwise, between the Sanskrit *kavi* and the old Persian *kai* and the Hebrew *ged*, or that the last can mean *a prophetic ruler?* It is really time that many of the wild vagaries of this wildest of men were exploded.

This rarity being autocratically asserted, it may be as well to say that the word נגיד occurs in the Pentateuch and book of Joshua alone some thirty times, almost as frequently as in all the other books together, and that among the prophets it is only used seven times by Isaiah, five by Jeremiah, once by Micah, and once by Malachi. How, then, can he assert that it is "rare in antiquity"? and what would that mean if it were, which it is not?

such a view, that we are right in attributing a future reference to the prophecy. The David spoken of is not the David of past history, but a David still to come, for whom sure mercies were reserved, with whom an everlasting covenant was to be made, and who should be a leader and commander of the people. But, if this is really so, and I think we must, upon consideration, allow that it cannot be otherwise, then surely the light in which it sets the person and the character of David is greatly changed. For not only is he seen to be the founder of the reigning family of Judah, the builder of the stronghold of Zion for whose sake the Lord had promised to defend the city of Jerusalem, and the king who stood in a peculiar relation to God in which none of his successors stood; but he becomes yet more the starting-point for fresh promises, the foundation of forward-looking hopes, the symbol of perpetual dominion, and the possessor of a throne that should know no end.

I want you specially to note that for the present I lay no stress whatever upon these supposed prophecies or promises. There may be no value in them whatever. They may be meaningless, baseless, and empty. But this, at all events, the prophet's language shows, that in the age of Isaiah, between two and three hundred years after the death of David, certain facts in his history were perfectly well remembered, and it was commonly believed that the house founded by him was destined to greater glory than it had ever yet attained, and that some special and mysterious privilege centred in and attached to his name and person. And we have seen that at all events to a certain extent the same conviction had been shared by the prophet Amos in the generation before Isaiah, and was familiar to the northern kingdom.

This, then, is the evidence that is producible from that period. Whatever else was believed concerning David three or four centuries later, cannot thus far throw discredit upon this, which was clearly in existence then.

Nor, on the other hand, is it reasonable to suppose that the estimate of David in the time of Amos and Isaiah was in any degree tinged with mythical colouring. There is nothing about it of the nature of myth. At an age when the recorder of public events was a high officer of state, as was the case in the reigns of both David and Hezekiah, and the reigning king was publicly acknowledged as the lineal descendant of David, there is not room for the exercise of myth at a distance only of some twelve generations, any more than there is room in our own history for myth to gather round or obscure the existence of Queen Elizabeth or the principal events of her time.

It is clear then, from written evidence, that in the age of Amos and Isaiah there was some unknown and mysterious property and privilege connected with the name and family of David, which, if we had no other sources of information, would seem to be of the nature of a covenant or promise made with him. It

is altogether a separate and distinct question whether
or how such a promise was made ; it is a matter of
fact that we are confronted with certain indications
in the national literature, which can only be understood as pointing to the conclusion that it was then
commonly and confessedly believed to have been
made.   The belief was older than the time of Isaiah,
because there are traces of it in the time of Amos.

The question, then, inevitably arises—What was
the origin of this belief?   From the writings of the
prophets alone it is not possible to answer this question.   They only afford contemporary witness to the
existence of the belief.   It cannot, however, for a
moment be alleged that they were the authors of
the belief.   Their allusions to it are too vague and
shadowy for that.   We are consequently thrown back
upon such historical records as are at our command,
and these are mainly the books of Samuel and Kings,
confirmed and supplemented as they are by the books
of Chronicles.   We are in profound ignorance as to
when these books were written or who wrote them.
With regard, however, to the books of Chronicles,
confessedly the latest of all, this point is worthy of
remark, that the compiler, whoever he was, is most
careful to give his authorities.   He makes reference
to no less than fourteen distinct treatises or works
which he cites by name.   It is true that these, for
the most part, exist no longer ; but it is obvious that
they existed in the time of the writer, and that he
was not afraid of appealing to, and therefore of being
judged by, their authority.   It must also be clear

that this appeal, though *we* can no longer apply the test, considerably enhances his authority. His value as a writer, being of a later date, is obviously much higher than it would have been had he given no authorities. The books of Chronicles cover the period embraced by the combined records of Samuel and Kings. As they differ in various details, it is plain that their testimony, not being identical, where it agrees or is not inconsistent notwithstanding disagreement, must be regarded as independent. But strange to say, throughout the books of Samuel, Kings, and Chronicles, which are the sole records at our disposal, there is no divergence whatever as to the position assigned to David. From first to last it is his throne and his family which is regarded as dominant and unique. It is represented as ruling by a kind of Divine necessity, or the obligation of a Divine promise. And as the books of Chronicles are supposed to date from a time subsequent to the captivity, when the throne of David had ceased to exist, and there was no prospect of its being restored, this is the more remarkable, because it is witness to a past condition of things, and witness that was apparently falsified by the actualities and contradictions of the present. And yet the books of Chronicles, no less than those of Samuel, record an alleged Divine promise given to David: *I will raise up thy seed after thee, which shall be of thy sons, and I will establish his kingdom . . . and his throne for ever.** It is not too much to say that the consciousness of

* 1 Chron. xvii. 11, 12.

this promise pervades the whole of the subsequent history. Somehow or other the whole of the history, if fabricated, was built upon this as a groundwork and foundation. But, in point of fact, it is absolutely impossible to regard the history as a fabrication, nor is it commonly proposed so to regard it. Accepting the history, therefore, as real, we cannot shut our eyes to this remarkable characteristic of it—the universal prevalence of the belief that perpetuity had been promised to David's throne, a belief which evidently survived the existence of the throne itself.

But it cannot be denied that a conviction such as that which pervades the historical books completely accounts for and explains the allusions gathered from Amos and Isaiah. It is exactly such a conviction as they embody to which these prophets testify. And we may surely ask whether there is any other imaginable cause which will account for these allusions. The historians, however, cannot have been in collusion with the prophets in thus representing the facts concerning David, because the materials thus supplied by their writings were too slender for them to work upon;* but both must be regarded as independent witnesses to the existence of a belief

---

* These remarks hold good, even if, as Kuenen (pp. 408 ff. and 429 ff.) and others suppose, the histories were the work of the prophets and the priests; for the writings of the canonical prophets were too obscure in their allusions to be the groundwork of the histories, and the histories, being, on that supposition, of far later date than the great majority of the canonical prophets, cannot have supplied the source from which these allusions were drawn.

which was common to the nation at large, and cannot have been absent from their history at any period from the time of David onwards.

The phenomenon, then, which meets us is the national belief concerning David, which is witnessed to by such writers as Amos and Isaiah, and the problem is how to account for it. If it is affirmed that the existing historical records were of later date, then it is evident that they cannot account for it in the sense of having created it. But it is no less certain that these records cannot have grown out of the meagre allusions in the prophets. The only conceivable hypothesis is that both must have been derived from some common source. Of this, however, we can form no idea, for we have no evidence as to its existence even. And so far as we can postulate the existence of any such common source, it would seem not improbably to be included among the authorities appealed to by the writer of the books of Chronicles. If, therefore, we would attempt to account for the national convictions concerning David, we cannot dispense with the information supplied by the existing records. Now we learn from them that David originally had no right to the throne of Judah; that the original king and his family were set aside for, and supplanted by, David; and that, as a matter of fact, for twenty generations his descendants ruled over the house of Judah. The evidence of events, therefore, at least for that period, seems to have justified an impression that we can trace in the prophets to about the middle of the third

century after his death.   There is even older and in
fact contemporary evidence afforded by the Psalms,
but this must not detain us now.   We can only dwell
upon the fact that *the sure mercies of David*, and the
other allusions to his name in Isaiah, point us conclusively to a yet earlier promise or pledge supposed
to have been given to him, the nature of which we
can only infer for the present from the existing
records which relate to it.   We cannot be wrong,
however, in supposing that it in some way concerned
the permanence of his throne.   Nor was the validity
of this promise supposed to have failed even after the
captivity.   The hope of it certainly still lingered in
Israel, and had penetrated far beyond the confines of
Israel at the commencement of our era.   Nor is it
possible to deny that, as a matter of fact, a large
portion of the actual foundations of the historic
Christian Church were laid in this hope.   The hope
itself, therefore, was a reality ; it may have been a
delusion and a dream, but there can be no question
as to its vigour and strength, for it was possessed
of inextinguishable vitality.   What, then, was the
origin of this hope ?   Is there any natural cause, or
combination of natural causes, that can adequately
account for it ; or does not the vast body of evidence,
when fairly considered as a whole, rather point us
to something for which no natural cause or causes
can be discovered to account ?   The answer to
these questions must be the subject of future inquiry.   For the present we must bear in mind that
the existence of the hope in all its features is a

unique phenomenon in history. There is nothing like it anywhere else. There can be no mistake as to the ultimate *form* it assumed, whatever mistakes we may make as to its growth and origin. The one is a matter of obvious fact attested by many witnesses, the other of theory and speculation. We may go astray in theory; we can only wilfully misinterpret facts. And it is a fact, account for it how we may, that the promises supposed to have centred in David's throne were the hope of a despised and oppressed nation for a thousand years; and that at the end of that time, so far from their intrinsic vitality being exhausted, they supplied the material for the foundation of a new religion which has already lasted for eighteen centuries, which has taken deep root downward in the soil of alien peoples, and has borne fruit upward in moulding their national character, their historical constitution, their arts and sciences, which has pervaded their literature, and developed their civilisation, and stimulated their progress, and of which two of the prophetic corner-stones, interpreted not after the flesh, but after the spirit, were these: *The Lord God shall give unto Him the throne of His father David, and He shall reign over the house of Jacob for ever, and of His kingdom there shall be no end. And as concerning that He raised Him up from the dead, now no more to return to corruption, He said on this wise, I will give you the sure mercies of David.*

7

ACTS II. 29—31.—*Men and brethren, let me freely speak unto you of the patriarch David, that he is both dead and buried, and his sepulchre is with us unto this day. Therefore being a prophet, and knowing that God had sworn with an oath to him, that of the fruit of his loins, according to the flesh, He would raise up Christ to sit on his throne; He seeing this before spake of the resurrection of Christ, that His soul was not left in hell, neither did His flesh see corruption.*

LECTURE VI.

THE HEIR OF DAVID'S THRONE.

HITHERTO we have seen, from an examination of certain passages in Amos and Isaiah, that there is clear evidence of the eighth century before Christ that the throne of David was regarded in a special manner as the centre of national hope and the subject of Divine promises. It remains for us now to investigate any further evidence that can be discovered, and to ascertain, if possible, the precise value of the evidence we may find, and the actual bearing of the facts relating to it. There are obviously many passages in the Psalms which speak of the promises that were supposed to centre in the house of David. The only question is the date which may be assigned to them severally, and the particular weight attaching to them in view of the uncertainty hanging over their date. The first of these passages is found, however, at the close of the eighteenth Psalm; and as that has been preserved to us in two versions — one in the second book of Samuel, and one in the first book of Psalms, and in both cases is ascribed to David, there seems to be strong *primâ facie* reason for accepting it as his. There are, indeed, those who will question it; for in matters of this kind it is not possible to get beyond the limit of debatable ground; but we may safely say that the reasons for believing it to be David's are stronger than those for rejecting it. We find, then, the last words of this Psalm running thus: *Great prosperity giveth He unto His king, and showeth mercy unto David His anointed, and unto his seed for evermore.* If, then, it is allowable to accept this as a Psalm of David, it is proof that he regarded himself as the Lord's anointed king, and that he expected his kingdom to descend to his seed for evermore. If it is not David's Psalm, or if this verse is a later addition, it becomes more difficult to decide about it, although even then we must acknowledge it as affording confirmatory proof of the national belief about him—of a doubtful age, indeed, but probably older than the time of Amos or Isaiah.

In the same sense we can alone understand words from the twenty-first and the sixty-first Psalms, both of which are ascribed to David: *He asked life of Thee, and Thou gavest it him, even length of days for ever and ever. Thou wilt prolong the king's life: and his years as many generations. He shall abide before God for ever.* This must surely mean that the life which could not in the course of nature be his should be prolonged in his posterity. It may be taken as contemporary evidence expressive of the prerogative of prosperity attaching to David.

The same may be said of the language of the

seventy-second Psalm, which, if not the work of David, is probably that of Solomon. Here the expectation expressed exceeds all natural bounds. It is said of the Prince of peace, who is to sit on David's throne, that *His name shall endure for ever; His name shall be continued as long as the sun, and men shall be blessed in Him; all nations shall call Him blessed.* This is probably not later than the commencement of the tenth or the close of the eleventh century before Christ. At that early time these extraordinary hopes had begun to cluster around the throne of David.

In the grand historical seventy-eighth Psalm, which is ascribed to Asaph, the contemporary of David, we have what may so far be regarded as independent evidence of the special right in virtue of which David was believed to reign: *He chose David also His servant, and took him from the sheep-folds . . . to feed Jacob His people, and Israel His inheritance.*

The two most remarkable Psalms, however, which bear most directly upon the supposed Davidic promise, are the eighty-ninth, ascribed to Ethan the Ezrahite, the contemporary of Asaph and Heman, and the hundred and thirty-second, which bears only the inscription, ' A song of degrees.' Each of these speaks in unmistakable terms of the oath that had been sworn unto David, from which the Lord would not shrink. Various dates have been assigned to these Psalms, from the age of David till after the return from captivity; and though in our judgment the former is far more probable, they at least show, on the other supposition, that at the latter date the national feeling with regard to David's house and throne was fully developed and mature. We have then a series of compositions extending from the age of David till possibly the return from captivity, or else from the age of David till the time of Isaiah, which must at all events be assigned to various writers who are unanimous as to the existence of some special honour or prerogative centred in David. It appears that he shared this belief himself, and it certainly can be traced to his age. In order, however, fully to understand the nature of the allusions made to him, it is necessary to refer to the history which is preserved to us in 2 Sam. vii. and 1 Chron. xvii. These narratives have this in common, that they are not at all likely to have grown out of either the eighty-ninth or the hundred and thirty-second Psalm. It is conceivable that either of these Psalms might have been a poetic version of the history; but that would necessitate the history being then in existence, which is perhaps more than would be granted, even though it may not be too much to assume. But, at all events, we are unable to explain the allusions in the Psalm, except by reference to the history, and there is no vestige of any history except that preserved to us in 2 Samuel and 1 Chronicles. But it is impossible to accept that history without admitting the operation of the supernatural to a degree that modern criticism cannot tolerate. What, then, is to be done? We must reduce, if possible, both history and Psalm alike to the limits of the merely natural. We must ascertain what it is in natural and modern language that is implied in Psalm and history. The attempt to reconstruct the history upon the basis of modern ideas has been undertaken by no feeble hand,* and with all the resources of an unlimited freedom of conjecture and hypothesis; but with what success? In no less than some eighty or ninety incidents we find our modern reconstructor drawing upon the existing records for his life of David without scruple, while he no less unscrupulously sets aside the entire principle upon which those records are framed. With marvellous ingenuity he applies the microscope of his self-consciousness and subjectivity to discover what the original writer does not express, in order that he may with the greater audacity ignore and overlook what he distinctly states. It must surely be by a misnomer that such a method of rewriting history is dignified and decorated by the epithet critical. If we are at liberty to make use of the records to such an extent as trustworthy, they surely deserve some credit when they vouch as they do for the operation of principles which the modern historian is at such pains to disregard.

It is doubtless possible in like manner to decline to perceive the operation of a Divine hand in the ordinary events of national or individual history. But this is exactly that which we all want to perceive

* Ewald's *History of Israel*, vol. iii., pp. 54—203, Eng. ed. See Note at the end of this Lecture.

if we can do so with truth and accuracy. Surely
there is no one of us who would not gladly and
thankfully know, if it were possible to ascertain, the
particular way in which the Divine hand has guided
us in the past, is guiding us in the present, where
it has interposed for our welfare, when we knew it
not, and where it has not less directly taught us
by leaving us to our own choice, in order that by
a late and too often bitter experience we might
learn the inevitable lesson. Could we but arrive at
authoritative knowledge upon such matters, it were
surely a boon to be desired. Now it seems to me
that the teacher who would eliminate from a professedly Divine history all the special elements of
the Divine, is acting like one who would eliminate
from ordinary human experience all the presumable
teaching and discipline of Divine providence. But
as a matter of fact, all the records of the Jewish
monarchy, without exception, and that not once, but
by continual iteration, represent the throne of David
as the inalienable heritage of him and his sons for
ever. And when we examine the entirely independent
evidence of the Psalms and prophets, we find the
expression of a like conviction, which seems to have
possessed the nation at large from a period coeval
with the rise of David's house. As it is clear that
nothing of the same kind is found to characterise
the house of Saul, but that, so to say, one effort
after monarchy seems to have satisfied the national
ambition, to the ideal of which in after times they
could never do more than recur, and could never

originate a fresh ideal; and as in no other history
is there anything like the kind of feeling to be discovered that is found to centre in the throne of
David, this is unquestionably an historical phenomenon that demands an explanation. Even if we
say that for some reason or other a profound conviction seized upon the national mind in relation
to David, and that this conviction expressed itself
in various ways, as we see it did in the national
literature and the national history, then there must
be some assignable reasons for the origin of this
conviction, there must be some discoverable cause
for its remarkable tenacity and depth. The history
and the literary monuments alike declare that the
reason for both was in the actual and express promise of God. The necessities of argument forbid us
to interpret such language literally; but certainly
if we reject the reason uniformly and consistently
assigned, then we are bound to suggest some other
which shall no less successfully account for all the
conditions implied. And beyond all doubt this has
not as yet been done, nor do we believe that it
ever will be done; but, on the contrary, we believe
that successive generations of men may point with
confidence to the known and obvious effects, literary
and historical, of the alleged promise to David, as
affording no slight evidence and confirmation of
some unknown and inexplicable reality underlying
and implied by that alleged promise. It is perfectly
true that we can have no merely natural proof of
the supernatural if we refuse to postulate something

beyond nature; but unquestionably the literary records of the Old Testament, both with regard to Abraham and to David, point us to the operation of unknown causes which defy all explanation if we decline to accept the possible operation of a Divine and superhuman, supernatural agency.

Hitherto we have been endeavouring to reason independently of any assumptions with regard to the documents of the Old Testament to which the most destructive criticism could demur. But if otherwise, the same conclusions are not really invalidated if we go yet further. Let us assume, for the sake of argument, that all the historical documents of the Old Testament are utterly untrustworthy, that none of the literary monuments can with certainty be referred to the writers whose names they bear. Then how do we stand with regard to a position so extreme, and we may add so monstrous? We stand thus. It admits of no shadow of doubt that the entire bulk of the Old Testament existed substantially and identically as we have it now, four hundred years before Christ. At that period, all, or at all events very nearly all the Scriptures that we now possess were not only written, but had assumed their existing form. The books of Moses were received as the veritable law given by him in the fifteenth century before Christ. The history existed as we have it now, in the same divisions, with the same names to the various books, with identically the same general features that we now discern. The Psalms were all collected and arranged as they are now, or at least

with a few small and unimportant differences whether
of text or of numeration; and the writings of the
prophets, if we grant, perhaps provisionally, the
possible exception of certain parts of Daniel, were
not only named and arranged as we have them now,
but presented the same well-known and characteristic features. These facts are mainly assured to us
by the existence of the Alexandrine version within
the first or the second century following, by certain
inferences suggested by the preface to Ecclesiasticus,
and more than all by the change of language which
in all probability took place in Palestine shortly after
the return from the captivity, when, therefore, it
would have been impossible for any man or for any
body of men in that company to have produced our
existing books. It follows, therefore, that in the
year 400 B.C., there was in existence a Hebrew Bible,
to all intents and purposes the same as that which
we now possess. Then in that Bible there were on
record—let us even suppose that they were a fabrication—certain promises to Abraham, standing exactly
as they stand now, and worded as they are now.
There were all the Psalms rightly or wrongly attributed
to David, to Asaph, to Ethan, to the sons of Korah,
and the like; there was the second Psalm verbally the
same as it is now, the sixteenth Psalm containing
the words quoted by Peter and by Paul on the day
of Pentecost, and in the synagogue at Antioch.
There was the same history of David, (if you please
an entire fabrication from beginning to end but for
all that) with identically the same features that we

have been now examining, the same professed selection of him in preference to Saul, the same declared
promise of perpetuity given to his house and throne,
the same extraordinary apparent revocation of it in
the case of his own grandson, for which, however,
verbal provision had been made in the terms of its
original grant.*   There was the same yet more remarkable and apparently utter failure of the promise
in the time of his latest royal descendant; there was,
nevertheless, the same distinct belief in the validity
of the original promise manifest in the people after
the captivity, which had characterised them before.
There were in the writings of the prophets the same
remarkable denunciations of future woe, which,
though indeed they might have been partly dictated
by the national experience as early as the fifth
century before our era, were nevertheless destined
to a far more striking and momentous fulfilment
hundreds and even thousands of years afterwards.
There were expressed in these writings the same deep
and ineradicable convictions that the God of Israel
was *de jure*, and would eventually become *de facto*,
the God of all the nations of the earth by the acknowledgment of adoration and submission; and
there were scattered up and down those writings
disjointed fragments, apparently the work of many
ages and of many minds, glimpses of an ideal por-

---

* 2 Sam. vii. 14, 15: " I will be to him a Father, and he shall be to
me a son, whom, if he commit iniquity, I will chasten with the rod
of men, and with the stripes of the children of men : but my mercy
shall not depart from him, as I took it away from Saul, whom I took
away from before thee."

traiture or character to which there was nothing that answered in the national history, and which yet was the absolutely unique and by far the most remarkable feature of the whole literature. I say there were all these elements patent and undeniable in the Jewish Scriptures of 400 B.C. What, then, on the supposition that the entire literature was fabricated, and fabricated as it must have been before that date, are we required to believe? Nothing less than this, that some unknown man, or since the broad divergence of style renders that hypothesis inconceivable, that a large body of unknown men agreed together to fabricate these remarkable documents, and to *inspire* them—I use the word designedly—to *inspire* and impress them with the particular features and characteristics, the particular elements and principles of spiritual truth, the apparent and mysterious insinuations and innuendos in which more is meant than meets the ear, to which I have referred, and which we cannot deny, are only too conspicuous in them. We have to believe that this was done with some undiscoverable and recondite motive, for under the circumstances there must have been a motive for the production of the result that as a matter of fact is produced; or, if there really was no motive, that then this was the chance and undesigned result of their purposeless lucubrations, a result which again, as a matter of fact, was not produced by the whole of the Greek and Roman literature combined, by the whole of the Hindoo literature combined, or by the whole of the Scandinavian literature combined. Is

this a conclusion which we can reasonably adopt as
on the whole more credible, more natural, more consonant with the laws of probability than the other
conclusion which after all has distinctly such evidence as exists, documentary and historic, in its
favour, namely, that the writings of the Old Testament, being as they are for the most part, speaking
generally, the genuine and authentic productions
they profess to be, were in some sense the natural,
though in another sense the no less supernatural,
productions of a most remarkable people; that they
are, to say the least, instinct with " startling originality," and that there are features characterising
them which defy our utmost ingenuity fully to account for, unless we postulate the operation of
another agency to which they professedly lay claim,
and to which unquestionably their distinctive phenomena seem to point ?

This fact then appears to be sufficiently plain,
that even if the Old Testament were a fabrication,
it must have been in existence four hundred years
before Christ, and in all material points in existence
as we have it now; and being so, its most peculiar
phenomena would be no more easy to account for
than on the supposition of its genuineness; clearly
therefore we gain nothing in this respect by shifting
its composition to the latest conceivable period. It
would in fact be more difficult to understand the
origin of these records as a fabrication, than to
suppose them to have been the gradual growth
of ages, and the work of their traditional authors.

Under all circumstances there would be evidence
that David's family and throne had been spoken of
in a very special and peculiar manner, which the
course of events had seemed to contradict rather
than to warrant. There would still remain all the
features of an apparent prophecy, all the foundation
ready at hand, upon which the superstructure of
an alleged apparent fulfilment might afterwards be
raised; and yet, from the circumstances of the case,
it is impossible that this could have been the purpose or object with which these writings were produced. Still the fact remains that they were produced,*
and therefore the only reasonable theory concerning
their production is that it was the gradual growth
of successive ages, from the fifteenth century to the
fifth century before Christ. During this period of a
thousand years there came into existence a national
literature, which cannot be assigned to less than

* If we suppose that the entire bulk of the history was the post-
captivity work of prophetical and priestly men, and the writings of
the canonical prophets the work of an earlier class of prophets from
the eighth century onwards, there still remain the distinguishing and
characteristic features of all those writings to be accounted for, and
the *possible* correspondence between them and the facts of the New
Testament, the acknowledgment of which correspondence, however,
is a matter of faith and converting grace, for *no man can say that
Jesus is the Lord* [Christ], *but by the Holy Ghost* (1 Cor. xii. 3).
The question is whether the theory of Kuenen is sufficient to account
for all the facts and phenomena of the Old Testament, and if, supposing it to be so, those of the New Testament can in like manner
be disposed of; if not, then the actual relation of the Old Testament
and the New, being what it is, is a fact that points us to the operation of the Divine will and the manifestation of the Divine purpose
in Jesus Christ.

some five-and-twenty or thirty different writers of
various ages, who wrote manifestly without collusion
or concert ; and the effects of their combined work
are what we see them now to be. We find in the
earliest book a distinct promise made to Abraham.
We find in the Psalms, the Prophets, and the historical books, indications of another promise made to
David. It is impossible to eradicate the tokens of
this latter promise from the existing monuments.
It is continually confronting us. There is no theory
that can adequately account for the indications of
this promise. We may not of course assume that
it was given, but we can most distinctly say that
had it been given, it would completely account for
all the indications that confront and perplex us,
as nothing else can account for them. Are we to
decide then that prophecy is a fact or a fiction?
As long as we stop at any period short of the
Christian era, it is only possible to decide that prophecy was *believed* to have been a fact; that there
was all the appearance in the records of very distinct
and definite promises; that these promises had been
persistently cherished, tenaciously clung to at various
periods, and for many ages; and that, though they
had never been abandoned, they had nevertheless
certainly not been fulfilled. This is as far as we
can go in the direction of proving the existence of
prophecy as a fact, in the cases we are now considering, at a period prior to the commencement
of the Christian era. But is it possible to have any
stronger proof short of absolute demonstration? We

have the existence of prophecy as a universal and persistent national belief; we have the *appearance* of it continually recurring in the several parts of a national literature; we have a variety of independent and necessarily undesigned coincidences and indications tending to establish and confirm the reality of that appearance; and we have the utter failure and complete inability of any theory to account sufficiently for the several phenomena as they exist, whatever may have been the actual circumstances under which the literature was produced. It becomes a question, therefore, whether we will accept the idea of Divine prophecy as the only adequate solution of the problem, or be content to leave it unsolved.

It remains, however, that we turn now to glance at another series of known facts. About thirty years after the birth of Christ, and after the national consciousness had acknowledged the cessation of prophecy for more than four hundred years, and after all the literary phenomena we possess had long been completed, there arose a man in the spirit and power of Elias, who declared that the mysterious kingdom of God, of which David and the psalmists had sung, and the prophets had spoken, was about to be revealed. He produced a profound impression on his age, the more remarkable because it was not himself to whom he directed the national attention, but another, in whom he declared the ancient prophecies found their meaning and were fulfilled. His ministry, as a matter of fact, was followed by another yet more remarkable, the ministry of One who not only took up the words of John, but announced Himself as the person of whom he spake, and as being at once the subject and the object of all ancient prophecy. This Person is admitted on all hands to have been the greatest moral teacher and the most perfect human character that the world has ever seen or literature ever invented. It is certain, however, that His recorded testimony concerning Himself in no degree falls short even of this high estimate, and it is equally certain that His death was mainly accelerated, if it was not entirely caused, by the persistency with which He maintained that He was the Christ of prophecy. It is certain, however, that while He persistently encouraged His disciples in their traditional belief in the ancient prophecies, He altogether revolutionised and reconstructed their conceptions of them. Nor can it be referred to any other cause than the influence of His teaching that we find His disciples after His supposed resurrection appealing to the ancient prophecies in an altogether enlarged and sublimated sense, by which they became enhanced in beauty, and even truer than before. Then it became manifest that the promise to David, if it had ever been a *Divine* promise at all, and exactly in proportion as the promise was God-given and from God, was not of any earthly and temporal, but of a heavenly and eternal kingdom—not of a changing and corruptible throne, but of one that was unchanging and incorruptible. *The sure mercies of David*, therefore, were mercies that could never

perish or pass away; not such as could be handed
on from sire to son, but such as would abide for
ever in the person of that son who he believed had
been promised to him, and for whom so many generations and ages waited. The contrast involved
throughout was one between corruption and incor-
ruption. There were wonderful words spoken by
David and by others, which, interpreted literally, went
to show that he and they had apprehended something
of that incorruptible and eternal spirit; and in whatever degree they had done so, they were the prophets
of the Most High; and in whatever degree their
prophecies had lent themselves to that interpretation,
they were not the offspring of their own minds, but
were prompted and inspired by the Holy Ghost.

This was their contention: the high argument and
contention of the apostles of Christ. Nor was it
either weak or vain. As no collusion had of old
produced the writings of the prophets, so no collusion or juggling on the part of the first disciples
had corrupted those writings, or had given them a
meaning which they would not bear. The words
to which they appealed had been there for ages;
they were known to have been there. If they ever
had been true at all, they were truer now than ever,
for their truth was revealed in Christ. If Christ
was indeed risen from the dead, if His own claims
concerning Himself were true, then He had demon-
strated the truth of prophecy; He had established
and confirmed its reality as an historic fact. It is
only as we refuse to acknowledge the Divine element

in prophecy that we reduce it to an inexplicable phenomenon, which is neither of heaven nor yet of earth, and are unable to account for it as it is. On the other hand, it is only as we admit that element that the actual phenomenon becomes intelligible, and the way is prepared for the stupendous results that were produced by prophecy, centuries after it had ceased, and for the gigantic edifice of the Christian Church, which was reared upon the sand, if it was not based upon the solid rock of an actual and antecedent Divine revelation. Undoubtedly the idea of any such preparation compels us to postulate the exercise and operation of the Divine foreknowledge. But if prophecy is a fact, it is the communication and expression of that foreknowledge, while assuredly the communication would seem to have been all the more authentic because the lapse of ages had declared that the promises had been fulfilled in a way far higher and more glorious than those who received them had anticipated. But if the appearance of man upon the earth was not till after long cycles of un-recorded time had fitted and prepared it for his habitation, although no eye was present to watch the process, and no voice existed to record it, how much more may we believe that the birth of the true Man, the crown and summit of human nature as man himself is of the works of God, could not take place, did not take place, till His coming had been prepared for by the long succession of promise, psalm, and prophecy which the Scriptures of the Old Testament present. We may, indeed, deny the

force of the teleological argument in the one case;
it is yet more patent in the other; and though the
earth, as the dwelling-place of man, bears witness
of long-continued preparation, we may say it was
not for *man* that it was prepared; but in view of the
preparation that is apparent in history, psalm, and
prophecy, we can only conclude that it was for the
advent of the Son of man that men's minds required
to be disciplined and taught, as they were subjected
to the education of long-continued and often baffled
hope and expectation; and that He who chose this
method of teaching and preparing them for the
advent of the Saviour of the world, the King of men
and the Prince of peace, was none other than the
Holy Spirit of God, who spake by the prophets.

NOTE TO LECTURE VI.

To take, for instance, one passage as a sample of many :—

" If we understand by this narrative (1 Sam. xv. 35—xvi. 13) that David was openly anointed king, with his own knowledge and that of his kinsfolk, it is difficult to conceive how either he or they could all remain so totally unconcerned, and how he could visit Saul's court with a clear conscience. [!]   But, according to the true significance of the narrative, although Samuel anoints him with his spirit, and knows what this means in the sight of God (the result, moreover, showing itself at once in the influence of the Holy Spirit), yet, as far as outward appearances go, he simply chooses him as his closest companion and friend in the sacrifice (comp. 1 Sam. ix. 22) without publishing aloud that the anointing has any further significance: but if, as the history developes itself, the truth is divined by one or two, such as Jonathan (xx. 13, xxiii. 17) and Abigail (1 Sam. xxv. 30), that is all the better.   The advent of higher life which prefaces the whole history is thus at the beginning loosely attached to what follows ; for the sequel, though developing itself quite in accordance with the introduction, yet implies that neither the young hero himself nor any one else knew all from the beginning, so as to be compromised by it.   The development of the subsequent history advances, accordingly, even if we set aside this previous revelation of the Divine destiny of the great hero, quite intelligibly in itself. It seems undeniable, even from a more strictly historical point of view, that Samuel had a most powerful influence over David (as the extant records of an early narrator know of at least one visit of David to Samuel at the time of his flight from Saul, 1 Sam. xix. 18— xx. 1), and also, that long before he was king over all Israel, David received prophetic intimations of his future greatness (compare 2 Sam. iii. 18, v. 2; prophets such as Gad were with him from an early period, 1 Sam. xxii. 5); but it is quite as clear that the narrative of the anointing of David by Samuel simply forms a lofty introduction to the whole history, and can be rightly estimated only in the light of the pure Divine truth which it embodies, and the lesson involved in it, which is drawn out clearly by the whole history " (History of Israel, vol. iii., Eng. Tr., pp. 66, 67).

Now on this we have to remark, (1.) that from history it is evident that neither Jonathan nor Abigail could have divined that David should be king, unless there had been something external in his history and circumstances pointing to this fact, besides his mere natural fitness and personal qualifications; and if they both were conscious of this something, it is the more likely to have been a reality; and that if there was this consciousness in David of his future destiny, it did not, as a matter of fact, hinder him from visiting Saul's court with a clear conscience, nor would it have done so if he saw in it the work of God's election, and not merely his own advantage, as he is always represented as seeing. (2.) There is no evidence whatever that the anointing in David's case meant nothing more than Samuel's choosing him as his closest companion and friend in the sacrifice, or even that the sacrifice was completed (xvi. 5—13). At all events, in Saul's case, the anointing was *subsequent* to the sacrifice, if such it was (1 Sam. ix. 22, x. 1), and in neither his case nor David's could have been confounded with it. By all means let us evolve the latent lessons of the narrative, but let us not ignore those on the surface, nor set them aside in favour of others we fancy we can read. One would imagine from the way in which Ewald writes, that no one had ever understood the narrative before. (3.) David was by no means compromised by what he knew, but was exposed to all the greater trial of faith in consequence of it, even as the Son of David was not compromised by His knowledge that He was the Son of God, but under the higher obligation to act as the Son of man. (4.) There is an impenetrable haze connected with Ewald's use of the words—God, divine, prophetic, and the like. Is there anything real in these words, or are they only forms of speech, jugglers' counters? The history is written, and so we read it, on the supposition that these words represent realities, and if they do, no critical manipulation, like that of Ewald's, will ever satisfy all the conditions of the problem involved.

In like manner, Kuenen tells us (p. 437) :—" This anointing of David by the prophet cannot be regarded as an actual occurrence. . . . his position at the court of Saul becomes false and unbearable, if from the very beginning he had to regard himself as a pretender (!) to the crown. . . . In the narrative with which we are engaged we neither see, nor may see, anything else than the palpable expression of the prophetical view of the manner in which Jahveh directs the fortunes of his people. It is no testimony regarding Samuel the prophet, but the garb in which a prophetical conviction is arrayed " (p. 438).

This theory still leaves unsolved the question What was the particular nucleus of *fact* which gave birth to Psalms like the 89th and 132nd, and Whence the allusions in Amos and Isaiah which imply a fact; and this is a question that inevitably suggests itself, but one also that it is by no means easy to answer adequately and satisfactorily.

Amos v. 25—27.—*Have ye offered unto me sacrifices and offerings in the wilderness forty years, O house of Israel? But ye have borne the tabernacle of your Moloch and Chiun your images, the star of your god, which ye made to yourselves. Therefore will I cause you to go into captivity beyond Damascus, saith the Lord, whose name is The God of Hosts.*

LECTURE VII.

THE THREATENED CAPTIVITY.

HITHERTO I have endeavoured to show that there are sundry features in the writings of the Old Testament which are of such a character that, when they are viewed in relation to events which happened long afterwards, it is impossible to deny that they receive an amount of unexpected illustration which is at once novel, striking, and unique. The notion that these features were previously moulded by the several writers with a view to any such collocation is wholly precluded by the date of the various writings, which, however uncertain, is known to be far too early for this. The notion also that the events themselves were in any way directed by natural or human agency so as to produce this correspondence, or the record of them modified so as to exhibit it, is inconceivable, because on the one hand it is beyond the compass of merely human power so to order events, and on the other because those who recorded them in this case were not the persons likely to adopt or invent such a method of modification, nor were the means resorted to likely to bring about the end desired. We are therefore constrained either to deny the alleged correspondence, which is not possible, or the significance of it, which is hardly less reasonable; or else to admit that the special features of it are not to be explained or accounted for on merely natural principles.

This is, of course, the broad and general statement of a very complex argument, the several parts of which may admit of considerable discussion, and the conclusion of which can only be allowed on one condition—namely, that we become *believers*. But that is the very point for which I contend, and I am the more willing to allow the utmost liberty of discussion because I feel sure that the issue of this argument thus broadly stated can be but one. It is precisely in this way that God has set landmarks for all time in the demesnes of literature and history, that may testify to His having wrought in them so as to lead us to the conclusion of faith, *This is the Lord's doing; and it is marvellous in our eyes.** We are well aware of the infinite variety of subterfuges by which the human mind will seek to avoid this conclusion, but for all that it may be, and we believe is, the only conclusion consistent alike with reason, justice, and the promise of life.

In pursuance of the method thus indicated, I have dwelt at large on the two instances of the words alleged to have been spoken to Abraham, and of the promise made to David. In the former case I showed that however we regard the narrative, it alone ac-

* Psalm cxviii. 23.

counts* for the known history of Israel, and therefore
supplies an indestructible foundation for the conclusions afterwards to be based upon it; and in the
latter we found so many traces in the literature and
history pointing to the influence of that promise as
to make it virtually impossible to doubt its existence.
But if so, then we not only have an instance of something that afterwards was turned to a prophetic
purpose and use, but strong evidence likewise in the
national literature of the exercise and operation of
a faculty in the nation which has the appearance of
prophetic and even of predictive power. It is to be
observed that the reality of this latter function is
entirely distinct from that of any other office of subsequently testifying to such a person as the Messiah.
It is conceivable that the royal line of David may
have been the recipients of Divine promises which
began and ended in themselves, and had no further
reference. Such promises might still have been real,
or on the other hand promises so given might con-
ceivably have had a meaning that the lapse of many
ages would alone reveal. In either case we might
acknowledge the operation of a more than human—of

* If we suppose with Kuenen that the history is merely the reflex
and expression of the national conviction of Israel, then that hypothesis leaves unsolved the very large question of the causes and
origin of that conviction which, when regarded in its nature and consequences, is still a unique phenomenon in history demanding a sufficient
explanation. Can any explanation be given more appropriate than
the one of old, *He sheweth his word unto Jacob, his statutes and ordi-
nances unto Israel. He hath not dealt so with any nation: and as for
his judgments, they have not known them. Praise ye the Lord.—*
Psalm cxlvii. 19, 20.

a Divine power, and there is reason to believe that with respect to David and the promise made to him, we have cause to acknowledge this twofold function ; but at all events the endeavour to establish the existence of prophecy as a fact must receive material aid in proportion as we can show traces of the existence and operation of such a power being felt and acknowledged among the people at the time, and impressing itself indelibly on the monuments of their literature. And such traces there seem to be in the various phenomena of the promise made to David and its effects.

With a view to the further illustration of this matter I proceed now to the consideration of another series of prophecies, in which one only of the two functions above mentioned is displayed—those, namely, which have reference to that marked feature in the national history of Israel which is known as the captivity. Supposing such prophecies to have been really uttered, and supposing that there is sufficient evidence to show that they existed and were on record prior to the event, I am not aware that it is possible or desirable to invest them with any ulterior Messianic significance. This is rather a case in which the prophecies, if they really existed, began and ended, so to say, in themselves and their immediate reference. The question is, What is the evidence that they really existed, and what are the consequences which flow from that evidence ? The determination of this question will affect the main argument in this way: the establishment of the existence of prophecy

as a fact will be more conclusive if we can adduce
contemporary evidence of its operation. If there is
proof of a supernatural predictive power at work in
the age of its supposed operation, we shall then
know that we are the less likely to be wrong in attributing to that power in certain cases the utterance
of words whose full and mature significance was not
revealed till many ages after they were uttered. Our
understanding of the nature of prophecy is often
clouded by a misconception of its necessary conditions. It is by no means necessary to suppose that
the prophet had a full and complete cognizance of
the circumstances under which his own words would
receive their ultimate fulfilment.* On the other
hand, we may almost affirm in many cases that it is
obviously impossible that he can have known them.
It is, perhaps, more than probable that David looked
no further than himself and his son Solomon for the

---

* Kuenen is continually seeking to disprove what he calls "the
foreknowledge of the prophets" (see *e.g.* 305, etc.), but this in truth
is not the point, but rather whether they were commissioned as special
agents of the Most High to make known His will, and whether their
words are not stamped with an impress which distinguishes their
utterances as a record of the Divine foreknowledge. And this, as it
seems to us, is undeniable in a multitude of cases. That it may not
be so in absolutely all cases is conceivable for various reasons, and by
no means invalidates the soundness of our position.

It is not, however, to be forgotten by those who acknowledge the
authority of Holy Scripture, that St. Peter expressly attributes "foreknowledge" to David, and that in a case in which "critics" would
unquestionably deny it. Acts ii. 30 ; cf. also ver. 23, where the same
speaker traces the existence and operation of God's "foreknowledge"
acting concurrently with the blindness and perversity of man's self-
will.

realisation of many of the hopes that the Divine promise had awakened in him. But it is precisely here that we detect the working of the Divine mind and the pre-arrangement and scheme of a Divine plan,— the evidence that prophecy was not a human device or delusion, but a Divine endowment, in that oftentimes no human intelligence could have anticipated the result which nevertheless, more nearly than any other, seems to have given the meaning that was intended to *the words of the wise and their dark sayings.** Prophecy is not to be regarded as a string of isolated and detached sentences, each of which had one definite meaning and no other, but much rather as a consistent and composite whole, which must be dealt with as a whole and interpreted as a whole.† When we so deal with it our difficulty is not to discover here and there marks of something unusual and more than human, but to shut our eyes to the broad, patent and innumerable indications which

* Proverbs i. 6.

† To admit the organic unity of prophecy is of course to go a very long way towards acknowledging its Divine origin, for only by a process of Divine superintendence and Divine supervision could the works of various writers in various ages form an organic whole, and therefore it is perhaps too much to assume this as a matter of course. And yet surely it must be self-evident that there is a unity in the canonical prophets which is totally distinct from anything of the kind to be found in the literature of Greece or Rome. And this unity consists in their common hope for the future, which becomes brighter and fuller and clearer: wider and yet more distinct and definite, as the stream of prophecy rolls on. Compare, for example, the progression from Hosea, Joel, and Amos, to Micah, Zechariah, and Malachi: and Why was this progression such as would allow of the Christian application made of it and to correspond therewith?

confront us everywhere of one vast design never lost sight of, never forgotten, but continually unfolding itself, continually expanding, and yet also continually contracting and converging, till it centres in one object, which gathers in itself all the many-coloured rays to reflect them again in multitudinous directions and a variety of forms. In fact, it is this feature and characteristic of the prophetic writings which is the most permanent and indestructible. After every individual prophecy has been dealt with separately, with an exhaustive and inexhaustible array of minute and ruthless criticism far more than sufficient to demolish it utterly were it not for an inherent principle of deathless vitality common to all, one has only to open the writings of the prophets to feel that they have been endowed with gifts of immortality and truth of which no criticism can deprive them. It is not what has been or can be said about them which is their strength, but much rather what they say for themselves and have been saying for five-and-twenty centuries. The danger is lest amid the din of discussion and the strife of tongues we should fail to hear what they say themselves, but if we hearken to it we need have no apprehension as to the result.

Take, for example, the prophecy of Amos, in the fifth chapter, *I will cause you to go into captivity beyond Damascus, saith the Lord, whose name is the God of hosts.** It is allowed to have been written soon after the commencement of the eighth century before our era, while Jeroboam the son of Joash was

* v. 27.

on the throne of Israel—during the period, that is, of its greatest magnificence and prosperity, some fifty years perhaps before the doom pronounced was executed. But it is not on the clear and unmistakable character of the prediction as a mere prediction that I would lay stress. Let it be granted that a thoughtful and far-seeing eye could detect under the outward splendour of the Israelitish throne the sure signs of approaching decay, could discern in the vast empire, rapidly growing on the shores of the Tigris and Euphrates, the destined conqueror and captivator of his nation.* This accounts only for one-half of the prophet's character, and that the most natural and human part. It has still to be explained how, being, as he was, the child of agri-

* Of course it is possible to see in the history of Israel no trace of a Divine hand—to maintain that when Israel went into captivity, it was a mere accident or incident in the natural development of human history. We should claim for it something more than that. But who shall prove such a view to be the true one? If, however, there was special Divine dealing in this episode of Israelitish history, would not that be consistent with the manifestation of the Divine will in prophecy, and will not our estimate of the one vary precisely with our estimate of the other?

It is prophecy only which enables us to understand the history. If we insist on our own interpretation of the history, how is it possible we should accept God's interpretation in prophecy? They stand or fall together.

"Our inquiry is in fact concerned with the very question, whether the asserted immediate intervention of Jahveh in the guidance of Israel's fortunes can be considered as historical or not."—Kuenen, p. 400.

The theory we maintain is that the record of God's dealings with Israel is so authoritative as to make it a sufficient standard for mankind, and prophecy is at once the key to its interpretation and the proof of its authority.

cultural labour, he should have found himself the
subject of a mission to the king and the nation;
how all his denunciations and threatenings took the
form, as they did, of moral rebuke and remonstrance;
how even the prospect of royal displeasure and persecution should have failed to shake his resolve,
though it is hard even to surmise any ulterior motive
of personal advantage that could have swayed him;
and how, finally, from first to last, he should have
felt himself empowered and authorised to adopt a
form of words so tremendously solemn as *Thus saith
the Lord, whose name is the God of hosts.** It is

* According to Kuenen, the prophets were not deceivers, but were
self-deceived—the victims of their own moral earnestness and religious
conviction (see p. 363).

The holiness of God and His hallowing of Israel were their
foundation principles, and His righteousness as manifested in the
dispensing of national and material blessings and calamities their
perpetual theme.   Their habit of prediction also is to be traced to
the same source, and regarded "as a result of the religious conviction
of the prophets" (*Ibid*).

But "while paying homage to the *earnestness* of the prophet's
conception of the righteousness of Jahveh, we must positively deny
its *truth*. We do so on the ground of experience; for experience,
in the most unequivocal manner, contradicts the assertion that the
outward fortune, either of a nation or of the individual, is determined
by the moral condition of the one or the other. It teaches that God
causes His sun to rise on the good and the bad, and sends rain on
the just and the unjust. That the sword, the famine, the noisome
beast, or the pestilence, should spare the pious and strike the godless
—of such a condition of things experience knows nothing—absolutely
nothing" (p. 354).

Strange that a progressive and partial revelation must perforce
be regarded as no revelation at all, and that the uniformity of God's
natural government is to disprove the reality of His moral and
providential government! (Cf. Matt. v. 45 and vii. 11, etc.)

this combination of features, which is more or less common to him with all the prophets, which gives the special significance to their mission, raising them altogether out of the category of ordinary self-styled prophets, and investing them with characteristics that are special and unique, and that require some other explanation than the facile and ready one which would include them in the terms of a classification to which they present the only exception, and which fairly and utterly fails when applied to them. What are the best and most striking instances of answers given by the Delphic oracle compared with the recorded prophecies of the sixteen Hebrew prophets? What is all the pomp and circumstance of Roman augury compared with the severe simplicity of these patriot champions of truth? Any method of induction which demands to sweep them all into one general heap and then base its conclusions on the heterogeneous mass, must stand self-condemned for the rashness and undiscriminating ignorance of the course pursued, and because it involves a radical error which must inevitably vitiate all its results.

If it were not for the inexorable requirements of the task imposed upon ourselves, which forbids us making assumptions as to the date of books which may not be universally granted, we might show that not improbably the prediction of Amos found its origin and prototype in the law of Moses, in the fierce denunciations poured out upon the people in Leviticus and Deuteronomy, if they should not fear the glorious

and terrible name of the Lord their God.*   In that
case the prophet would be but carrying out a far-
reaching plan which had its commencement in the
Law; but however this may be, no one will deny to
Amos the clear assertion of a captivity hanging over
Israel in the future.   And there is no cause to doubt
that this prophecy was uttered in the reign of
Jeroboam the Second, even as that cognate one
which was spoken apparently a little later, *Israel
shall surely go into captivity forth of his land,*† and
was addressed to the king himself; and a point
which does not seem to have been considered with
the full importance due to it is assuredly to be
discerned in the fact, which no one disputes, that
these prophecies were put on record.‡   It is even
conceivable that they might have been spoken, and
then have passed away, like so many other winged
words of which no trace remains; but in this case
it was otherwise.   They were, for some reason or
other, committed to writing in the eighth century §

---

* Deut. xxviii. 58.   † Amos vii. 17.

‡ This is the more remarkable when we bear in mind the great
number of persons who exercised the prophetic office whose existence
only is implied, while no trace of their work remains.   What was
the relation of the canonical prophets to those others?   Why is it
these alone whose writings remain to us, and why are they canonical?
We find no answer to these questions in Kuenen.   Is canonicity the
mere arbitrary verdict of the Jewish Church, or is it not rather itself
the necessary consequence of a fact?

§ This is not, indeed, denied (see Kuenen, p. 150): but at the
same time I am at a loss to know how it is to be proved, if all our
records are of post-captivity date (see Kuenen, p. 416); or why it
is assumed, if the records themselves in other respects are not to be
trusted.

before Christ, most probably by Amos himself, or with his authority, for they are accepted as genuine; and having been so preserved, their message and meaning is imperishable. It is, however, not only imperishable, but likewise unmistakable. Here we have a deliberate assertion in the name of God, made by one who was plainly recognised as holding a certain office (for Amaziah, the priest of Bethel, called him *seer*), uttered, moreover, in the presence of the king and in defiance of his power, and affecting the very existence of their common nation. This prediction was preserved, and after king and prophet both had passed away it was found to vindicate itself, and we now are witnesses to its truth. A few more kings of brief duration sat on the throne of Israel, and then came the hosts of Shalmaneser and carried off the nation of Israel into final and hopeless captivity. As to the mere matter of correspondence between the words recorded and the subsequent issue of events in this case, there is and can be no dispute.* It is too notorious and patent

---

* Kuenen's representation of the matter is as follows: "If, however, the question is asked whether the prophet had formed to himself a clear conception of the realisation of this threatening which agreed with the subsequent reality, we must return an answer in the negative" (p. 152). Mainly because he nowhere names the Assyrians who conquered Samaria about eighty years afterwards, whereas he imagined the time to be close at hand (vii. 17); and because he has not abandoned the hope that Israel may be brought to repentance (v. 14, 15). "If the prophet is in earnest in what he says here—and how can we have any doubt of his sincerity?—then he can have had no *certainty* with regard to the future course of Israel's fortunes, though it be true that, for the most part, he does not venture to

to be called in question. All we can do is to deny
that it affords us any clear case of fulfilment. The
correspondence may be accidental. It is perhaps
possible to find some parallel cases* hardly less
striking, but better calculated to direct our judgment
in the matter for the simple reason that they have
never been suspected of being charged with any
supernatural meaning. Or more likely still, it will
be quite possible to show that the prophet uttered
other predictions with no less assurance, but of whose
fulfilment no record has been preserved. Take, for
instance, this very denunciation addressed to the king.
It was accompanied with the threat of personal
chastisements no less tremendous, of which, however, we know no more than that they expired for
the time on the prophet's tongue : *Thus saith the
Lord, Thy wife shall be an harlot in the city, and
thy sons and thy daughters shall fall by the sword,
and thy land shall be divided by line, and thou*

hope, and scarcely doubts any longer, that the extreme inflictions which
he from time to time anew depicts are indispensable." We are not
concerned to maintain that Amos had formed to himself a clear
conception of what he threatened, but that he had an unclouded
conviction of the authority with which he spake, and that this
conviction was based in *fact*,—which is what Kuenen will not allow.
According to him the prophet's commission began and ended with
himself. This is not strictly speaking, and ultimately, the subject of
proof. In either case there must be a substratum of faith. Kuenen
believes it did ; I believe it did not. The question is whose belief is
most consistent with *all* the facts before and afterwards.

* See, for example, those suggested by the Dean of Westminster,
in his *Lectures on the Jewish Church*, vol. i., p. 468, which, however,
have been adequately disposed of by Dr. Pusey, *Daniel the Prophet*,
p. 637 sq.

*shalt die in a polluted land.** Are we to argue
from the accidental silence of history here, and to
say that as we do not know that these particulars
came true they were not improbably unfulfilled, and
that therefore, as the prophet's predictions were unverified in the one case, their apparent fulfilment
must be held to go for nothing in the other? This
would, indeed, be a method of criticism that would
be most uncritical. It would surely be more reasonable to infer that, because the denunciations were
recorded and preserved, the jealous watchfulness of
contemporary observation could discover no dis-
crepancy between the record and the history of
events. At all events, the same possibility of suspicion does not attach to the case in point. We
have, then, to deal with a distinct assertion that
Israel should go into captivity. This was not only
declared, but the declaration was committed to
writing. It was made publicly before the nation and
in the face of the royal family. The effect produced
by it at the time was correspondent with its intrinsic
importance, for the prophet was accused of high
treason, and *the land*, it was said, was *not able to
bear his words*. It is plain, therefore, that the
circumstances of the prophet's mission were such
as to lend weight to the prophet's words. They
were at all events not treated with contempt. It
was felt that there was in them a force and solemnity
not derived from him or his antecedents. This was
an evidence that they woke a response in the con-

<hr>

* Amos vii. 17.

science of the people. And the reason was not far
to seek. For the whole basis of the prophet's
denunciations was laid in the charge of national
idolatry: *Ye have borne the tabernacle of your
Moloch and Chiun your images, the star of your
God, which ye made to yourselves. Therefore I will
cause you to go into captivity beyond Damascus, saith
the Lord, whose name is the God of hosts.** It was
because they had broken the Divine covenant, because
having been the recipients of a Divine revelation
they had nevertheless chosen to make gods for
themselves after their own devices, that judgment
was to go forth against them. The national punishment was to be on account of the national sin. But
there was no national sin in this respect if there
had not been any Divine covenant with the nation—
if there had not been, that is, any Divine revelation
vouchsafed and entrusted to the nation. If the
supposed relation of the people to their God, as
attested by the earlier literature, was only the fiction
of their own imagination, where was the enormity
alleged in violating it? There was no departure
from the truth involved in so doing, but only the
exchange of one delusion for another. And yet as
a matter of fact, steeped as the people were in
idolatry and its brutalising effects, they nevertheless
shrank before the threat of national punishment that
was to overtake the national sin. The national conscience pleaded guilty to the sin when confronted
with the shadow of the punishment. In other words,

<hr>

* Amos v. 26, 27.

the foundation of the prophet's message was laid in the moral sense of the people. In spite of themselves they were witnesses to the truth of it. The remorseless and irresistible current of events soon testified to the actual truth of the prophetic denunciations, and that in a way which will last for ever; but the question is to what was that truth owing? Is it merely to be regarded as an instance of natural illumination, or has it any claim to be reckoned as supernatural? That is to say, was the prophet informed by special communication from the Divine mind of the special intentions of the Divine will? or did he merely guess and guess rightly what they were? He may have done so, but then I conceive there is an end to any claim that can be preferred for a really Divine mission entrusted to him. On the contrary, there was falsehood mingled with the very foundation of his assumed mission. The solemn asseveration *saith the Lord whose name is the God of hosts* becomes not only unmeaning, but blasphemous. While he was invoking the name of the Lord his God to attest the reality of what he threatened, he was violating one of the first principles of the Divine Law. He was taking the name of the Lord his God in vain even while rebuking the nation for their idolatry. He was charging them with the breach of the first two commandments while he himself was breaking the third. This is the dilemma in which we find ourselves, if we refuse to recognise the inherent features of the supernatural in the various circumstances of the prophet's mission.

It may of course be asked, and not without some show of success, How are we to conceive of any Divine communication being actually imparted to the prophet's mind? But it may perhaps be accepted as a sufficient answer to reply: It is not more difficult to understand or conceive of illumination on the subject of a future historic event like that of the national captivity being conveyed supernaturally to the prophet's mind than it is to accept the reality of any Divine covenant subsisting between God and the nation of which the knowledge, distinct, definite, and unmistakable, was imparted to the nation. And yet we find this same prophet declaring, *You only have I known of all the families of the earth: therefore I will punish you for all your iniquities.** And it may be presumed that there was a certain response in the national conscience to the truth of this indictment. At all events, the very form of it warrants us in implying no less.

But how was it that Israel believed that the relation between God and His people was a unique relation among all the families in the earth? The context of the same passage supplies the answer. Because He had *brought up the whole family of Israel out of the land of Egypt.*† The witness of the national history was notorious and unimpeachable. God had espoused His people to Himself in that memorable episode. The reception of the Law as the token and memorial of those espousals could not fade from the

---

* Amos iii. 2.   † Amos iii. 1.

national recollection. There had been a channel of intercourse established between the Most High and His people; their knowledge of the moral Law as *His* Law was the proof of it. That very law itself was based on the revelation of Him: *I am the Lord thy God, which brought thee out of the land of Egypt, and out of the house of bondage. Thou shalt have none other gods but me.** Unless the Person thus speaking had revealed Himself, there was no meaning in any covenant with Him. Nor could the covenant be known unless He had spoken.

How it is possible for Him to speak is not for us to decide. But the decision of that abstract question involves other considerations than those which are immediately concerned with the endeavour rightly to weigh the evidence on which it is to be decided. The denial of the fact that God has spoken involves also virtually the denial of those faculties to man which would enable him to hear His voice if He were to speak. If we have no spiritual faculties capable of holding intercourse with our Maker who is a Spirit, then it is of course useless debating the question whether or not there is sufficient evidence of His having spoken. But it is this evidence, and this alone, with which we have to deal. Not only Scripture as a whole, but pre-eminently the writings of the prophets, come to us at once as a proof of the existence of such faculties in man, and also as vouchers for the reality and genuineness of the message with which these documents are fraught.

* Exodus xx. 2, 3.

Our immediate concern, therefore, is with the just
estimate of this evidence, and not with the preliminary questions whether and how it is possible
for it to exist. Suffice it, therefore, to say that we
believe the origin of the words now under consideration is revealed and witnessed by the words
themselves. The ultimate proof of the revelation
is in the thing revealed.* At all events, we can
have no moral relations to a person who has
not made known himself nor told us what those
relations are. And in order that God may thus
make known Himself, and establish moral relations
with us on a solid and secure basis, He must speak
to us, He must reveal Himself, whatever difficulties
that may involve for which we are not now prepared
to account. But if He does this at all, there is
surely no way in which He can do it more worthy
of Him than by the revelation of a moral law of
which the very foundation principle must be alle-
giance to Himself. But no sooner is this done than
a covenant is established, which has its root in the
unseen and the supernatural, and for the breach
of that covenant those who are admitted to it must
be responsible. This, according to the ancient

* The further consideration and discussion of the question here
touched upon, inevitable and important as it is in relation to the
whole argument, is too wide and extensive in its bearings to be adequately disposed of in this place. by the way. For a more complete
and thorough investigation of the entire subject, which really lies at
the foundation of the theory not only of prophecy but also of revelation at large. the reader is referred to Note D, at the end of this
volume, on " The Credentials of Revelation."

prophets, was the position of Israel, and this was
the ground of their denunciations, and this was the
source of their moral and predictive knowledge; but
the streams were co-ordinate, and the source of both
identical.

LECTURE VIII.

IT is not doubted that this is a genuine utterance of the prophet Micah, who is stated to have prophesied in the days of Jotham, Ahaz, and Hezekiah. Like the prophecy we last considered, it in no way relates to the Messiah, but concerns the future of the nation. It admits, therefore, of being tested by subsequent history, and may serve also, in some degree, to show how the declarations of the prophets were regarded in their own day. For though in the writings of Micah himself we have no such indication, yet there is this remarkable feature about this prophecy, that it is expressly alluded to in a later book. About a hundred years afterwards, in the reign of Jehoiakim, the prophet Jeremiah had expaserated the people by declaring that the Temple should be like Shiloh, and the city should be desolate without an inhabitant; whereupon *the priests and the prophets and all the people took him, saying, Thou shalt surely die.** Howbeit, certain of the elders of the land rescued him by quoting the example of

* Jer. xxvi. 8.

10

Micah the Morasthite, who prophesied in the days of
Hezekiah the words of the present text, and the
conduct of the king, who did not put him to death,
but on the contrary feared *the Lord, and besought the
Lord*, so that *the Lord repented Him of the evil
which He had pronounced against* * the nation. We
have, then, the very remarkable fact that the age and
genuineness of a particular prophecy are established
incidentally beyond all possibility of doubt from its
being referred to by way of precedent a century afterwards. At that time, also, it is plain that it was
recognised as a Divine communication and appealed
to as a Divine oracle.† It is of these words that
Professor Kuenen observes that "they were quoted
by the elders of Judah exactly in the same sense in
which they had been recorded by Micah. The elders
of Judah also judged correctly on this point," he
continues, "that Micah speaks of a judgment which
should befall Jerusalem *in the reign of Hezekiah*."
And further, that "the reproach addressed to the
chief men of Jerusalem that the city would be
changed into a ruinous heap *for their sake* makes
us hesitate to ascribe to Micah the idea that this
destiny would not overtake Jerusalem till a considerable time, about a hundred and fifty years
afterwards." Now, here it is to be observed that
Micah is silent about the times and the seasons. He
says nothing as to the when or the how : all that he
says, however, is perfectly explicit as to the fact. It

---

* Verse 19.

† *The Prophets and Prophecy in Israel*, p. 163, Eng. edit.

is entirely gratuitous,* to imply that he expected his
words to be fulfilled in the reign of Hezekiah.　Of
this we know nothing.　It is, indeed, only natural
to suppose that in proportion as he was believed to
be really speaking in the name and by the authority
of the Lord the men of his own time would be appre-
hensive that the judgments threatened would overtake them shortly, but we are not at liberty to import
their apprehensions into the literal meaning of the
prophet's words.†　All we have to do as critics is
to take their words as we find them, and to examine
what they say and to inquire what the sequel of them
was.　We entirely reject the notion that the personal
intelligence of the prophets is in every case the suffi-

---

* Equally groundless and unreasonable is the remark: " It is
evident that Micah's threatening had made a deep impression and
had not been forgotten above a century afterwards in the capital of
Judah, which certainly would not have been the case if other prophets
had announced the same judgment before him or along with
him " (p. 162).

And yet seventy or eighty years before Amos had said, ii. 5, " I will
send a fire upon Judah and it shall devour the palaces of Jerusalem,"
and he only echoed the words of Hosea, viii. 14, " Judah hath
multiplied fenced cities ; but I will send a fire upon his cities, and it
shall devour the palaces thereof,"—if indeed, as seems probable, this
was the original and earlier prophecy.　Kuenen places Hosea later
(p. 153).

† Neither may we infer with Kuenen that " the narrative of
Jeremiah shows us that his contemporaries applied the prediction of
Micah—not to events which were then, in Jehoiakim's reign (608—
597 B.C.) still future; but to disasters which would have befallen
Jerusalem at a much earlier period if the threatening had not been
recalled at the prayer of Hezekiah " (p. 162, see also p. 334); for
they may have misapprehended the true nature and Divine intention
of the prophecy no less than many of our modern critics.

cient measure of the significance of their own words.
If that could in every case be clearly assertained,
which it cannot, it would still be found incomplete
and inadequate. The prophets have left on record
certain writings which on certain points, as those for
instance of the captivity and the return, are definite
and distinct. If in the known course of subsequent
history a broad and general correspondence is discerned between their writings and the events, the fact
would even be more remarkable if we could be sure
that this correspondence differed in some respects
from the personal expectation of the prophets. .
Indeed, we can hardly imagine a more significant
proof than this, that they spoke under an authority
not their own and an influence they could not
absolutely control. And again, to suppose that in
the words "for your sake" we are justified in discovering any indication of time is surely most
uncritical.* Is it not obvious to the most casual

* No less gratuitous and unwarrantable is Kuenen's assertion that
in the words of Micah iv. 10, *and go to Babylon*, the prophet " *must have
intended*" Assyria and not Babylon, or at all events only " Babylon
as the capital of one of the provinces of the Assyrian kingdom, and
not the Chaldean monarchy, of which he knows nothing" (p. 164).
Nor is it surprising to find him clutching at the straw that the words
may have been interpolated : " The conjecture, therefore, is not
unnatural that one of the later readers of the prophet should have
added the verse in which Babylon is named, or at least the second
half of it. Perhaps we do not require even to go to this length (!).
Just as, two verses before, the words ' out of Babylon ' are interpolated
in the Greek translation (iv. 8*b*), so the tenth verse may have
been completed by the one clause, 'And thou shalt go to Babylon.'
There would, in that case, remain for the prophet himself the expectation that Jerusalem should fall into the hands of the enemy (Assyria),

reader, as well as consistent with the constant tenor of Scripture, that the punishment denounced upon a people "for their sake" (that is, because of their sins) oftentimes overtakes them in their posterity and not as soon as it is denounced? Once, indeed, it was declared, but it was by the Prophet of Prophets, and is for the most part unusual in the language of prophecy, *All these things shall come upon this generation,*[*]—*This generation shall not pass till all these things be fulfilled.*[†] But otherwise, for the most part, as regards the times and the seasons, the Father hath reserved them under His own authority.

We pass on, then, to examine this prophecy of Micah, and the application that was made of it in the time of Jehoiakim. And first it is absolutely certain that it was regarded in his own days, and a hundred years afterwards, as not only spoken by him in the name of the Lord, but as really having the Divine sanction and authority. It may be said that this was merely in accordance with the opinions of the time and the people. But that is the very point I am anxious to enforce. There is and can be no ambiguity as to the way in which the prophets of Israel were regarded by the people of Israel them-

and the citizens, expelled from the city, should dwell in the open fields, where Jahveh should intervene on their behalf, and deliver them out of the power of the enemy," etc.—*Ibid.*

And yet we are asked to accept this as the certain result of scientific criticism. Alas for the science, if not the criticism! It is too often forgotten that science means knowledge and not conjecture.

[*] Matt. xxiii. 36.

[†] Matt. xxiv. 34.

selves. It may have been altogether a delusion on both sides; but at all events, the high estimate in which they were held was not the creation of after-times, when a halo of glory had gathered round their memory and the vagueness of distance had made them great. In their own day they were acknowledged as the mouthpieces of the Most High, as specially and wonderfully commissioned by Him to make known His will; and not seldom the faithfulness with which they did this exposed them, as in the case of Jeremiah, to persecution and the risk of death. What were the means by which they thus became the channels of the Divine communication, it is useless to inquire. It is sufficient to remark that the unique character of the writings they have left, as a whole, bears permanent and conclusive evidence that their mission was unique. If this is denied, argument becomes impossible, because a deficiency is evidenced which can only be compared to that of a sense or a faculty. It is impossible to discourse on music to one who lacks the perception of harmony, or to speak intelligibly of colours to the colour-blind. And so, if any one is disposed to maintain that the volume of prophecy is not essentially distinct from others of analogous character, and is not raised above them by intrinsic and unalterable features of difference, it is hopeless to reason with him. To us it appears simply obvious that the characteristic features of this volume are such as have no true parallel elsewhere, and are sufficient to mark it out from all others in kind as well as in degree, and therefore to warrant us in dealing with it—nay, rather to compel us to deal with it, as a special and exceptional book. It is certain, moreover, that the writers of the New Testament regarded the volume of prophecy as a collection of Divine oracles, to the accomplishment of which the honour and faithfulness of the Divine Being stood pledged.

If, therefore, we are asked to deal with these writings as though they were not entitled to any such claim, we must not shut our eyes to the fact that this is to ask us to concede the very point that has to be proved. To admit that we have no prophecies in our possession is to prejudge the case at issue by suggesting an hypothesis at variance with the facts. By much the fairer and more equal course is to take them as they were universally accepted, and as we ourselves have received them, and to inquire patiently, impartially, and honestly, whether there is ground for the estimation in which they have ever been held. And therefore I would ask boldly whether it is in the power of any one to affirm, on reading the words of Micah for example, now under consideration, that they were ultimately falsified by the event. It matters not whether that event took place in the age of Hezekiah; or a century afterwards, in the time of Zedekiah ; or even six centuries later still, under the emperor Titus. What I ask, and what I am warranted in asking, since it is ostensibly a prophecy that I have before me, is— Did the ultimate issue, or did it not, correspond in substance with the words of the prophecy ? And

to this question there is and can be but one answer.
The only subsequent question, therefore, that can
be asked, is—How far are we warranted in pointing
to this correspondence in vindication of the claim
advanced on behalf of the prophecy? How far does
the known course of events show it to have been a
prophecy? Is it possible that it can have been only
a successful guess? And with regard to this matter,
it may be observed that in the time of Jeremiah the
immediate danger which threatened in Micah's days
was thought to have passed away. Consequently, as
a mere guess, the wisdom and supposed foresight
of the prediction notoriously failed. Micah had to
endure the trial which fell so often to the lot of
the true prophets—the apparent proof, namely, that
his prophecy had miscarried, that he had uttered
lies in the name of the Lord. It is to be observed,
however, that though in the time of Jehoiakim
Micah's prophecy was supposed to have failed in
this respect, it was nevertheless regarded as valid
and genuine; it was not for a moment thought that
Micah's claim to the gift of prophecy was unsound,
but that *the Lord had repented of the evil which He
had pronounced against the people.* And on the

---

* The following is Kuenen's statement of the matter: "The
contemporaries of Jeremiah see in Micah the organ of Jahveh; his
prophecy is Jahveh's word. They cannot, therefore, form any other
opinion than that Jahveh retracted his threatening, and think this
the more reasonable as they know—or at least are persuaded—that
Hezekiah prayed that the judgment might be averted. This view
of theirs is neither supported nor contradicted by the prophecies of
Micah. These prophecies teach us that he encountered much oppo-

supposition of a really Divine scheme for the education of Israel conducted by the agency of prophets, there is surely nothing inconsistent or inconceivable in the punishment thus being threatened and then withheld, and then again threatened, till at last it fell upon the impenitent nation. Rather, on the contrary, the conditional suspension of a threatened calamity might well be taken as confirming the reality of the threat; and certainly it would be beyond the power of merely human wisdom so to frame a prediction of punishment as to allow of such conditional suspension, and yet to be in strict accordance with the subsequent issue of events. But this was manifestly the case with the prediction of Micah. There are, however, certain special features characteristic not only of this prophecy, but of Hebrew prophecy in general, which serve to take it altogether out of the category of successful guesses.

In the first place it does not stand alone. It is one of a long series of prophecies and part of a sition among the people, while other prophets, who flattered the passions of the masses, were listened to with applause. But the possibility remains that the popular disposition altered at a later period. The denunciation itself is, moreover, very positive. It purports not that Jerusalem may, indeed, be some time laid waste, but that it *shall* be laid waste. Then the elders of Judah do not assert that the prediction of Micah was conditional, but that 'Jahveh repented him of the evil which he had pronounced'" (p. 165).

The evidence of prophecy lies in the interpretation of phenomena. Where there is a determination not to acknowledge that evidence, the phenomena will be interpreted in one way; where the moral weight of the evidence predominates, they will be interpreted in another. But to appreciate moral evidence a certain condition of mind is requisite, just as sight is requisite to see the sun.

vast whole. Amos, Isaiah, Micah, Jeremiah, seve
rally and together, bore witness to the coming doom.
It has to be explained how these independent writers
were all animated by the common spirit of anti-
national foreboding. There is no evidence that one
was under the influence of another, or intentionally
adopted his tone; but the effect produced by all is
the union of harmony, the mingling of many voices
in concert; the concert and harmony, however, not
being simultaneous, but spread over a considerable
period of time, and maintained notwithstanding the
influence of very diverse circumstances. In like
manner the phenomenon of prophecy generally is
the supernatural counterpart of an exceptional and
supernatural history. No one can survey as a whole
the long stream of Hebrew history, even when its
main features are stripped of all supernatural ad-
juncts, and not be constrained to allow that the
undoubted framework of historical fact that still
remains is akin to the supernatural. That a nation
of feeble and oppressed bondmen should be rescued
from the thraldom of Egypt, and after a series of
vicissitudes and adversities should be securely established in Canaan, a land to which they had no
natural right; that they should be able to maintain
their hold on it for many centuries in the midst
of nations vastly more powerful than themselves;
that they should, in consequence of their very
position, be alternately exposed to the assaults of
the Assyrians on the north and the Egyptians on
the south, and yet once and again should survive

both; that they should eventually be carried captive
to Babylon, and yet, contrary to all likelihood and
historical precedent, be again restored to national
independence, or at least to national existence,—is
a series of undeniable facts so remarkable that they
may well serve for the natural and appropriate framework of incidents possibly supernatural. But the
idea of the events thus sketched in outline having
been fictitiously invented, or even substantially
altered in their broad features, is preposterous and
absurd. Now, it is as the fitting concomitant of a
history such as this that the complex and remarkable
phenomenon of prophecy confronts us. The main
features of the history are what they are, and the
marvellous works and words of the prophets are now
before us. It is sufficiently evident that the writers
themselves, like most other writers, had comparatively little influence in moulding the history of
their time. Judah and Israel were both transported
*beyond Damascus,** notwithstanding that their prophets declared they would be. The stream of prophecy flowed on side by side with the stream of
history, but the current of each was independent
of the other. The prophets did not make the history,
though the history produced the prophets; both alike
were the work of an unseen Master-mind, but the
completeness of His design and the relation of its
several parts could not be seen till the scaffolding

---

* This was one of the cases in which the national action, or, rather,
the national destiny, was not "compromised" (as Ewald would say)
by the nation's knowledge of the Divine purpose.

of contemporary events had been taken down and the proportions of the completed structure stood out on the background of the past. To deny that there is this relation between the history and the prophecy, or between the various independent prophecies, or that each and both alike are parts of one vast whole, is to shut our eyes to facts. And to deal with the several writings of the prophets as though each were an independent entity and responsible for the life of the whole is assuredly unphilosophical, if it is not uncritical. The question is not whether our very scanty knowledge of contemporaneous history does or does not enable us to substantiate and verify every utterance of the prophets; but whether the phenomena of prophecy, regarded as a whole, are so remarkable as to justify the assertion that they are unique;* and whether being so they can be explained merely by the application of principles that govern other historical and literary phenomena; or whether they do not rather suggest very forcibly

---

* " Yes, truly, the Israelitish prophet *is a unique phenomenon in history.* It does not disown its human origin ; that is borne witness to both by its gradual ripening and by many imperfections which cleave to it. Every attempt to derive it directly and immediately from God must therefore fail." (Kuenen, p. 591.) The italics are his.

Without venturing to maintain that every prediction of the prophets can be *shown* to have been fulfilled, and without offering to affirm that all the sentiments uttered by them were equally Divine, we yet are willing to declare that the existing phenomena of prophecy, as a whole, are such as to stamp it as a divinely appointed agency in the education of mankind, and attest it as a record of Divine foreknowledge ; and this is a position which Kuenen does not touch, and seems quite incapable of comprehending.

the operation of a higher principle working in a special and exceptional manner, this principle being the will of God declaring itself in an express and intentional way in which it has not declared itself in any other history and literature. The thesis is one which perhaps does not admit of actual demonstration; but there can surely be little doubt in which direction the logic of facts points us. We must either forcibly distort them in order to reduce them to the measure of the insignificant and the ordinary; or we must accept the witness of their extraordinary character which points us to the conclusion of faith —of faith, that is, in the ministry of prophecy as a select and authorised Divine agency for making known the Divine will for a special and ordained purpose, which, though faintly grasped by believing minds at the time, could only be perceived in its completeness when the purpose was fulfilled.

And this brings us to the second indication that this prophecy like others was not a successful guess. For it is not possible for any reverent or attentive mind, carefully noting the features of prophecy, to fail to discover the marks and tokens of a progressive scheme. One has only to mention the Prophets in order—Amos, Isaiah, Micah, Jeremiah, Ezekiel—to see at once that their writings have a corporate unity, and that there is a progression and a development running through them. The first note of the coming doom of captivity was sounded by Amos; and the message of Ezekiel was delivered in exile, far from his native land, while the abominations perpetrated therein were revealed to him in vision. And whatever difficulty there may be in setting one prediction over against another as its natural complement arises from the fact that each prophet wrote in entire independence of the rest, so that the effect of unity is produced notwithstanding all the freedom of individuality. If Amos speaks of *a fire being sent upon Judah which shall devour the palaces of Jerusalem,** Micah declares that *Zion shall be plowed as a field, and Jerusalem become heaps, and the mountain of the Lord's house as the high places of the forest;* † and Isaiah tells Hezekiah that all that is in his house which his *fathers have laid up in store shall be carried to Babylon, and his children be eunuchs in the palace of the king;* ‡ and Jeremiah goes so far as to say, *I will make this house like Shiloh, and will make this city a curse to all the nations of the earth.*§ Shall we say that there is here nothing more than the cuckoo cry of imitation? Or shall we not rather confess, bearing in mind the circumstances under which each menace was pronounced in different ages and to different persons, that they resemble rather the reiterated thunder-claps of one gathering storm, which become louder and more awful as the crisis approaches. It is hard indeed to demonstrate such a matter to the reason, but we may safely leave it to

* Amos ii. 5.

† Micah iii. 12.

‡ Isaiah xxxix. 6, 7. Kuenen has no hesitation in referring this narrative to "about 150 years later than the events which it records." (p. 287.)

§ Jer. xxvi. 6.

the judgment of the unbiassed. As a matter of fact, the tremendous calamities which befell the Jewish nation at the close of its monarchy had been for generations before not obscurely predicted by many independent prophets, whose writings of unquestioned authenticity and genuineness still remain to us; and the question is whether these were only so many successful guesses. The traces of unity and growth which they present, notwithstanding their individual originality, the tokens of a progressive scheme gradually and successively working itself out, is distinctly against such a notion. Besides, if the menaces of Jeremiah were the outcome of those of Amos, to what shall we refer the denunciations of the herdman of Tekoah which were uttered a century and a half before, in the palmy days of Israel and Judah? Was he nothing more than a rash enthusiast, and was his tone gratuitously adopted by subsequent prophets whose instinct and penetration foresaw the calamities that were coming on their nation and who determined to establish their own reputation for prophetic wisdom by building upon his? Such a theory has not the advantage of being more in accordance with probability than the facts with which it must deal and which it would endeavour to explain.

It is contended that there are no supernatural or divine features in the phenomena of prophecy; that there is no evidence that the prophets spoke with any other skill than that of a natural prevision; that their predictions were partly fulfilled and partly falsified, so that the effect of any apparent fulfilment is

vitiated and neutralised by actual falsification; and
that the writings which contain them, when critically
examined, serve to show that they are simply human
productions of no higher authority or value than any
others. There can be no doubt that a great deal of
the foresight with which the prophets are credited is
owing to the completeness with which *we* see that their
predictions were fulfilled. The retrospect of the past
and the clear knowledge of it leads us to think that it
must have been equally clear before the event. But
was this so, or can we reasonably think that it could
have been? Take, for instance, any one of the leading
countries of Europe, at the present time, and let any
man attempt to declare, in language as clear and intelligible as this of Micah's, what shall be its particular
position or crisis in ten years' time. Is there any one
who would venture to predict the particular phase of circumstances through which our own country will then
be passing? And when we look forward yet further,
for fifty or a hundred years, how utterly inconceivable
does it become! But are we prepared to say that in
the time of Hezekiah it was any more within the
limit of Micah's unaided capacity to put on record
words which should be found to be literally true a
century or a century and a half afterwards? It matters
not the least how he understood the words, whether
or not we have any evidence on this point, because
the moment they were written down with the
authority of a recognised prophecy, they appealed
with the significance of a deliberate challenge to
the issues of time and to the judgment of posterity.

And if a Divine prophecy they really were, it is more than probable they would transcend the widest imaginings of their human author. The calamities in store for the Jewish nation were by no means exhausted by the captivity, and though the first instalment of verification may have been dealt out then, there was yet more to follow, for prophecy is to be regarded as embodying and enforcing principle, and principle which is not omitted or lost sight of even here, in the already noted and notable words *for your sake.* If the human utterance of the prophet was the declaration of the Divine will, there must have been a purpose and a plan in it, and this purpose is not obscurely indicated. God is not dealing with His people in an arbitrary manner: He is about to chasten them for their sins and for their good; for both these meanings seem to be included in the words *for your sake.* Now, it is simply impossible to deny that prophecy as a whole presents to us this double aspect. The prophets, as a class, were the reprovers of national vice. They were the natural, or if you will the supernatural, regulating power which tended to redress the variations of the social and ecclesiastical machine. They ever recalled the nation to the imperative demands of a higher standard than they were willing to accept, and which they were prone to neglect or to deny. This was one of their obvious functions, which they to a man discharged, and it must not be lost sight of in estimating the moral value of their claim to be prophets in the name of the Lord. But they had another function too.

And this was a function as little to be questioned
as the other. They were ministers to the nation's
highest good. And they aimed at being this by
elevating its aspirations and inspiring it with the
highest hopes. More than one prophet expressed
his idea of this function in well-known language:
*How beautiful upon the mountains are the feet of
him that bringeth good tidings, that publisheth peace.**
To estimate the effect and influence of their dis-
charge of this function we need only to imagine one
contingency—namely, that it had happened to the
entire volume of Old Testament prophecy as Jeremiah
was bidden to do with his denunciations against
Babylon. What would be the aspect of human literature, and what the condition and prospects of
mankind, if all the writings of the prophets and the
record of their alleged fulfilment were drowned in
the depths of the sea?

* Isaiah lii. 7, Nahum i. 15.

JEREMIAH XXIX. 10—14.—*For thus saith the Lord, That after seventy years be accomplished at Babylon I will visit you, and perform my good word toward you, in causing you to return to this place. For I know the thoughts that I think toward you, saith the Lord, thoughts of peace, and not of evil, to give you an expected end. Then shall ye call upon me, and ye shall go and pray unto me, and I will hearken unto you. And ye shall seek me, and find me, when ye shall search for me with all your heart. And I will be found of you, saith the Lord; and I will turn away your captivity, and I will gather you from all the nations, and from all the places whither I have driven you, saith the Lord; and I will bring you again into the place whence I caused you to be carried away captive.*

LECTURE IX.

THE PROMISED RETURN.

WE have already seen that there is sufficient evidence to show that the destruction of the city and the temple had been not obscurely foretold in the writings of the prophets many years before those events had taken place. And indications are not wanting that the correspondence between the written predictions and the subsequent history is not to be explained by the supposition that the former were merely successful guesses.

I purpose now to consider another class of predictions referring to the national history, of which the passage just read may be taken as a typical instance.

Not only have we reason to affirm that the captivity in Babylon had been the subject of prophetic announcement generations before it occurred, but the yet more improbable event of restoration from that captivity had been similarly declared. I proceed now to examine the evidence of this.

It is a matter of undeniable fact that the writings of Jeremiah contain no less than three distinct assertions of such a restoration. The first occurs in the twenty-fifth chapter, to which the date is assigned of the fourth year of Jehoiakim, which was the first of Nebuchadnezzar. This has reference to the duration of the power of Babylon rather than to the return of Israel, which is only implied; but taken in connection with the other prophecies it may fairly be said to imply it. *And it shall come to pass,* says the prophet, *when seventy years are accomplished, that I will punish the king of Babylon and that nation, saith the Lord, for their iniquity, and the land of the Chaldeans, and will make it perpetual desolations.**   The second is the last verse of the twenty-seventh chapter, which has reference to the vessels of the house of the Lord and the house of the king, of which the prophet says, *They shall be carried to Babylon, and there shall they be until the day that I visit them, saith the Lord; then will I bring them up and restore them to this place.*†   This was apparently in the reign of Zedekiah.   The third is the present text, which must also be referred to the reign of Zedekiah.   Two, therefore, of these passages distinctly assign the period of seventy years to the dominion of Babylon, and two of them connect the restoration with the end of that dominion.

Needless difficulty has been raised with regard to the period of seventy years, which is mentioned in the two passages that must be assigned to different dates, as though the *terminus a quo* must be shifted accord-

---

* Jeremiah xxv. 12.

† n LXX., ch. xxxiv. 19, 20, 22 : ὅτι οὕτως εἶπε Κύριος. καὶ τῶν ἐπιλοίπων σκευῶν, ὧν οὐκ ἔλαβε βασιλεὺς Βαβυλῶνος, ὅτε ἀπῴκισε τὸν Ἰεχονίαν ἐξ Ἰερουσαλὴμ, εἰς Βαβυλῶνα εἰσελεύσεται, λέγει Κύριος.

ingly. But as the date of the latter passage, which is that of our text, is not precisely defined, though it must clearly be referred to the reign of Zedekiah,* and as the date of the former passage is distinctly assigned to the fourth year of Jehoiakim,† it seems reasonable to accept that date and to suppose that when the prophecy was virtually repeated somewhat later the seventy years intended were the seventy years before mentioned, as the prophecy manifestly affords us no means of fixing them more accurately. It is at all events gratuitous to assume that as time went on the prophet deliberately removed his *terminus a quo* in order to give his prediction the additional chance of fulfilment; and whatever difficulty there may be in adjusting this date and bringing it into

---

* See chs. xxviii. 1, xxix. 2. Kuenen refers it to the fourth year of Zedekiah, p. 309.

† "This repetition is regarded as proving that Jeremiah foresaw, not merely a long continued captivity in general, but a slavery of exactly seventy years. But such a view is unjust. If Jeremiah had wished to state the definite duration of the Chaldean rule, he would not have named in his letter the very same number that he had given in his prophecy eleven years before. He could repeat his previous announcement without alteration only if it was his sole object to express the idea that *a long time*, more than a generation, must elapse before Israel could be restored."—Kuenen, 310.

We are not told, however, what authority he had or could have for declaring that Israel should be restored. Nor is it anything to the point to say (p. 316) that "*by its moral influence his prophecy of Israel's restoration effected, or at least very powerfully promoted, that restoration itself*," for that surely under the circumstances would be a very remarkable influence for it to have.

Was it, moreover, easier on natural principles for Jeremiah to predict that the captivity would last for *a long time* than that it would last for seventy years? I fail to apprehend the difference.

correspondence with other systems of chronology,* there is not the slightest reason for rejecting it as the actual date of the deliverance of the prophecy. It is to be observed also that the period of seventy years is probably intended to be taken as more or less of a round number † equivalent generally to the length of two generations, or the standard limit of human life according to the ninetieth Psalm. If this is the case, we are relieved from the necessity of making the actual period of captivity at Babylon tally to the month and the day with the exact period of seventy years, whatever means we may have of determining this. At all events, the language of the prophet in this place may serve to show that he was speaking not only to the men of his own time but to posterity likewise, inasmuch as the majority of those addressed could not expect to be among the number of the remnant who should return from the land of their captivity. This also may serve to illustrate the sense, different from that of Professor Kuenen, which is to be put upon the words *for your sake* in the prophecy of Micah that we last considered. But the point which

* Cf.. *e.g.*.. Dan. i. 1.

† "The number seventy is simply a round number." (Davidson, ii. 460.) See also the previous note.

"Dr. Rowland Williams is inclined to assign the whole prediction to the later readers of the prophecies of Jeremiah ("The Hebrew Prophets," ii. 183, 239 f.) But if that were the case, how are we to account for the number seventy? Instead of that round number, an interpolator would rather have given accurately the true duration of the captivity. Besides, there is nothing whatever in chap. xxix. to justify the supposition of interpolation." (Kuenen, p. 311.)

I wish now to insist upon is the clear evidence we have that Jeremiah, as early as the commencement of Jehoiakim's reign, distinctly assigned the limit of seventy years to the Babylonian captivity already commencing, and promised the people a restoration out of it.   Nor does this evidence stand alone.   It is confirmed to us from other sources.   At the end of the second book of Chronicles we are told that *the Lord stirred up the spirit of Cyrus, king of Persia, that the word of the Lord spoken by the mouth of Jeremiah might be accomplished.*   It is true that we do not know when the books of Chronicles were written,* but as this statement is identical with that at the beginning of the book of Ezra, we are probably warranted in referring it to his time, or about the middle of the fifth century before Christ, or little short of a hundred years after the decree of Cyrus. At that time, then, the prophecies of Jeremiah contained these predictions about the seventy years' captivity, because otherwise Ezra would not have referred to them, neither could he possibly have alluded to them as promises of the Lord to be fulfilled unless they were known and recognised as such, not only by his contemporaries, but at the time to which his words referred—that, namely, of the proclamation of the edict of Cyrus.† Again, in the ninth

* Kuenen refers them to the middle of the third century B.C. (p. 388.)

† It is all very well of Kuenen (p. 319) to speak disparagingly of Josephus and the testimony he so clearly gives (Ant. XI., i. 1, 2), and to say, " In his days criticism had not yet been born, and exegesis was in its infancy. But what was permissible to him is now no

chapter of the book of Daniel, we find that prophet saying, *In the first year of Darius the son of Ahasuerus, I Daniel understood by books the number of the years, whereof the word of the Lord came to Jeremiah the prophet, that He would accomplish seventy years in the desolations of Jerusalem.* Although for the present we may not assume for the book of Daniel an earlier date than the second century before Christ, yet even on that hypothesis this passage is evidence that the writer of the book believed, and knew that others believed, the prophecy of Jeremiah referred to was in existence at the time assigned to Daniel.[*] As a matter of fact, however, it is not commonly disputed that the passage in question is a genuine utterance of the prophet Jeremiah, nor that it is rightly assigned to the early part of Jehoiakim's reign. Indeed, to imagine that the prophecy was

longer allowed. We must examine more keenly and discriminate more accurately." By all means : but let us not shut our eyes to evidence : and the testimony of Josephus, as far as it goes, is of the nature of valid external evidence, not to any opinion of his own, but to the tradition of his time, which tradition has to be accounted for historically, and not simply set aside as an obsolete opinion which we have learnt to despise. Similar evidence in the case of any other documents would have its due weight acknowledged at once. The catena of Ezra, Zechariah (i. 12), Daniel (admitting its latest date), and Josephus, is one of considerable strength. If external evidence is thus lightly to be set aside, verily we need tremble for no hypothesis.

[*] Hitzig and Graf suppose the number seventy to have been inserted by Jeremiah in ch. xxix., but that some one else introduced it in ch. xxv. Kuenen thinks the *repetition* "exceedingly doubtful" (p. 312); but see his remarks in the last note. None but subjective reasons can be assigned for these conjectures. Davidson, following Hitzig, "pronounces" Jeremiah xxv. 12 "suppositious." (iii. 98.)

first of all fictitiously ascribed to Jeremiah, and then, in order to make the fiction current, that it was quoted as authoritative by the writers of Ezra and Daniel, with all the assumed appearance of reality, would be to allow such an amount of license to criticism as would fairly deprive it of all title to the name. Besides, how is it that these writers, being themselves, on this hypothesis, untrustworthy in matters of fact, were nevertheless able to vouch for and establish the trustworthiness of another writer whose position in the canon was higher than their own? A thing such as this would be far more improbable than the simple fact that a genuine prophecy of Jeremiah was fondly cherished by the nation throughout the dreary period of its exile, and more than once appealed to by subsequent and independent writers like the authors of Ezra and Daniel. Unless we suppose the writings of Jeremiah to have been most unwarrantably tampered with (and the fact that the version of the Seventy, differing as it does from the Masoretic text very largely, nevertheless contains these three prophecies with a variation in that only which refers .to the vessels of the Lord's house, which it says shall be taken to Babylon,* is distinctly against any such supposition), we must face the fact that a prediction such as this we are now dealing with was recorded in the writings of Jeremiah and tenaciously preserved by the Jews in Egypt. If not, we can only imagine that it was interpolated after the return from Babylon and deliberately in-

* See note on p. 166.

serted in order to show well, and to look like a prophecy; and that, being so inserted, the writers of Ezra and Daniel no less deliberately acquiesced in the barefaced forgery, and helped it on by their quotation of it as genuine—a supposition which no one laying claim to the judicial faculty of criticism would venture to make. If, on the other hand, we suppose these writers to have been themselves deceived by the interpolation, it must furthermore not be forgotten that whoever is responsible for the addition of the last chapter of Jeremiah was specially careful to warn his readers against supposing it to be the prophet's own by adding to the former chapter the statement, *Thus far are the words of Jeremiah,* thereby suggesting the unavoidable inference that all the rest was his. The evidence, however, of Zechariah, reaching back as it does to within sixteen years of the edict of Cyrus, may be said to be conclusive on this point; for to what else can he refer if not to this prophecy of Jeremiah when he says, *Then the angel of the Lord answered and said, O Lord of hosts, how long wilt Thou not have mercy on Jerusalem and on the cities of Judah, against which Thou hast had indignation these threescore and ten years?* *

If, therefore, we are constrained to accept these prophecies as integral portions of the book of Jeremiah, belonging to the times of Jehoiakim and

* Zech. i. 12. Cf. Hag. i. 2, which not improbably refers to some uncertainty about the period at which the seventy years began and therefore ended.

Zedekiah, as the great preponderance of evidence and probability clearly determines, what is the inference to be drawn from them? First, that it is altogether gratuitous to assume that distinct and definite prediction was not an actual and legitimate branch of the functions of prophecy. On no naturalistic principles can it be explained that a statement such as this was made at the time supposed, so long before the occurrence of any event answering to it. To all human intelligence and skill the thing was an absolute impossibility. It may perhaps be characteristic of some of our modern and popular notions on the matter, that we are at times prone to confound the two functions, in themselves distinct, of prophecy and prediction. But the point for which I contend is this: that the books of the Old Testament, and notably the writings of the prophets, do contain most unmistakable instances of the prediction of events yet future at the time when they were written ; that these instances of prediction, specimens of which have been dwelt upon at length, cannot by any fair or reasonable process be explained away or accounted for as the result of natural foresight ; that they were uttered as predictions communicated by the foreknowledge of God and universally received as such ; and that being what they profess to be, they do serve in their degree to make good the claim on behalf of the Old Testament to be the channel of· a Divine message, and of the prophets to have spoken under the influence of the Holy Spirit as men without that influence could not have spoken.

The position thus maintained is by no means an extreme one. We admit that there are prophecies of whose fulfilment we have no record; that there are others which as far as our present knowledge extends may even seem to have been falsified by the event; but neither fact, so far as it is established, will suffice to counterbalance the yet more distinctly undeniable fact that there are those characteristic features about the Hebrew prophecy as a whole which mark it out as among the means specially chosen by God for making known His will to man, and for showing to all ages that He had so made it known, and thereby sealing the record in which it was enshrined as the depository of a special revelation of His mind and will. We do not, therefore, bring any theory of inspiration to bias the discussion of this matter, but maintain that the honest contemplation of all the phenomena presented tends distinctly to the establishment of inspiration as a fact.

Nor can there be any doubt that the unwillingness which many persons manifest to recognise the truly predictive element in prophecy arises mainly because of its obviously demanding the exercise of a supernatural agency. But not the less is the exercise of such an agency demanded if we duly note the existence of other features which are more commonly recognised. I said at the conclusion of my last lecture that one function discharged by the prophets was that of being ministers to the nation's highest good by seeking to raise its aspirations and holding out the promise of future hope. Conspicuously is that the case with the words before us—*I know the thoughts that I think towards you, saith the Lord, thoughts of peace and not of evil, to give you an expected end*, or more literally, *an hereafter and a hope.* Now, there is no one probably, whatever his views about the supernatural in prophecy or elsewhere may be, who will not at once acknowledge the extreme beauty of the sentiment here expressed. But I would venture to ask in what does its beauty consist ? Is it merely in the collocation of harmonious words and the association of pleasing images? Or does it not consist in a far higher degree, if not simply and solely, in its *truth ?* I may even say that to my mind there is comparatively speaking no beauty in it if it is not true or was not true. If the prophet was merely uttering from out of the resources of his own imagination that which he believed he might reasonably state with respect to the intentions of the Most High towards His people, then I maintain we have no guarantee that he may not have been deceived. Nay, can we have any sufficient assurance that he was justified in saying what he did ? He was speaking as one who was privy to the secret thoughts of the Most High. We may think that what he says sounds very well, and may ourselves agree with it, but how can we be sure that it expresses the truth—and this is my point—unless the prophet was really authorised to say what he did ? But if this was the case, there was a more than ordinary, a superhuman and a supernatural means of communication, instituted between the Divine mind and the prophet's mind. That is to say, he was, as a prophet, not one who laid claim merely to supernatural communications from God, but one who was selected, chosen, and ordained by God to declare His will to His people. If so, I can clearly understand that the juxtaposition of a prophecy, like that of the seventy years as the limit of Babylonian power, with the sentiment here expressed, would tend wonderfully to confirm its reality and truth; and I cannot understand how it could be more effectually confirmed otherwise, if indeed it could otherwise to us be confirmed at all. For the record of a physical miracle would to *us* have less force than this prophecy, inasmuch as the record of a miracle would itself require confirmation, whereas the record of a prophecy possesses it. Given the fact that the record of this prediction is genuine, as it most unquestionably is, and we ourselves are judges as to whether or not it was substantially fulfilled in fact; and what is more, there never will come the time when this, the moral weight of the prophecy, will be less than it is at present. It will appeal with equal force to the conscience and the judgment of generations yet unborn as to our own. In this respect prophecy has an evidential advantage not possessed by miracles, inasmuch as we accept the miracles because of the authenticity of the narrative relating them, but an established prophecy is a witness for all time from its very nature.

I take it, then, that if we are really and authoritatively to know that the thoughts of the Almighty towards His people are verily thoughts of peace and not of evil, as here stated, it can only be by our having valid reason to believe that He has Himself told us so: but when or how has He done this if not by revelation—if not by prophecy? Prophecy, however, implies a prophet, and the proof of prophecy is prediction; but if prophecy is truly prophecy, that is the authoritative declaration of the Divine will, it involves the operation of the supernatural no less than prediction does. The prophet who makes known the Divine will, whether by prediction or otherwise, can only do so by the exercise of a faculty not given to man as man, but to man in virtue of his being the chosen agent of the Most High to make known His will. It follows, consequently, that those benevolent thinkers who would smooth over the difficulties felt by some minds in accepting the Scriptures as documents to which the very greatest respect is due by eliminating therefrom the traces of any supernatural predictive element can only do so—and this ought to be clearly and distinctly understood—by removing at the same time therefrom the traces of any authoritative declaration of the Divine will. All that we are supposed to know about this from Scripture is nothing more than so much human speculation, which may be right or may be wrong. The Bible, as a matter of fact, not only is not the word of God, but it does not in any true sense contain that word if the message which it gives us about God, and as from God, is not actually from Him but only from some misguided enthusiasts who thought they spoke with His authority. I am quite aware, brethren, that I am treading on very delicate ground and dealing with a matter of profound difficulty; but it is one on which I have not myself the slightest hesitation, because on it I am prepared to base my own prospects for weal or woe for all eternity. Either we have an actual communication from God by His chosen agents, or we have not; if we have not, then reason, or philosophy, or experience, or what you will, it matters little what, must be our guide : but if we have, and that communication is the message of life, then we may assuredly, confidently, and implicitly trust it, and live by it as we can live by nothing else. God has actually spoken to us, we have heard His words, and *the entrance of His words giveth light, it giveth understanding unto the simple.**

But this is the supernatural claim of the Scriptures as the word of God, and more particularly now of the prophets as the heralds of that word. And I fail to perceive wherein the difference lies, if we really believe that word, between allowing that the moral sentiments of the prophets were not only very beautiful but likewise Divine, and allowing that there is evidence in their writings that the Lord was pleased by their agency to make known events or ever they came to pass which no human foresight could have enabled them to foretell. It is a very simple, a very definite, and an all-important issue, but I do not see how sooner or later it is to be avoided, nor do I believe that there is any solution of the issue but one. The Jewish nation went into captivity knowing

* Psalm cxix. 130.

as clearly as prophetic language could tell them—
whether or not they understood it in all its bearings
—that the limit of that captivity would be seventy
years: as a matter of fact the interval of time from
the first year of Nebuchadnezzar to the promulgation
of the edict of Cyrus was seventy years. But there
are several ways in which the same period of time
may be computed.* It is not upon a detail of this

---

* It is at least curious and interesting to observe that from 606 B.C.,
the approximate date of the delivery of Jeremiah's prophecy, to
536 B.C., the approximate date of the edict of Cyrus, the first termination of the captivity, was a period of seventy years.

Again, from 598 B.C., the approximate date of Jehoiachin's captivity
(2 Kings xxiv. 12), to 528 B.C., the approximate date of the close of
the first period of amnesty and of the counter efforts against the decree
of Cyrus (Ezra iv. 6), which were virtually a renewal of the captivity,
was a period of seventy years. Thus the captivity was eight years in
progress, as was also the return. Also from 588 B.C., the approximate
date of the completion of the captivity by the destruction of the city
and temple (2 Kings xxv. 8), to 518 B.C., the approximate date of the
decree of Darius (Ezra vi. 1), which was a second termination of the
captivity, was a period of seventy years. Also from 527 B.C., the
approximate date of the second renewal of the captivity (Ezra iv. 6),
to the decree of Artaxerxes in 457 B.C., which was the close of the
captivity, was a period of seventy years.

It is undoubtedly hard to prove or disprove the exactitude of
these several periods within a year or so, but for those who insist that
the seventy years are a round number it is plainly needless to do so ;
while, at all events, the recurrence of the number seventy in connection with the history of the captivity and the return of the Jews is,
to say the least, striking.

We have contemporary evidence from Zech. i. 12 that the Jews of
that age were themselves in doubt as to when the seventy years ended,
because they did not clearly know from when to date their commencement. It is reserved for us, in looking back over all the history,
to see that the very uncertainty attaching to the determination of
the seventy years is itself a confirmation of the reality and genuine-

kind that we base the reality of the prophecy, but upon the undoubted and indubitable broad historical fact, that, contrary to all precedent, a remnant of the nation, according to prophecy, did return from Babylon and again take root in the land of their fathers. So it had been foretold, and so it came to pass. The course of the captivity was turned like that of the rivers in the south.

Nor is there wanting evidence that through the long dark night of exile the promise given by Jeremiah was remembered and watched with eager eyes like a beacon shining from afar, because the appendix to his book, which was probably not added till long after his death, and perhaps by Baruch, mentions the circumstance of Jeremiah's release from prison in the seven-and-thirtieth year of his captivity, which was, roughly speaking, about midway in the period of the seventy years. Now, the occurrence of this fact must have served as a reminder that the Lord had not forgotten His people, but was mindful of His promise, even if this was not the very purpose for which it was mentioned. And unless the statement in Daniel is a gratuitous forgery, it is evident

ness of the prophecy concerning them, inasmuch as not in one way only but in several it may be shown to have fulfilled itself, and therefore may be justly regarded as a record of Divine foreknowledge, an expression of God's intention with regard to His people; while for those who choose to affirm that there is nothing in it, there is, of course, abundant opportunity for doing so. Here, as in so many other cases, we cannot arrive at anything absolute, but must be content with the balance of probability, which will vary in accordance with our own appreciation of facts.

that as the term drew on he was eagerly watching for the fulfilment of the promise.

It is clear, therefore, that we may not exclude the predictive element from the legitimate functions of prophecy, because in so doing we equally destroy the foundations of any certain expression of the Divine will. It requires a supernatural agency to convey to us the knowledge of any Divine purpose like that of goodwill no less than it does to impart to us a knowledge of the future. One is, humanly speaking, impossible, but so also is the other. And this serves to show the legitimate place of prediction in what purports to be a revelation from God. If all our knowledge of the Divine will is not to be merely tentative and conjectural, it is reasonable to suppose that the manifestation of it would be accompanied by special instances of prediction. And as a matter of fact, the prophets not only laid claim to this faculty, but pointed to it in confirmation of their claim to be prophets: *Let them bring forth and show us what shall happen: let them show the former things what they be, that we may consider them and know the latter end of them, or declare us things for to come. Show the things that are to come hereafter, that we may know that ye are gods.** Can any challenge be more explicit than that, or at the same time more reasonable and conclusive?

---

* Isaiah xli. 22, 23. " Proceeding," says Kuenen, " on the twofold supposition that the Israelitish prophets were the interpreters of Jahveh, and that Jahveh, the only true God, governed the world with a view to and in the interest of ' Israel His servant and Jacob

But though prediction is thus important and indispensable, if we are to have any prophetic message from God that we can really trust, it is nevertheless subordinate and subsidiary to a higher function. Prophecy regarded as prediction is not an end in itself, but a means to an end. The end is the direct and immediate recognition of the will and voice and word of God. God's purpose is to lead us to Himself, to reveal to us Himself. It was more for Judah of old to know and to believe that His *thoughts* . *towards them were thoughts of peace and not of evil* *

whom He had chosen,' he must have written exactly as he does write, about Cyrus and his victories, the destiny which Babylon had to expect, and the future of Israel." (p. 317.)

Our position is exactly the reverse of this—namely, that God governed Israel with a view to and in the interest of the world, and that the history of Israel and the ministry of the prophets is the record of this government. " It is self-evident that if Isaiah the son of Amos foretold not only the Babylonish captivity, but also the liberation of the Jews by Cyrus, he possessed a foreknowledge more than human : and in the contest on behalf of Jahveh and against the idols he could with the fullest right appeal to this prediction, *as soon as it was confirmed by the issue.* Before that time he could not of course do so. What man proves his gift of prediction by an appeal to the supposed fulfilment of his anticipations? How could Isaiah, about 700 B.C., triumphantly maintain the omniscience of Jahveh on the ground of facts which were to take place 150 or 160 years afterwards?" (Kuenen, 318.)

According to this author, no man has, or ever had, any "gift of prediction" he would care to "prove." And certainly there would be no "omniscience" to "maintain triumphantly" in the case of *vaticinia* confessedly written *post eventum.* To satisfy the requirements of this hypothesis, the writer must have been deliberately perpetrating pseudo-prophecies, which were as deliberately accepted as real ones by the nation at large. Is this probable?

* Jer. xxix. 11.

than it was to be quite sure that the captivity would last for seventy years. But how could there be a greater proof of the real nature of the Divine thoughts towards His people than the national future He had yet in store for them, notwithstanding their national sins? And how could there be any certain knowledge of such a future being in store for them unless He was pleased to make it known? And if known, as it manifestly was, how could it have been made known except by Him? It is all very well to attempt to base the evidence of the Divine word upon the nature of that word itself; but a time will come when our own estimate of that nature will itself vary, and there will always be those whose estimate of it will differ intrinsically from ours, nor shall we ever succeed in persuading them that our estimate is more just than theirs. And though possibly in such cases the evidence of predictive prophecy will not be of any more avail than the self-evidencing nature of the Divine word itself, yet the effect of it upon hearts already disposed to believe, or upon our own wavering hearts, will surely be to confirm and re-establish them.

But however this may be, if there is reasonable evidence, as there undoubtedly is, that prediction is one of the agencies selected and employed by God, and to all appearance for the express purpose of confirming our belief in Him, it will not be for us to reject or to disparage such an agency, but rather to use it as He designed it to be used—not, indeed, as the sole or even the principal foundation of His truth, but as one of those aids He has Himself vouchsafed, and to which He has assigned its proper place and function. Great harm is done when we insist at all hazards on the supernatural element in prophecy being recognised as the ground on which its moral and spiritual message is to be received; but not less harm is likely to accrue, if, out of professed deference for the spiritual message which we affect to regard as its own evidence, we surrender altogether the solid groundwork of confirmation and proof which may verily be found in the contemplation of actual phenomena which cannot satisfactorily be explained upon any principles of merely natural interpretation or as instances of merely casual coincidence. And such instances, I venture to think, are to be found among many more besides in the specimens of predictive prophecy which have been adduced. Not one of them can be adequately explained on the assumption that there is nothing in it of a more than ordinary natural or human character. Of no other nation under similar circumstances was it ever declared many years before the event that it should be carried into captivity by a definite power; and of no other nation was it ever declared on the very eve of such a captivity that after seventy years were accomplished the captivity should have an end and the nation be restored to the home of its ancestors—a promise, be it observed, which was never given to the ten tribes. But we have incontrovertible evidence that this was the case with Judah, and we have incontrovertible evidence

that in process of time the events predicted were
brought about. Now the prophecies containing these
predictions are numerous, independent, systematic.
They are universally accepted as the genuine works
of a race of men who professed to be the bearers
of a message, however communicated, from the Most
High. We may go so far as to say that they were
nothing at all if they were not this. It is the
prominent and predominant feature of their character
by which they must be judged. If they were true
men, they were charged with a superhuman and a
supernatural message from God. If they were not
so charged, they were wilful deceivers and arrant
impostors.*   It would be no slight test of their
character in this respect if it were made to turn
upon the broad and patent verification of their predictions thus indicated. Were these predictions a
substantive part of their prophecies, or were they
not? Did they themselves challenge the verdict of

* This supposition is indeed indignantly denied (see note on
Lecture VII., p. 131), by those who reject the Divine authority of the
prophets. But the real question is whether we can find a satisfactory
and solid standing-ground in the intermediate position that the faith
of the prophets created their facts. This is *the* question with which
the religious thought of our age has to grapple. It is a very wide
question ; and as regards the Hebrew prophets, is only one part of a
much larger whole. We cannot logically stop with the prophets, but
shall have to ask and answer the question, Is the Christian faith
self-originated, or is it fact-begotten—that is, originated by the fact
that Christ rose from the dead? If this was a fact, and not a
Christian fancy, then there is no reason why the fancies of the
Hebrew prophets should not have been facts, but every reason why
they should. But if facts, then they were also " supernatural " facts,
and the prophets themselves charged with a " supernatural " message.

posterity upon the fulfilment of them, or did they
not? Is there reason to believe they were fulfilled,
or is there not? If there is, does not the sublime,
moral, and spiritual character of their writings lend
its weight to the authority of their predictions, and
do not their predictions irresistibly tend to show
that the moral and spiritual character of their
writings was indeed stamped with the authority of
Him in whose name they were recorded, and that,
in fact, it was none other than He "who spake by
the prophets"?

LECTURE X.

IN endeavouring to show that Old Testament prophecy is a record of Divine foreknowledge, I
have dwelt at present mainly upon two features of it
—namely, its apparent witness to a Person to come,
who may with more reason be supposed to be our
Lord Jesus Christ than any one else, since His
coming lends to it a significance of meaning which
it otherwise lacks, though still seeming to demand it;
and, secondly, its apparent reference to two great
national events, the captivity and the return, which
no fair treatment of it can refuse to recognise. If
the one of these features may be regarded as in the
highest sense prophetic, it seems, I confess, almost
impossible not to regard the other as predictive.
At all events, we may safely say that those who are
prepared to acknowledge the presence of Divine
characteristics in Scripture which cannot be adequately represented · as merely human and merely
natural will have no difficulty in admitting the
evidence of prediction here. Of course, if we are
determined that the Bible shall be reduced to a
merely natural literary phenomenon, we must at any

cost get rid of, or refuse to acknowledge, whatever tokens of prediction it may contain; but this will be a very different thing from establishing satisfactorily the non-existence of any such tokens. That there have always been those who believed them to exist, and that from the very first, it is impossible to deny.

I propose, in my remaining Lectures, to consider at least one other famous prophecy which there seems good reason to believe is not only prophetic but predictive, and which combines in itself the features I have named of reference to a Person to come, and also to some great national crisis which was future when it was written : I mean Daniel's prophecy of the seventy weeks.

We have to bear in mind that the book of Daniel has been the subject of the most vehement assaults— that it has been, and is, stoutly denied to be genuine —that it is distinctly declared to have been written in the year 165 B.C.,* and the like. Our task, there- fore, will be no easy one, for we must argue upon and not against these assumptions. If we could assume that we had in the book of Daniel a genuine produc- tion of the sixth century before Christ, it would then, I conceive, be absolutely impossible to deny to pro- phecy its predictive element. But this we must not assume. All we can hope to do is to show that on the assumption of those who deny its genuineness there is less appearance of probability that their theory is correct than there is in favour of the tradi-

---

* Kuenen is quite certain about this, though he confesses to "assuming" it. (pp. 145, 266, 268.)

tional view that the book is genuine, and that therefore this balance of probability is itself in favour of
the predictive character of prophecy.

I start, then, with the distinct statement of St.
Mark that our Lord began His ministry in Galilee
with the emphatic words, *The time is fulfilled*, which
he as distinctly states occurred after that John *was
delivered up*,* and not, as our version erroneously has
it, *was put in prison*. St. Mark is the only evangelist
that records these words. St. Matthew, however, is
equally precise in marking the reference to the same
event in the career of John † in connection with the
commencement of our Lord's ministry. And in St.
John's gospel we have continual reference by that
evangelist, and also by our Lord Himself, to His
hour not being come, or the reverse. In the seventh
chapter we are told,‡ *Then they sought to take Him,
but no man laid hands on Him because His hour was
not yet come;* and again in the next chapter, as He

---

* According to St. John ii. 1, 12, 13, 17, Jesus had disciples with
Him at Cana, at Capernaum, and at the feast in Jerusalem, and for
some months was baptising in Judæa, before John "was cast into
prison" (John iii. 24). Whereas, according to St. Matthew and St.
Mark, John was "delivered up" before Jesus went to reside at Capernaum, before He preached at all in Galilee, and before Peter and
Andrew and James and John had received a commission to "follow"
Him—that is, soon after the temptation. I infer, therefore, that
this delivering up must have reference, not to John's imprisonment
by Herod, but to some previous examination or inquiry, by the
Sanhedrim possibly, to which John had been "delivered up," being
afterwards acquitted.—See Pound's "Story of the Gospels," ii. 137.

† St. Matt. iv. 12.

‡ St. John vii. 30.

taught in the treasury, *No man laid hands on Him, for His hour was not yet come.** In the twelfth chapter Jesus answered Philip and Andrew, who told Him of certain Greeks that they desired to see Him, *The hour is come that the Son of man should be glorified. . . . Now is my soul troubled; and what shall I say? Father, save me from this hour : but for this cause came I unto this hour.*† The next chapter opens : *Now before the feast of the Passover, when Jesus knew that His hour was come that He should depart out of this world to the Father;* ‡ and our Lord's last prayer continues, *Father, the hour is come. Glorify Thy Son, that Thy Son also may glorify Thee.*§ In St. Matthew also we have Him saying, just after His agony, *The hour is at hand, and the Son of man is betrayed into the hands of sinners.*‖ As also similarly in St. Mark's corresponding narrative. It is true that we are accustomed, perhaps, to understand these passages in a somewhat lower and more ordinary sense than the strict and emphatic one which they will undoubtedly bear; but if we remember who spoke them, and the solemn event to which they referred, I think it will be hard to deny that they are such as to lend countenance to the idea that our Lord regarded His end as an hour which could neither be hastened nor deferred, or at least that the Gospel writers have represented Him as so regarding it.

Nor is the idea one which is in any way peculiar

---

* viii. 20.   ‡ xiii. 1.   § xvii. 1.

† xii. 23, 27.   ‖ xxvi. 45 ; St. Mark xiv. 41.

to them. St. Paul tells us distinctly in his epistle
to the Galatians that it was *when the fulness of the
time was come,* and therefore not till then, that *God
sent forth His Son, made of a woman, made under the
law, to redeem them that were under the law.** In the
epistle to the Ephesians he speaks of *the dispensation
of the fulness of the times.*† In the epistle to the
Romans he speaks of *the mystery which was kept
secret since the world began, but now is made manifest
and by the scriptures of the prophets made known.*‡ In
writing to Timothy he calls the ransom of Jesus Christ
the testimony in its own times; and to Titus he says
that *the God who cannot lie promised eternal life before
eternal ages, but had manifested* and so fulfilled *His
word in its own times.*§ In like manner, we find St.
Peter representing the prophets as eagerly *searching
what, or what manner of time, the Spirit of Christ
which was in them did signify when it testified before-
hand the sufferings of Christ and the glory that
should follow;* ‖ and, lastly, the writer of the epistle
to the Hebrews says that *once for all in the end of
the world,* or upon the consummation of the ages,
ἐπὶ συντελείᾳ τῶν αἰώνων, *Christ hath been manifested
to put away sin by the sacrifice of Himself.*¶ Now,
from all these passages it would seem that we are
warranted in saying that the writers of these several
epistles regarded the manifestation of Christ as
appointed for a particular time (χρόνος as well as
καιρός is used in them), that this time was either

* Gal. iv. 4, 5.   ‡ Rom. xvi. 25, 26.   ‖ 1 Peter i. 11.
† Eph. i. 10.   § 1 Tim. ii. 6; Titus i. 3.   ¶ Heb. ix. 26.

hidden deep in the counsels of God, or that it was obscurely intimated by the prophets, and that St. Peter, apparently referring to the conduct of Daniel in the ninth chapter, regarded the prophets as eager to know *what manner of time the Spirit of Christ that was in them did signify.* The question is not now as to the amount of authority we are to assign to their opinion thus expressed; but that this was the opinion they expressed there can be no question. And when, in consideration of all these facts, we find our Lord beginning His ministry with the statement *the time is fulfilled,* we naturally ask, what time did He refer to, and have we any means of ascertaining what that time was?

It seems, then, that we must either consent to eviscerate His words of their natural meaning, or we must suppose that He had a definite time in view, and that He spoke to the impressions of those who heard Him, who believed, as we know from other sources, that that time was then at hand. It seems, I say, that we cannot duly estimate the burden and force of John the Baptist's and our Lord's early proclamation, *the kingdom of heaven is at hand,* without supposing that both speakers and hearers alike had in their minds and memories the kingdom which Daniel declared *the God of heaven should set up; which should be given to the Son of man, and to the people of the saints of the Most High, which should be an everlasting kingdom, and should never be destroyed.** If any

* Dan. ii. 44, vii. 14, 27.

one is prepared to maintain that there was no
association perceived or intended between the statements of the prophet on the one hand, and those
of John the Baptist, our Lord, and His apostles,
on the other, it is simply hopeless to discover any
common ground upon which we can reason. At
all events, while the several statements are what
they are—no matter how they came to be what
they are—it is certain that till the end of time
there will be those who will not fail to perceive
this association, and who will, rightly or wrongly,
deduce certain inferences from it.

Our first contention, therefore, is that Jesus Christ,
when He began His ministry with the words *the
time is fulfilled*, referred not merely to what He
knew of the counsels of the Most High, for which
none who at first heard Him could be expected at
once to give Him credit, but to a definite and
well-known period, which for some reason or other
was commonly understood to be then at hand. Now
if this be so, (and whether it is or not I must leave
for you, brethren, to determine; for myself I cannot
conceive it is open to ·question,) but if it be so,
there is only one passage in the whole compass of
Scripture which had any bearing on the matter, and
this passage is Daniel's prophecy of the seventy
weeks. If our Lord and His hearers had any one
definite time in view, it can only have been the
time which within certain limits had been in mysterious prophetic language defined by Daniel. The
book of Daniel was known to contain the statement,

*Seventy weeks are determined upon thy people and upon thy holy city, to finish the transgression, and to make an end of sins, and to make reconciliation for iniquity, and to bring in everlasting righteousness, and to seal up the vision and prophecy, and to anoint the Most Holy.** I leave out for the present all verbal emendation or criticism, and merely take the passage as it stands in the authorised version, which is sufficient for my purpose. These seventy weeks, according to a principle † commonly recognised and laid down in the prophets, are all but universally acknowledged to indicate seventy weeks of years, or

---

* The first intimation of this principle is given in Numb. xiv. 34; cf. also Ezek. iv. 5, 6, where it is expressly laid down. But as Dr. Pusey says, " There could not be any ambiguity in the people's mind. The period could not be 'seventy weeks of days,' *i.e.* a year and about four months. The events are too full for it." (Daniel the Prophet, p. 167.) But in point of fact interpreters are all but unanimous on this point (see *ibid.*, p. 197). It is strange, however, that there should be this unanimity, since the acknowledgment of the principle involved implies the recognition of a certain unity in Scripture. Why, for instance, should the writer of Daniel make use, without explanation, of a method defined in Ezekiel? With reference to the same subject, compare also Lev. xxvi. 34, and 2 Chron. xxxvi. 21, where the principle of reckoning by Sabbath-years seems to be implied. It has been pointed out that from the period of first asking for a king (cir. B.C. 1096) to the commencement of the captivity (cir. B.C. 606) was seventy hebdomads, or 490 years, while from the time of the first plundering of the temple by Shishak (cir. B.C. 970) to B.C. 606 was a period of fifty-two hebdomads, corresponding to the fifty-two years from B.C. 588 to B.C. 536, the period that the land lay desolate. Thus in the history of Israel there were two marked periods of 490 years—one measuring the duration of the temporal kingdom, and the other that between Daniel's fervent prayer and the manifestation of the True King. Is this fancy or is it chance?

† Dan. ix. 24.

seventy times seven years; if for no other reason,
yet for this, that here at least they can have no
other meaning if the passage has any sense at all;
and only on this principle can it for a moment be
supposed that the national anticipations of the
coming of the Christ were in any degree influenced
by this prophecy, or can they be understood as
culminating at that time, as they manifestly did.
Now it must distinctly be borne in mind that whenever the book of Daniel was actually written, it is
perfectly obvious to what age it professed to refer.
The date of this ninth chapter is patent and explicit:
*In the first year of Darius the son of Ahasuerus,
of the seed of the Medes, which was made king over
the realm of the Chaldeans; In the first year of
his reign I Daniel understood by books*—that is to
say, the books of Scripture, which as far as they
then existed were the sacred books to Daniel as
they are to us—*the number of the years whereof
the word of the Lord came to Jeremiah the prophet
that He would accomplish seventy years in the desolations of Jerusalem.* Then follows the statement
that the prophet set his *face unto the Lord God
to seek by prayer and supplications with fasting
and sackcloth and ashes;* and then his prayer is
given in full. That is to say, the prophet represents
himself, or is represented,—for my present purpose
it matters not which,—as knowing from his study of
the prophecies of Jeremiah that the seventy years
of which he had spoken were nearly accomplished.
He did not know how nearly, for to him as to us

there was the same difficulty, which to him before
events had unfolded themselves must have been even
greater, about fixing the exact time when the seventy
years began. But at all events he knew, or was
supposed to know, that he had himself been nearly
the prescribed time in captivity.* Poring then
anxiously over prophecies which he believed to be
Divine, he knew that the allotted time was almost
run out, and he longed eagerly for its accomplishment. He prayed that the Lord would *hearken and
do, and defer not, for His own sake, and for the sake
of the city and people that were called by His name.*
Daniel, believing that the time was at hand, is represented as praying most earnestly that it might fully
come. Upon this we are told that while he was
praying and confessing his sin, and the sin of his
people Israel, *the man Gabriel*, whom he had before
seen in vision, *being caused to fly swiftly, touched
him about the time of the evening oblation*, and spake
unto him in answer to his prayer. And this passage
about the seventy weeks is part of the man Gabriel's

---

* From about 607 B.C., apparently the year before Jeremiah's
prophecy, to 538, the first year of Darius. It has been rightly
observed that the mention of this date, 607, the third year of
Jehoiakim, Dan. i. 1, which perplexes all the commentators, is no
slight indication of the genuineness of the book, because what writer
of a fictitious narrative which was intended to pass for a true one
would venture to deviate from the known authorities in such a point
as this, and to deviate so slightly? while on the supposition of
genuineness the discrepance is capable of explanation in various
ways—as, *e.g.*, either by the use of another method of computation,
or by the possible occurrence of an incursion of the Babylonians not
otherwise recorded in the recognised authorities.

communication. It cannot, therefore, be doubted that what is thus given is given as the result of an angelic communication under the most solemn circumstances, and in special answer to a very solemn prayer. Of course, if it is a matter of no importance whether or not we are grossly deceived and imposed upon in things relating to God, it is a matter of entire indifference when and under what circumstances this narrative was written. It may be true or false, and matter not. Only, and this is my point, if it was written in the second century before Christ, then of course it cannot possibly be true; it was to all intents and purposes a romance and nothing more. It may have been a tale with a high and elevating moral, written with the best intentions, but a tale it was and could be nothing else. But then we are surely warranted in asking ourselves whether it is likely that being such a tale, a merely edifying story referring to a person of whom *nothing whatever was known* except the mere mention of his name in a few places in Ezekiel,* and who must have lived, if he lived at all, nearly four centuries before,—whether it is likely, I say, or even possible, that such a pure romance should have sprung suddenly into note, should have been commonly received, made more generally available by means of translation by the Seventy, have become associated with other books of which we know from the history of the Maccabees,† and from

* Ezek. xiv. 14, 20; xxviii. 3.

† 1 Macc. i. 57; Jos. c. Apion. i. 8; cf. Philo in Euseb. Præp. Ev. viii. 6, p. 357; Pusey, p. 295.

Josephus, that for them many were prepared to die rather than give them up; and what is more, in the short space of a century and a half should have produced such a marvellous effect as to be the main if not the only known cause of the general expectation of the coming of the Messiah at the time of our Lord's manifestation; that expectation upon the hypothesis having been altogether in abeyance, if it had not practically died out,* at the time when this narrative is supposed to have been produced.

For we must not forget that but for the book of Daniel we ourselves should know nothing of Daniel, and it is *entirely gratuitous* to suppose that in the year 166 B.C. any one knew or had ever heard any more than we should have known apart from this book. It is difficult in these matters to rest on one hypothesis only, and not unconsciously to borrow something from the counter hypothesis. Of course if in the second century before Christ the tradition about Daniel was in substance such as we have it now in the book of Daniel, then it is conceivable that a book like the book of Daniel might then have been written. But this is a pure presumption for which there is no evidence whatever; that is to say, in order to give the present book of Daniel its existence, we are obliged to postulate a condition of things which but for that book had, and for the most part could have had, no existence. We are obliged to postulate a tradition, which tradition is itself the product of this book. In our minds the idea of

* Cf. Psalm lxxxix. 49—51.

Daniel is clear and vivid, but how about the men who lived in the second century before Christ? They knew no more of Daniel than Ezekiel had told them, that he was a wise man, and for some reason or other might be ranked with Job and Noah. But when he lived was as uncertain as when they lived.

And yet it is from such a shadowy, nebulous, impalpable germ as this that our present book is supposed to have sprung. Certainly to propound such a theory is to anticipate by many centuries the age of the historic romance. Shakespear and Walter Scott are known to have made use of materials ready to hand, and to have worked them up into their magnificent ideal creations; but where were the materials ready to hand out of which a Daniel might have been created? They were hewn from a quarry which is to be found only in the book of Daniel itself. This is not making bricks without straw, but making the straw too for the bricks to be made with; or, as Dean Milman felicitously puts it, making them entirely of straw.* The hypothesis, then, of the late origin of the book of Daniel is not to be maintained without the further hypothesis of the existence of traditions which we have no reason whatever to believe existed. Thus it is clear that if Daniel is a late production, it is and can be nothing more than a pure romance, alike untrustworthy in all its details.

But then, adopting this hypothesis, what was the object with which the book was written? It was

* " History of the Jews," vol. i., p. xxv.

written in the year 165, to encourage and sustain the Jews under the severe persecutions of Antiochus Epiphanes.* We are told that the writer thought " Jeremiah could not have spoken of seventy years, for " that, " if he had, his prediction would have been fulfilled." "The opinion that seventy Sabbath-years or year-weeks had been meant forced itself upon him, and in connection with this the belief that that period was now drawing to a close."† By way, therefore, of gaining the time, like the Chaldean magicians of whom he had spoken, he takes the prophecy of Jeremiah and expands his years into weeks of years. The former prophet had made a mistake, as the event had proved : he will hazard another prophetic conjecture by way of correcting it. But then, surely, if he was not writing prophecy, but only history that should look like prophecy, he would make the prophecy agree with the history. But the difficulty is to do this.

If, however, it is granted that seventy weeks of *years* are meant, that gives us the definite number of 490 years to deal with ; and as the angel Gabriel, in the vision of Daniel, is clearly speaking in the first year of Darius the Mede, the most natural idea would be that those 490 years would be counted from that first year of Darius the Mede, or else, possibly, on the supposition that he was modifying the prophecy of Jeremiah, from the date of *that* prophecy.

---

* See " Essays and Reviews," p. 76, quoted by Dr. Pusey, *Daniel the Prophet*, p. 224.

† Kuenen, p. 273.

But the date of Jeremiah's prophecy was the fourth
year of Jehoiakim, or about B.C. 606. One would
suppose, therefore, that if the writer had intended to
sustain the men of his time with the hope of prosperity and deliverance soon to come, he would have
chosen a date near at hand. But 490 years from
B.C. 606 brings us to the year B.C. 116, an altogether
fruitless result, and manifestly one of no bearing at
all on the national calamities of his own day, B.C. 165.
What present relief would be given by the thought
that in some fifty years to come the trials of that
time would have passed away? No fictitious or
apparent prophecy was wanted to tell them that
which they all knew, nor would this have been a
sufficiently worthy object for the writer of an historical romance to aim at.

But if we count, as it seems more natural to do,
the 490 years from the supposed time of the vision,
that will bring us to the year 48 B.C., or thereabouts.
And here, as before, the result is entirely nugatory,
and even more inappropriate as regards the supposed
temporary purpose with which the narrative was
written ; while it certainly does, strange to say, bring
us within one generation of that particular generation
in which our Lord was born.

If, therefore, the book of Daniel was written in the
year B.C. 165, or thereabouts, it seems at all events
reasonable to assume that this remarkable declaration about the seventy weeks, which is given with all
the solemnity of a prophecy, would have some discoverable application to the time at which it was

given, and to the generation for whose benefit it was announced. But no such application can be found. Like the arrows of Jonathan, this apparent prophecy has altogether missed the mark. On the hypothesis, it surely ought to have agreed with the history : as as a matter of fact, it altogether disagrees with it; and one cannot understand why it does. And is it not natural that the manifest failure of an assumed prophecy like this in corresponding with current events would utterly damage the character of the document in which it was found, when its only claim to attention would be the tokens it presented of fore-knowledge? We are asked to believe that a book is produced at a certain period, by an unknown author, gathering together and consolidating certain supposed floating traditions about Daniel, embellishing and adding to those traditions, making a connected story of the whole, and venturing certain statements under the form of prophecy which were to seem to predict the striking events of the writer's own time. We are asked to believe that this book acquired great notoriety, and produced an enormous effect in consequence of its being at once supposed to be nearly four centuries older than it was, though there was no evidence of its continuous existence, and more especially because it was thought to contain wonderful prophecies which the course of current events was day by day fulfilling. One of these prophecies declared that within 490 years from a certain time the transgression and sin of the nation would be finished and iniquity atoned for, that everlasting righteousness would be brought in, and vision and prophecy concluded, and a holy of holies anointed. Whatever these mysterious phrases may mean, they would serve to point to a great crisis which should be unique, which could be confounded with nothing else; and this crisis was to occur at a definite period, and that period was the writer's own time. Surely the men of that generation and of the following generation must have known how far events had justified these prognostications, and surely they would have judged of them and the book containing them accordingly.

It seems perfectly inconceivable that a book should have been put forth in the midst of events then going on, of which it could be said that it was "not prophecy, but history, which in consequence of the drapery is represented as prediction," * and yet that one of the most prominent of its apparent prophecies should be not only hopelessly at variance with the history, but apparently no less incapable of application or adaptation to it by any process of manipulation. The notion of the writer holding out the hope that within fifty or a hundred years the golden age of Israel should arrive, and that this was *the* hope which was fraught with special elements of strength and consolation for *the men of that day*, then smarting under the persecution of Antiochus IV., and that it was owing to the felt appropriateness of the comfort thus administered that the book became so popular as to be confounded with the traditionally

* Kuenen, p. 147.

sacred books, and to be thought Divine, is, when we fairly realise all that it involves, a notion that on the face of it is absurd. Whatever may have been the actual fortunes of the book of Daniel, this at all events cannot be a fair representation of what they actually were.

And if we are disposed to think that it was not the verisimilitude of prophecy in the book, but the mere assumption of the guise it wore that was the secret of its fascination,—that it was not because it seemed to be prophecy, but because it pretended to be so, that men were attracted and deceived by it,—that is indeed a notion very easy to be conceived, but we may question whether on the whole it is one so likely to have been realised in fact. If the prophecy of the seventy weeks had any fitness for the time when it is alleged to have been written, one can understand its producing a certain effect and gaining a certain influence, but if it was neither prophecy nor history, one is at a loss to comprehend the secret of its strength. If it did not suit the history, where was the evidence of its being prophecy, or why was it likely to pass as such, or to be confounded with it?

And yet it is at once obvious that no possible manipulation of the 490 years will make them fit the requirements of the last years of Antiochus. Here, then, was a crucial test to which a person writing at the time supposed would surely have taken care not to expose himself, being as it was, moreover, one which he might so very easily have avoided. Why not choose a number which would suit the exigencies of his case, and not one which would seem to court failure from its manifest incongruity?

But it is said that the writer had no definite system of chronology. " We are not sure that he follows the same chronology as that which has now been fixed for us by the scientific study of history. He may have thought that some periods were of shorter or longer duration than they were in reality. Nay, there is no probability in the expectation that his reckoning should exactly coincide with ours. How could he determine accurately what space of time separated him, for example, from the Babylonish captivity? " * To which I reply, this is surely to credit him most gratuitously with an unnecessary and improbable amount of ignorance, in order to save our own hypotheses. That his reckoning and ours may not have coincided to the year is conceivable; but if he was altogether at fault, why should he hazard so definite a number as 490 years, and what right have we to assume that his calculation should need correcting by centuries and half-centuries? Surely before assuming his ignorance, of which there is not the slightest proof, seeing that, on the contrary, recent investigation and discovery have combined to establish the accuracy of his information in other respects,† it would be as well to question our own honesty, or at least the wisdom of our hypotheses, which cannot anyhow be made to tally even with his supposed mistakes.

* Kuenen, p. 265.

† This is admitted by the Dean of Westminster, " Jewish Church," vol. iii., p. 73.

Furthermore, the writer of the first book of Maccabees three times over refers to the extinction of prophecy in his own day as a fact; * and, strange to say, the first of these is in connection with that very year when it is confidently asserted that the book of Daniel appeared; but twice afterwards, during a period of five-and-twenty years, he speaks of the want being still felt. May we not fairly ask whether this language would have been possible if in the interval a book had appeared which had been utterly unknown before, but was then at once and so suddenly popular

* The first of these is with reference to the altar of burnt-offerings which had been profaned by Antiochus Epiphanes, of which the writer says: "They thought it best to pull it down, lest it should be a reproach to them because the heathen had defiled it: wherefore they pulled it down, and laid up the stones in the mountain of the temple in a convenient place, *until there should come a prophet to show what should be done with them*" (1 Macc. iv. 45, 46). This was obviously in the very year B.C. 165, in which various modern critics are agreed that the book of Daniel sprang into existence.

Again, after the death of Judas, "there was great affliction in Israel, the like whereof was not *since the time that a prophet was not seen among them*" (ch. ix. 27).

And once more of Simon, after the Romans had entertained his ambassadors honourably: "The Jews and priests were well pleased that Simon should be their governor and high priest for ever, *until there should arise a faithful prophet*" (ch. xiv. 41).

It is perfectly clear from these passages that the writer of the first book of Maccabees was acquainted with no prophet of his own date. It is also plain that he supposed it impossible that the people of the time of which he wrote should be acquainted with any contemporary with themselves. This, of course, might be the case even if the book of Daniel had been produced in the year 165 B.C. But had that book then appeared and taken the place in the national literature which it must have taken to become canonical, then it is impossible that the writer, living perhaps some fifty or sixty years afterwards, as to be mistaken for the work of Daniel? That the writer of it was not accepted in his own name is absolutely certain, for it has utterly perished. Is it the least likely, or is it reasonably probable, that his own individuality could have been lost in his identification with the great prophet of Babylon, who but for himself and his book was manifestly otherwise unknown?

I have purposely abstained from treating the prophecy of the seventy weeks in greater detail because I was anxious to deal with broad and general principles. I have also confined myself at present to trying to show that that prophecy by itself presents very serious and as I believe absolutely fatal obstacles to the theory of the late origin of Daniel. Into its actual meaning I have no time now to enter. Suffice it for the present to say that I believe when our Lord began His ministry He had this prophecy in view, for there is no other He could have had; and that it was to the mysterious promise of the angel Gabriel that there should be an interval of 490 years between His own advent and

should have spoken as he did, because there was then a patent and notorious instance of one who, if not reckoned among the old prophets, had yet 'eclipsed them by the fame and importance of his predictions bearing upon times still recent.

In connection with this matter it should also be borne in mind that ages before the time of the Maccabees the history and literature of the Jews had borne witness not indeed to the cessation of prophecy, whatever traces there may be of that, but to the failure of other gifts of a kindred nature which had once been the glory of Israel. See, *e.g.,* the statement made (Ezra ii. 63) and repeated (Neh. vii. 65): " The Tirshatha said unto " the priests whose genealogy was incomplete, " that they should not eat of the most holy things till there stood up a priest with Urim and Thummim."

some period we have as yet not determined, and which was designedly left obscure, that He referred when He began to preach : *The time is fulfilled, and the kingdom of God is at hand. Repent ye, and believe the Gospel.*   And may we not fairly question whether we can in any true sense believe that Gospel if we are not prepared to accept it as given by God, and not merely invented and proposed by man ; and, if given by God, as not impossibly or improbably prepared for and even promised by Him in the *sure word of prophecy ?*

Daniel ix. 24.—*Seventy weeks are determined upon thy people and upon thy holy city, to finish the transgression, and to make an end of sins, and to make reconciliation for iniquity, and to bring in everlasting righteousness, and to seal up the vision and prophecy, and to anoint the Most Holy.*

LECTURE XI.

THE theory of the late origin of Daniel is, as a
theory, beset with certain difficulties, from
which the opposite theory of the genuineness of that
book is undoubtedly free. For instance, not only is it
impossible on the former hypothesis for one moment
to regard the narrative as in any sense true, but considering the entire absence of information respecting
Daniel, which on this hypothesis there obviously
was in the second century before Christ, the interest
attaching to his name, no less than the details of his
history and character, would have had to be created
by the writer; whereas if the book was genuine we
are delivered from any difficulty as to its origin,
because it was the natural and spontaneous record of
very remarkable events. In this latter case all the
difficulty centres, and I desire by no means to disguise its magnitude, in the acceptance of the events
recorded. After we have surmounted the difficulty
of the book being genuine, there arises the yet greater
difficulty of its authenticity. If it is the work of a
writer in the sixth century before Christ, is it after
all an authentic record of historic fact? This, no

doubt, is a very momentous question. But it is to be observed that whereas in the former case we have to account for certain facts,—for example, the existence and influence of the book under known conditions of probability,—in the other we have not to account for the facts, but only to accept them, it being previously allowed that they violate all the known conditions of probability. They are recorded as in the highest degree exceptional, and they are accepted or rejected as such. Given the supposition that they occurred, there is no further difficulty attaching to the record of them. In the one case, on a natural basis, there is a great natural difficulty; in the other, on a basis admittedly above and beyond nature, there is no further difficulty at all. The difficulty, therefore, lies *in limine.*

It is at once manifest that this difficulty is so great that it is likely to overshadow and conceal the other, and in either case very seriously to affect our judgment. We should, however, be especially careful to guard against its doing so as long as we desire to regard the question as a purely literary one, to be decided by the rules of literary evidence. If we start with a prepossession against anything transcending the experience of our own ordinary daily life, and make that the test of genuineness, then there is not one of the books of the Bible that can stand. The questions of genuineness and authenticity must be kept perfectly distinct. It is easy to see how readily they may become confused. Daniel is not authentic because it is not genuine, and as we have seen in that

case it cannot be ; that is a perfectly valid inference :
but, Daniel can hardly be genuine because it is so
replete with the marvellous ; that is an inference no
less easy and natural, but by no means valid.

At the present time, then, we are not at all concerned with the question of the authenticity of Daniel,
but merely with that of its genuineness. We must
be specially careful that the free discussion of its
genuineness is not in any way affected or influenced
by our prepossessions as to its authenticity.

We have already seen that if this book was written
in 165 B.C., there are certain grave difficulties to be
disposed of which may otherwise prove fatal to the
theory. Nor is it easy to dispose of them. As long
as we confine ourselves to *à priori* considerations
apart from the contents of the book, it is undoubtedly
more easy to explain its existence if genuine than
the reverse ; and taking the prophecy of the seventy
weeks as a crucial instance, it is absolutely impossible
to assign any meaning to that prophecy which will
make it applicable to the time supposed. It remains,
therefore, to inquire whether it has any meaning at
all, and what that meaning is.

And first it must be remembered that there is no
question as to the date of Daniel, if it is not a late production. It was either written in the second century
before Christ, or it was written in the sixth. No one
proposes any other alternative.* If, therefore, the

* See Pusey, "Daniel the Prophet," p. 43. Edition 1869. If
Daniel was not written cir. 165 B.C., no object is gained by the hypothesis of any other date after cir. 530 B.C., for place it where we will

theory of a late origin leaves this particular prophecy unexplained, is the opposite theory more promising in this respect ? I shall endeavour to discuss this question as far as possible on broad principles, and independently of minute verbal details.

I assume, then, that in the first year of Darius, or about 538 B.C., Daniel was told that seventy weeks were determined upon his people and his holy city for a particular purpose afterwards explained in the remainder of the verse; and I make this further assumption, which will hardly be denied me, that the seventy weeks so determined are afterwards split up into seven weeks, and threescore and two weeks and one week ; but I do so merely because, if this is the case, then it becomes no longer a matter of doubt as to when the seventy weeks began, or at least only so far as it depends upon *the going forth of the commandment to restore and to build Jerusalem.*   That is to say, we are apparently intended to count them, not from the time when the angel was speaking, as we might have thought most natural, but from the time of which he subsequently spoke.   The first sub-division of seven weeks manifestly began from *the going forth of the commandment to restore and to build Jerusalem*—if, that is, the seven weeks, and threescore and two weeks and one week, are identical (as, being equivalent to them, none can doubt they are) with the seventy weeks.   It is entirely gratuitous to

during the interval it contains statements as to the future manifestly inexplicable on any human principles. As a matter of fact, however, no intermediate theory has been formulated.

suppose that these seventy weeks are to be counted from the year of Jeremiah's prophecy; and though we might at first suppose the present moment was the one referred to, yet when a definite *terminus a quo* is afterwards given for an equivalent period to commence from, it is at least reasonable to suppose that *that* is the *terminus* meant in both cases.*

But now arises a much greater difficulty. What was the commandment which went forth to restore and to build Jerusalem? and when did it go forth? We must not forget that the angel was speaking before the issue of the edict of Cyrus. If, therefore, the narrative is authentic, everything was as yet unknown and unaccomplished. Daniel himself was perplexed and anxious as to the termination of that captivity, which he believed was limited to seventy years. He thought the end of those years could not be far off. He is told that there is still a future in store for his people and city of seventy weeks of years—supposing, that is, that by the weeks were meant years. He is not told anything as to the termination of the captivity, which was his chief subject of anxiety. But we know that he lived to see the cause for that anxiety removed. Its removal came in the natural course of events. And this being

* If otherwise, however, it must not be forgotten that then the computation, however made, leads us to no satisfactory result. This is the point: on one hypothesis a consistent and intelligible result is obtained ; on any other, none. The difficulty is that the first hypothesis points us inevitably to prediction : any other holds out the hope of escape from that conclusion ; but in every case the hope is delusive.

so, the spirit of prophecy did not concern itself with that immediate source of anxiety, but reached on into the far distant future, and spoke of the ultimate destiny of the people and city, which was after all at the bottom of the prophet's thoughts, aspirations, and anxieties, however legitimately they were interested likewise in the immediate fortunes of his nation.

And here we may pause for a moment to notice a mark of reality in the narrative on the supposition of its genuineness and authenticity. The last date given in Daniel is the third year of Cyrus.* We know that he was alive then: he could not have lived long afterwards. As, therefore, he witnessed the promulgation of the edict of Cyrus, he witnessed at all events an issue and answer to his prayer which received no elucidation from the communication of the angel, however much it may have served to elucidate the prophecy of Jeremiah, and yet the record of that communication remained. It was far too precious to be cancelled. Events had made it even more obscure; but it was the message of an angel, and therefore of inestimable value. The present distress and problem of the national fortunes had been relieved and solved by the development of circumstances; but a pledge of vast magnitude and importance had been given to the future, which embraced five centuries to come. This is at all events consistent with the ordinary dealings of Providence, which leaves our perplexities to be solved by the process of events, however much it may be fraught

* Dan. x. 1.

with principles of far wider import concerning even
the distant future. What was uppermost in Daniel's
mind was virtually passed over by the angel, but a
communication was made to him which involved not
only the solution of the immediate present, but bore
the promise also of centuries to come. Our prayers
are not answered as we expect or wish them to be,
but in a manner at once inscrutable and far more
abundant.

The angel, however, spoke of a *decree to restore and
to build Jerusalem*. But it is to be observed that the
edict of Cyrus, gladly as Daniel must have hailed it,
in no degree fulfilled the conditions of this decree as
here given. The terms of that edict, as it is preserved
to us in Chronicles and Ezra,* have reference only to
the house of God at Jerusalem. It was in no sense
a decree to *restore and to build Jerusalem*. And the
same likewise applies to the decree of Darius, which
confirmed in similar terms the suspended decree of
Cyrus. The only decree which was capable of any
wider application than the temple merely, and the
text of which is preserved to us in the historic records
of Scripture, is the edict which was given to Ezra in
the seventh year of Artaxerxes,† or B.C. 457. This
decree in its express terms provided not only for the
embellishment of the temple, which had been completed since the sixth year of Darius,‡ but also for
the political organisation and government of the

---

* 2 Chron. xxxvi. 23, Ezra i. 1—4, v. 13 *seq.*, vi. 1—12.

† Ezra vii. 7, 11—26.

‡ Ezra vi. 15.

nation. It was by far the most important act of recognition performed by any foreign monarch in relation to the Jews, and the most complete and comprehensive in its nature of which we have any record in Scripture; and to it are to be referred not only all the reconstructive operations of Ezra, but those also of Nehemiah,* who was furnished with subsequent authority by the same king in the spirit of his former decree. As far, therefore, as the sacred history of the Jews enables us to determine when the commandment went forth *to restore and to build Jerusalem*, there seems little doubt that we must refer it to the decree of the seventh year of Artaxerxes, of which the original Aramaic text is preserved to us in the book of Ezra. It is unquestionably a fuller and wider decree than that either of Darius or of Cyrus, important as those decrees, and more especially the former of them, undoubtedly were.

Of course it is obviously impossible that Daniel could have lived to see this decree, or have known anything about it. We are supposing now that his narrative is authentic, and consequently there is nothing inconsistent in supposing also that the Spirit of God made known by Gabriel that which Daniel himself could neither have known nor understood. If, therefore, *the going forth of the commandment to restore and to build Jerusalem* may fairly be referred to the decree of Artaxerxes, then it is plain that that decree becomes the starting-point of the seventy weeks, or 490 years.

* Neh. ii. 1—8.

What, then, is it to be the work of these 490 years to accomplish? This is stated in a very full and complete manner under several heads. First, it is *to finish*, or to restrain, or shut up *the transgression*, and *to make an end to* or to seal up *sins*. There is a twofold uncertainty here as to the exact reading,* the verb in each case at all events suggesting the alternative signification; an uncertainty which seems to bear silent testimony at once to the felt importance and obscurity of the prophecy which is inconceivable on the supposition of its origin in the time of Antiochus Epiphanes, but not at all unnatural on the other supposition. The mention also of *the* transgression, apart from the indefinite word *sins* which follows it, might suggest at first thought some possible reference to the cruelty of the Chaldean oppression † under which the nation was still suffering, though the context would almost immediately show this to be impossible. Transgression and sin, then, it would seem, were to undergo some special restraint or limitation as the first result of these seventy weeks of years.

A second result was the *atonement* or reconciliation that was to be made for *iniquity*. As sins were to be made an end of, so iniquity in general terms was to be atoned for, to be ceremonially cleansed, covered over, and put away. Broad and universal in its bearing as the language is, it nevertheless does not seem

* The reading dubitates between כלא and a suggested כלה, and between חתם and התם. In favour of the second, Davidson, " Hebrew Text, etc.," says, " Cdd. mult. Nachmanides. all vss.," and of the fourth, which is the Keri, " Cdd. mult. LXX. Aq. Sym. Syr. Vg."
† Cf. Hab. ii. 5, sq.

to be altogether and absolutely incapable of a possible and primary reference to the immediate circumstances of the time, and to the approaching emancipation, though that is indeed a reference which would at once be felt to be merely transitory and wholly inadequate. And in this connection it is barely conceivable that even the seventy weeks may themselves have had literally an immediate and passing reference to the promulgation of the edict of Cyrus in the year but one following the message of the angel, in the same way that the loftiest and farthest-reaching of the prophecies had their natural genesis in the human emergencies of the time, though their very unfitness to the mere limitations of those emergencies was the proof of their truly prophetic character and heavenly origin. It is the lapse of time alone which brings the true solution of the prophecies, while it shows at once the way in which they transcend all primary application, and reach forth in the plenitude and natural expansiveness of their language to some ultimate and possible verification and fulfilment even yet far distant. While, therefore, we insist mainly upon the far-off meaning of this great prophecy, it seems right nevertheless not wholly to lose sight of the transient reflexion of meaning which may have been cast on the all but immediate present, or of the way in which it thus displayed its generic albeit faint resemblance to the rest of prophecy as a whole.

But we pass on. The next result of the seventy weeks is *to bring in everlasting righteousness.* Here it is at once plain that, however this may have been anticipated as a consequence of the return from captivity, it was an expectation that would speedily be disabused. The times of Zerubbabel, Ezra, and Nehemiah were no times of everlasting righteousness, neither were *they* personally exponents of it equal to many whom the nation had already known. Nor, on the other hand, would the times of the Maccabees answer more accurately to this description. And yet *to bring in everlasting righteousness* was a promise —unless the writer was singularly ignorant of or singularly reckless in the use of words—fraught with very solemn and tremendous issues. Moreover, Jeremiah, who on any theory preceded this writer, had spoken of *the Lord our righteousness*, and of *a righteous branch* being raised unto David ;* and Isaiah also, to whom the same remark applies, had spoken of the Lord as *bringing near His righteousness.*† Surely, then, to *bring in the righteousness of ages*, or *everlasting righteousness* like *everlasting strength*, ‡ was an expression of unfathomable significance, even if it was not intended to bear a correspondently profound meaning. To talk of *bringing in everlasting righteousness* as a thing imminent 165 years before our era, when the hope was forthwith to be falsified, and he who gave it stultified by the event, was surely not the way to commend a forged production to the notice and acceptance of his own generation, still less of the generations following. We have heard of prophecies lying dormant for many years till events have

* Jer. xxiii. 5, 6.   † Isaiah xlvi. 13.   ‡ Isaiah xxvi. 4.

suddenly brought them into note, but here there is
no analogy discernible in the process, for we can
trace the immediate influence and effect, permanent
and widespread, of this prophecy, although for many
generations no fulfilment of it was alleged.   Here
we find an attitude of suspense and expectation
created by the prophecy, and not a borrowed glory
of accidental renown attaching to the prophecy in
consequence of the unexpected development of events.
To bring in everlasting righteousness was verily a
hope worthy of a nation calling itself the holy nation,
and which alone of all the nations of antiquity has
left us memorials attesting the justice of the claim,
and establishing the imperishable and unalterable
standard of an ideal righteousness which must at
once dwarf and condemn every other standard that
would compare with it.   But this was the hope that
the prophet Daniel held out to his people, and, what
was more, within certain limits he fixed the advent
of its dawn.

Nor was this all.   The seventy weeks were also *to
seal up vision and prophet.* The language is obviously
figurative, but we can hardly err in interpreting the
figure.   It must either mean to *close up* and so *conclude* or *put an end to*, or, which seems even more
vivid and therefore more probable, to *put the seal to
and attest:* in this latter sense the former one also
would be virtually included; and indeed in an age
which was, as the few surviving fragments of its literature conspicuously proclaim,* especially conscious of

* See, *e.g.*, 1 Macc. iv. 46, ix. 27, xiv. 41.

and sensitive to the cessation of prophecy as a fact, it seems strange that a promise should have been given, and as we must suppose eagerly grasped at and mistaken for prophecy, that a period of 490 years should infallibly witness the cessation of vision and prophet. On the other hand, therefore, I infer, as seems more probable, that the special meaning of the figure was that the entire dispensation and phenomenon—for as manifested in Israel it was a unique phenomenon—of prophecy should receive a special completion and verification in that which should finally and conclusively set the seal to all that the prophets had spoken, should once and for all show that they as a race were not impostors or enthusiasts, but men who had the fear of God before their eyes and the message of God as hidden fire shut up in their hearts and struggling to be delivered, as well as the professed words of God on their hallowed lips. And if this was the promise of Daniel, he assigned the limits within which it should be fulfilled.

But that promise is not exhausted yet. The time specified was determined concerning the *people* and the *holy city*, not only *to seal up vision and prophet*, but also *to anoint a Holy of Holies, or a Most Holy.* We allow all possible latitude to the meaning here, whether it is personal or local,* about which authorities are divided, and which is unquestionably obscure. We try simply to understand the words as they seem to be by any means capable of being understood. If the meaning was local, and referred to *the* Holy

---

* See Pusey, p. 1~1 ; Tregelles on Daniel, p. 98, etc.

of Holies in the Temple, then on the supposition
that the writer himself witnessed the reconsecration
of the Temple after its defilement by Antiochus,
and was writing, not some seventy natural weeks
before, but apparently in the very year that it was
thus reconsecrated,* where was the special appropriateness of such a promise as this, that within
a definite and given time the anointing of a Holy of
Holies should take place?   Surely the known events
of the year 165 B.C. do not provide us with a natural
historic basis broad enough or strong enough or
real enough for the possible foundation of this prophecy; nor is any supposed correspondence between
its language and the circumstances of those events
likely to have furnished the reason why this book,
being spurious, should at once have been accepted as
rendering specially opportune and Divine consolation,
and because of the help so rendered have been at
once, or very shortly afterwards, as it must have
been, assigned to the time and authorship of Daniel
four centuries before.   Truly an hypothesis such as
this, in the strength of its desire to avoid the miraculous, has summoned the miraculous to its aid,
and while professing to deal only with natural causes,
has postulated the operation of causes absolutely
unnatural and wholly improbable.

If the book of Daniel was the product of the times
of Daniel, then we know what we have to accept;
but if it was, as we are asked to believe, the spurious
and parasitical growth of the age of Antiochus

* 1 Macc. v. 25 : and Pusey, p. 220.

Epiphanes, then verily not even the unlimited fertility in hypothesis of the unrestrained and irresponsible critical faculty seems capable of imagining circumstances that could naturally have produced it, or at least of giving such consistency to those circumstances as shall be consistent with one of the most conspicuous and crucial utterances of the book.

If, on the other hand, Daniel wrote it, and if this was really the heaven-sent communication of the angel which he recorded, then the last work of the seventy weeks, or 490 years, was *to anoint the Holy of Holies*, or *a most Holy one*. We know that Haggai, writing after Daniel, declared plainly that the latter glory of the house he witnessed should exceed all the glory it had known before,* and therefore it is not inconceivable that some special and peculiar sanctification of the material Temple may have been intended, or at all events understood, by the words, more especially when we consider how prominent a place the Temple held in the national thoughts and affections.   But there is reason to believe that this local sense does certainly not exhaust their meaning, which is capable of a personal reference; and they may therefore be interpreted as corresponding with the *everlasting righteousness* before mentioned.   The anointing of one who is a holy of holies, or all holy, is the complement of bringing in everlasting righteousness; and the subsequent prophecy of Malachi, that *the Lord should suddenly come to His Temple*,† seems, if not written in view of this promise to Daniel,

* Haggai ii. 9.   † Malachi iii. 1.

at all events to combine the personal and local sense of this particular phrase, and to suggest that the coming of *the Lord our righteousness* might prove a consecration of the Holy of Holies never before experienced. Once regard the narrative as genuine and authentic, and the suggestiveness and possible significance of the language here becomes simply inexhaustible; whereas, relegate it to the second century before Christ, and it is absolutely hopeless to assign to it any meaning that shall fit in with current events, or that shall seem likely to have gained for this prophecy its known popularity and distinction in consequence of its supposed correspondence with those events.

Whereas, if it is really a Divine communication that we have here to deal with concerning events beyond the reach of Daniel's natural faculties to discern or to comprehend, then we have to face the fact that he was told, obscurely indeed for him, but with sufficient clearness for all subsequent generations of men when the limits assigned had been reached, that from the going forth of a certain decree as yet undetermined, a period of 490 years should witness the accomplishment of transgression and the filling up of sin, the reconciliation of iniquity, and the bringing in of everlasting righteousness, should set the seal to vision and prophet, and anoint a Holy of Holies. If the words were in any sense true, a most remarkable charge was entrusted to the unknown future, to the tender care and ultimate accomplishment of five centuries to come.

And how was it executed ?   Let history declare.
If we compute the 490 years from any conceivable
date from the first year of Darius the Mede to the
twentieth of Artaxerxes, the two extreme limits possible, we are brought to within fifty years of the birth
of Christ, whether before or after it.   The knowledge
that in the last half-century before Christ the seventy
weeks of Daniel must nearly have run out, was surely
to those who believed the prophets sufficient to
generate an eager expectation of a crisis at hand, and
of a person soon to come,—an expectation of which
it may be said that the aggregate of human history
presents us with no parallel to it,—an expectation
which arose, indeed, in the midst of an insignificant
and despised people, but which spread from them
throughout the civilised globe.   And the more we
contemplate this expectation, the more unable shall
we be to account for it, if we leave out of our calculation the influence of prophecy, rightly or wrongly
interpreted, and in particular the influence of this
prophecy, which alone of all others gave the note of
time, but which, had it first been published in the
second century before Christ, would have carried with
it the promise of its sure detection, because of its
obvious discrepance with current events.

As we have seen, however, the only edict in
Scripture not exclusively limited to the Temple is
that in the seventh year of Artaxerxes,* or 457 B.C.,
from which the computation of 490 years brings us

---

* The reign of Artaxerxes Longimanus was from B.C. 464 to
B.C. 425.

to the year of our Lord 33.   After this date, in the reign of Artaxerxes we read of no edict, but only of certain letters given by that sovereign to Nehemiah. Consequently, as a matter of fact, on the supposition of the genuineness of Daniel, we are confronted with the remarkable circumstance that 490 years after that edict of the Persian monarch, in virtue of which Jerusalem was restored and built again after the captivity, a person had been born and died whose influence on mankind has been unique in the world's history, and events had happened which not only have changed the face of the earth, but to the range of whose possible influence we ourselves cannot even now set the limit.

If these events are of the nature of which those most conversant with and influenced by them declare them to be, then it is undoubtedly true that transgression and sin were ended by the death of Him whose death, although the crowning sin of all, yet took away the sin of the world; then reconciliation for iniquity was made by Him who prayed in His last moments for His murderers, *Father, forgive them, for they know not what they do;* * then everlasting righteousness was brought into this sin-stained world, never more in the brightness of its example and the power of its influence to leave it, by the life and character of Him in whom *the Father was well pleased,*† and who *abideth a priest for ever after the order of Melchizedek;* ‡ then the ministry of seer and prophet was once for all vindicated and

* Luke xxiii. 34.   † Matt. iii. 17.   ‡ Heb. vi. 20, vii   4.

verified by the career and office of Him who was
Himself greater than the greatest of the prophets ;
then was the sanctuary of the Most High sanctified
by the presence and teaching of Him who *spake as
never man spake ;* * and then was a Holy of Holies,
or one Most Holy, anointed among the sons of men
in the person of Him to whom *the Spirit without
measure was given.*†

Of course it is open to us to deny that these
events had this significance, while it is not open
to us to prove to demonstration that they had ; it
is open to us to say that there was no Divine
message of forgiveness in the death of Christ, no
assured promise of pardon sealed in His blood ; that
the marvels of His life and the mystery of His death
stood alone in their isolation without any bearing
on the history of the Old Testament or on the lofty
utterances of the ancient prophets ; that the promise
of the Spirit whom He undertook to send was but the
naturally explicable phenomenon of a merely physical
sensation,—while it is not open to us to prove conclusively the opposite ; but at least it is not possible
for any man to deny that these were the only
events in the history of the world to which this
significance was ever assigned, or that they themselves were inherently unworthy of it ; nor is it
possible for us, do what we will with it, to shut
our eyes to the singular correspondence in point
of time between the seventy prophetic weeks of
Daniel who spoke of some such events as these,

* John vii. 46.   † John iii. 34.

and fixed the date for them, and the age in the
world's history at which our Lord appeared as the
promised One

> " Who came to break oppression,
>   And set the captive free ;
> To take away transgression,
>   And rule in equity."

Rev. xix. 10.—*The testimony of Jesus is the spirit of prophecy.*

LECTURE XII.

THE SPIRIT OF PROPHECY.

IN dealing with Daniel's prophecy of the seventy weeks, I was concerned to show that it had no possible bearing on the events of the second century before Christ, when it is assumed to have arisen; but that, if it was a really Divine communication, it had, notwithstanding much inherent uncertainty, a very remarkable correspondence in point of time with the known historic rise of the Christian Church and with the advent of the Son of man. I did not care to follow this correspondence into minute particulars, not only because of the natural dryness of the subject as a matter of discourse, but because of the many points that upon any such treatment of it must ever remain open to question, and also because of the great difficulty in bringing home conviction to the mind by such a method, which is my first and only object. If I fail in other respects, it is a matter of no importance; if I fail here, I shall have spoken and wrought in vain.

I tried, then, to show that if our religion is what it professes to be, and if Christ had really a Divine mission, then the language of Daniel, while it could apply to nothing else, would accurately and exhaustively apply to Him; that what the angel Gabriel declared to Daniel should happen at a certain time, did actually happen when Christ came; that the interval between the edict of Artaxerxes and the birth of the Christian Church, leaving out minor details into which we cannot here enter, was as nearly as possible seventy weeks of years,—neither one week more nor one week less.

I am myself by no means insensible to the marvellous correspondence which may be traced yet further when we closely examine the prophetic language,* but I prefer to deal broadly with the

---

* I regard it as absolutely certain that the seventy weeks of Daniel ix. 24 are split up in the next verse into seven weeks and threescore and two weeks and one week, which, being commensurate, are intended to be identical with them, and that by "after the threescore and two weeks" of ver. 26 we are intended to understand, after the second of these periods so divided; while ver. 27 gives us the events of the last week, and of the period concisely alluded to in the former verse. In this way, the death of Christ took place in the middle of the last year-week, after His ministry of three years and a half: while the remainder of that week was occupied with the events succeeding His death till the closing of the covenant with Israel and the admission of the Gentiles to the Christian Church. It is true that our chronology fails us in this last particular from the want of details, but there is no reason to think that if it were complete it would not correspond. That the death of Christ happened in the middle of the last of the seventy weeks from 457 B.C., I think may be regarded as virtually *proved.* (See Pusey, ch. iv.) And the time that elapsed from the crucifixion to the vision of Peter and the baptism of Cornelius, or the death of Stephen and the conversion of Saul, may very probably have been between three and four years. (See Pusey, p. 178.) I may add that since the seventy weeks can only be regarded as identical

seventy weeks themselves, which, though sufficiently
definite, yet, from the very fact of their being *weeks*,
seem to suggest a certain latitude of computation
which may serve to render us practically independent
of more minute calculations, which, however accurate,
seem to challenge our adherence on the ground of.
their accuracy which must therefore be withheld if
that fails.

While, then, it is admitted that the theory of the
late origin of Daniel cannot explain the prophecy of
the seventy weeks, we find it impossible to deny
the fact that the life and death of Christ, and the rise

with the 7 + 62 + 1, and the work of ver. 24 was that which Messiah
was to accomplish when He came, unless His coming was an empty
dream, it is a matter of comparative indifference where we place the
principal stop in ver. 25. Dr. Pusey does not scruple to say that the
Jews must have placed it dishonestly after *seven weeks*. But seeing that
the events of ver. 24 were only to be accomplished with the accomplishment of the seventy weeks, it matters not whether " the building
of street and wall in troublous times " is assigned to the seven
weeks or to the threescore and two weeks, though unquestionably the
history would favour the former. This is a point entirely independent
of the work of the seventy weeks so fully described in ver. 24. And
as on no theory of the origin of this prophecy can it be shown that
after the first seven year-weeks any person arose to whom the term
Messiah could be justly applied, we conclude that not only the
seven but the threescore and two weeks also were to precede the
coming of Messiah, and that the last week was to be occupied with
His career and its immediate consequences, in accordance with verses
24 and 27. The statement, therefore, of ver. 24 seems to us to decide
the punctuation of ver. 25 to be that which the English authorised
version and the Seventy (virtually) have followed. It is, moreover,
simply preposterous to attempt to distinguish between the Messiah
of ver. 24 and ver. 26. This being the only passage in the Old Testament where this peculiar use of the word is found, it is surely
obvious that it must apply to the same person in both.

of the Christian Church, present a remarkable correspondence in time with the words of the angel: *Seventy weeks are determined upon Thy people, and upon Thy holy city, to finish the transgression, and make an end of sins, and to make reconciliation for iniquity, and to bring in everlasting righteousness, and to seal up vision and prophet, and to anoint a holy of holies.*

It may be there is no meaning at all in this language, only then we have to account for the history of its influence on the world; but if it has any meaning, then Christ has done more than any one to reveal this meaning. And the time at which He did it corresponds with remarkable nearness to the time assigned. It is even possible that it may correspond with minute accuracy; but at all events the correspondence is so near that, failing any other possible meaning, the question arises naturally whether this may not be its meaning. We cannot answer this question in the affirmative without believing in Christ. But if we believe that He really did all that the angel spake of to Daniel, is it then absolutely incredible, we may ask, that an angel should have been sent to speak of it? If, however, this is the case, then we have here a clear instance of prediction in prophecy, and then is the record of this prediction a record of the Divine foreknowledge.

It has been my endeavour throughout these Lectures to show that Old Testament prophecy is such a record; that from the times of Abraham and David to those of the captivity there are features in it which cannot adequately be explained as the subsequent development of history certainly has explained them; that while the outlines of the features were undoubtedly there before, the course of events has invested them with colouring and expression; that these prophecies seem to point to a person to come in whom they converge, but far from being, as in this case they might be, merely vague and general, they also had reference to great national events yet future, such as the captivity and the return, so that justice would not be done to them if they were not allowed to be, strictly speaking, predictive, and that in one especial instance they not only had the prophetic characteristic of referring to this Person, but had also predicted and defined the proximate time of His appearance.

It will at once be obvious that it is impossible to prove all this to demonstration, but it is as well to observe what it is we can prove. We can prove a sufficient antiquity for all the prophecies—that they were certainly not written after the events alleged to have fulfilled them—that is, after the Christian era. We can prove that they were neither altered nor modified to make them more applicable to those events. We can also prove that the events as a whole were not historically moulded by those who recorded them so as to correspond more closely with the prophetic writings. We can also prove that both in their origin, their nature, and their influence, those events stand alone without any parallel in history. We can also prove that if those events were intrinsically what the New Testament represents them as being, then the obvious correspondence between them and the prophecies is so great as to justify their claim to have fulfilled them. We can also see that there is nothing inherently more difficult of belief in the supposition that the true meaning and intent of the prophecies was revealed in those events than there is in the nature of the events themselves: in fact, that on this hypothesis both events and prophecies become in some respects more simply *natural*, inasmuch as the events in that case do not stand in utter solitude, but are anticipated by exceptional phenomena leading up to them, while the phenomena of prophecy have at once a sufficient and adequate object to account for and demand their occurrence.

Every step here is perfectly legitimate and sound. The conclusion arrived at or suggested is undeniable on two conditions,—first, that we postulate the existence of a God like the God of the Bible, and allow that He has spoken in a special and exceptional manner for a special and exceptional purpose— namely, to make man acquainted with His will as the mere investigation of nature will not reveal it ; and, secondly, that we acknowledge the will so revealed, and bend ourselves to comply with it. If either of these conditions is unfulfilled, it is useless and hopeless to argue about prophecy, for that we are told *serveth not for them that believe not, but for them which believe.**

The question for us to determine is whether or not

* 1 Cor. xiv. 22.

there is evidence to show that God has made use of prophecy to declare His will, or whether all the special and peculiar features of it can be explained away and got rid of so as to reduce it to a mere record of human error and extravagance, of exaggeration, self-delusion, or imposture. If this is the case, then is our religion verily a thing of the earth earthy : it is merely one more of the futile, erring, and abortive efforts of man's natural sense of religion towards self-development ; efforts which are necessarily destined to failure, inasmuch as they are directed towards that which may not be—namely, recognised intercourse with the Infinite.

Such is the counter theory which is deliberately advanced and elaborately maintained in the present day. In permanent and irreconcilable opposition to it there are two conceptions which underlie the whole of Scripture, and pre-eminently prophecy: one is the idea of the spoken Word of God, and the other is the idea of that Faith in the heart of man to which it appeals. Where the latter does not exist, the former may be never so distinct and authoritative, but it will speak in vain.

Now we may say that prophecy, which implies this spoken Word of God, is witnessed mainly in two ways: partly by the self-illuminating nature of its communications, as when the prophets " boldly rebuked vice and patiently suffered for the truth's sake,"—they were to a man the preachers of the highest and purest morality, not only of their own but of any times, and they were for the most part

tried in the furnace of affliction,—and partly by prediction.

The declaration of events yet future is a faculty
not given to man. Whenever there is clear evidence
of its existence we are compelled either to resort to
the hypothesis of a lucky chance or to postulate
Divine foreknowledge. The predictions of the
Hebrew prophets cannot be ascribed to chance.
Where they exist, they are only to be ascribed to
Divine foreknowledge.

We must beware, however, that we do not ascribe
that foreknowledge to the prophets themselves.
The predictions of the prophets were frequently
verified in a way far different from that which they
themselves expected. The written record of their
sayings is the witness to their prophetic power, and
not their anticipations as to its fulfilment, which may
have been partial or even false. It is Divine and
not human foreknowledge of which prophecy is the
record. And we affirm that there are those broad
features in the Hebrew prophecy which warrant us
in regarding it as a record of Divine foreknowledge,
and that a wide and general survey of all the circumstances forbids, and emphatically forbids, us otherwise regarding it.

Who can read the fifty-third of Isaiah in the light
of the cross of Christ and not feel that the Divine
Spirit intended the prophet to speak of Him, and has
declared to us His intention by the utter hopelessness
of discovering any one else to whom his words are
half so applicable? But this appropriateness is no

less miraculous than if the prophet had been transported mentally into the distant future, and had
depicted what he saw. This may have been so or it
may not. We cannot tell, and it is useless to inquire.
All we know is, here is a prophecy of the eighth
century before Christ, and when we stand beneath
His cross we can only see in it a prediction of His
healing and atoning death. That His death has
given it a meaning that it never could have had before
is our warrant for claiming it as a record of Divine
foreknowledge. But we can only recognise the
accuracy of the record when we are content to see in
the cross of Christ the only adequate expression of
the Divine love. Nevertheless, at all events, the
accuracy of the correspondence between the record
and the great event is a fact that to a large extent
is independent of our acknowledgment either of the
foreknowledge or the love.

Such a prophecy as this, however, only becomes
predictive when we acknowledge it as prophecy. I
have endeavoured to point out that there are other
prophecies which are shown to be prophecies because
they are predictions. Indeed, if we deny to prophecy
its power to assume the character of prediction, we
lower it to a mere shadowy and sentimental function.
Evidentially there can be no direct proof of prophecy
but prediction. If the volume of prophecy contained
no predictions, then its sentiment and morality might
be never so high, but it would still lack something
that should show it to be more than human.

It is indeed true that we may bow down in blind

acknowledgment or contend in dogged assertion of the existence of this power, and yet be unelevated by the morality and untouched by the sentiment of the prophets, and remain, in fact, unpenetrated and unquickened by their spirit;—that is not the point; the question is whether we can truly acknowledge the Divine authority of prophecy, and yet deny its predictive power.

To acknowledge, however, the predictive character of prophecy is not an end in itself, but only a means to an end, the end being to accept the message of prophecy, whether conveyed with or without prediction, as the message of God. If there are real predictions in prophecy, then they must be the work of the Spirit of God. We may be sure that if that is the case, He desires us to acknowledge His work, but only that we may adore *Him.* If we lose ourselves in stolid wonderment at His work, or in the excitement of contending for it, instead of giving our hearts to Him and conforming our wills to His will, we shall miss the true end of prophecy; but none the less may we miss that end if we are content with vague generalities as to the glory, the beauty, the dignity, the grandeur of prophecy, and the like, and after all refuse to acknowledge the patent and conspicuous evidence it bears of being the special and distinct utterance of the mind of God conveyed in a highly exceptional and superhuman way, and bearing superhuman credentials.

In short, the object and design of all prophecy is that we should imbibe its spirit; and the evangelist apostle has told us that *the testimony of Jesus is the spirit of prophecy*,—that the spirit which animates the faculty is the spirit that bears witness to Jesus and about Jesus.

Nor can there be a more exhaustive or distinguishing mark of the character and functions of prophecy than this. It at once explains and accounts for the several features we have been considering. If Jesus was indeed the Christ the Son of God, then, if He was to spring from the seed of Abraham, there is nothing unreasonable in its being declared to Abraham that in his seed should all the families of the earth be blessed; nor is it unintelligible that in the sacred narrative of that promise there should be put on record that which should afterwards show it to be more adequately than anything else a record of the Divine foreknowledge. Then there is nothing inconceivable in a promise being given to David that his throne should be established for ever; and if the record of that promise, whenever it was written, was manifestly at variance with the known history of David's throne, and its only too conspicuous overthrow, then it becomes all the more evident that if there was any warrant for the promise at all, and if the record of it was in any sense a record of fact, then it could only be regarded as, humanly speaking, an undesigned record of Divine foreknowledge. Then also it becomes conceivable that the nation of Israel, being the elect and holy nation in consequence of the promise which it bore of producing the Holy Seed, should be the nurse also of a race of prophets who should not only indicate from time to time the characteristics of the coming Messiah, but should also forewarn the nation of its own destiny, and predict the more important and typical crises of its history—such as the captivity and return, significant and prophetic as those events not improbably were of a yet greater captivity under which the nation still suffers, and of a yet greater return that may still await it; and then, lastly, it becomes conceivable that after the hope of a great deliverer had been implanted deeply in the nation, and its destiny to bring him forth not obscurely revealed, the message should be conveyed to the *man greatly beloved*, which should prescribe within certain limits the actual time when He should be given to the world, who was consciously or unconsciously the desire of all nations, and in whom all nations should be blessed; and then most conspicuously the record of that message, if authentic, would be a standing witness to the Divine foreknowledge, while the utter impossibility of explaining it otherwise would constitute no unwarrantable or slight presumption of its authenticity.

We are dealing here, indeed, as we must deal, with presumptions. The being and providence of God are presumptions; the future life and immortality of man are presumptions; the correct interpretation of history is a presumption; the recognition of the voice of God is a presumption; but the question is whether we have caught aright the utterance of the voice of God in our interpretation of this history, and whether the marvellous promises enshrined in its records and literary remains are or are not prophecies, and whether the great and exceptional events connected with the life of Christ did or did not fulfil them. If they did, then is prophecy a record of Divine foreknowledge, and then are we warranted in saying that the spirit of prophecy is the testimony of Jesus, for the testimony of Jesus is an adequate object, and the person of Jesus is a sufficient goal.

But more than this; for it is not only the function of prophecy to lead up and on to Jesus, but *the testimony of Jesus is the spirit of prophecy*. It is not only that the spirit of prophecy bears witness to Jesus, but that the testimony of Jesus and concerning Jesus expresses itself in and by the spirit of prophecy, that it chooses and has chosen that particular manifestation, and enables us to enter into and to sympathise with, and in our degree to partake of, the spirit of prophecy.

And it is this thought which will lead us to the profitable gathering up of all the lessons that have been inculcated, and will point the moral of the whole.

If we would be in sympathy with prophecy, we must be in sympathy with Jesus. There is no more important or essential truth in relation to this matter. The age boasts of being a critical age, and forgets that it will itself become the subject of criticism. It is not only our privilege and right, but far more as honest men it is our bounden duty, to judge as critics of the records and foundations of our faith, whether they are to be discerned in the writings of the prophets or in the records of the life of Christ and the works of His apostles. By all means let the writings of the prophets be weighed and tried to the uttermost : by all means let the sacred records of the Christian Church be weighed and tried to the uttermost. It is when the Lord's *word is tried to the uttermost* that His *servant loveth it.** As that love will breathe no syllable to make the trial less, so neither will that trial countervail to deaden or chill the love, if only we be the Lord's servants. *If any man willeth to do His will, he shall know of the doctrine whether it be of God or whether I speak of myself.†* But as *the testimony of Jesus is the spirit of prophecy*, so is the spirit of Jesus all-essential and indispensable if we would apprehend, and still more appreciate, the spirit of prophecy.

And there are certain characteristics of Jesus which are characteristic also of prophecy. *He hath no form nor comeliness, and when we shall see Him there is no beauty that we should desire Him*, is no less true of the prophets as a class than it is of Him who was at once their cynosure and their anointed Head. We may criticise the life and character of Jesus Christ as long as we please, but if we would be Christians we must unreservedly give in our allegiance to Him first or last. *For he that is not with me is against me, and he that gathereth not with me scattereth.‡*

* Ps. cxix. 140.　　　　　　† St. John vii. 17.
‡ St. Matt. xii. 30 ; St. Luke xi. 23.

And it is the same with prophecy. We may criticise it as long as we like, but if we believe in Jesus we shall find little difficulty in believing that the prophets spake of Him. The one phenomenon no more transcends the condition of the human and the natural than the other, for both are alike unique, and after criticising without limit or restraint, we must sooner or later determine whether or not there is any testimony to Christ in prophecy. And if there is any testimony at all, we must sooner or later determine whether it is human or Divine, whether it is of man or of God. If it is of man, I hesitate not to say that it is altogether an unparalleled and solitary, and, that being the case, an unaccountable exhibition of human foresight; but if we decide that it cannot be of man, then we must sooner or later acknowledge that its testimony, being as it is a written and ancient testimony, is the record of Divine foreknowledge. And then our decision will make it for us a matter only of degree whether or not we recognise prediction in this or that form as part of the substantive essence of prophecy, as one of those veritable and emphatic characteristics by which God has stamped it, once for all, as a real thing, and not merely as a vague and impalpable floating sentiment.

And then we can hardly fail to see that if we are prepared to admit the production, in the *sixth* century before Christ, of such a passage, for instance, as the fifty-third of Isaiah, and to allow that the writer, whoever he may have been, was enabled and virtually overruled to speak, not *of himself*, but *of some other man*, who was even Jesus, then there is not really in this a less marvellous exhibition of the Divine will, a less remarkable putting forth of the Divine power, than there would be if, in the *eighth* century before Christ, the prophet Isaiah was enabled to write as he did in the spirit of prophecy, for in both cases the testimony of Jesus would confessedly be the *spirit* of the prophecy. And then, as this spirit was truly apprehended, we should be the less likely to see in the exceptional features of the confessedly prophetic and Divine record, a reason for imagining, in opposition to all evidence, that the record was falsely attributed to Isaiah. For at all events it would be a question merely whether we should make the record one degree more human or one degree more superhuman, seeing that in either case we accepted it as intrinsically Divine.

And in like manner with the book of Daniel, stupendous undoubtedly as many of its features are, if we really believed that the innermost spirit of that book was one of unfaltering trust in the living God, and of assured conviction that He had historic glories in store for His people, and would set up in the end of the days a kingdom that should never pass away, and that the only sure foundation of such a kingdom was Jesus the eternal King and eternal Priest, and were also prepared to admit that this belief and the knowledge of these facts was not and could not be *of men, neither by man*, it would surely be to us a matter of comparative indifference whether, acknowledging all this, we were willing to go one step further, and confess, on the strength of the external evidence, and the reasonableness and consistency of the internal claim, that it was possible for one who had spoken by the spirit of prophecy to testify also of His Son, and to determine the times before appointed, even in such a marvellous prediction as that of the seventy weeks, so that when His ministry began He could preach saying : *The time is fulfilled : repent ye, and believe the Gospel.*

Yes, verily the age is too far advanced for us to stand debating whether we will have one degree more or less of what is called the supernatural. The question is eagerly asked nowadays whether we will or must or can have *any* of it. Those who would make a compromise, and retain prophecy by giving up its predictive element, will find the attempt a mistake and a failure. It will satisfy no one. Least of all will it satisfy the exigencies of the case. Either prophecy is a record of the Divine foreknowledge, distinct, permanent, and unalterable, or it is nothing. If it is a record of the Divine foreknowledge, it is impossible to deny to it a predictive element; for only as we acknowledge that predictive element will it lead us to Christ.

The first evangelist has told us of certain magi, wise men from the east,—who or what they were we know not, and whence they came we know not,—who, moved unquestionably by the fame and influence of the ancient prophecies, prophecies which we have in our hands now, journeyed from their distant home to seek the infant Saviour in His cradle at Bethlehem, and when they had found Him they worshipped Him, and presented unto Him their treasures of gold and frankincense and myrrh. If it was a Divine King they had found, it was surely a Divine guide that had led them thither. That guide was the spirit of Prophecy. It had testified of Jesus, it had led them to Him. It could not have led them to Him if it had not foretold His coming. But the prophecies that foretold His coming, whichever they were, the prophecies which guided them, were a record of the Divine foreknowledge; and if we would be led as they were, the prophecies must be no less to us. To breathe their spirit is to be prepared for the spirit of Christ, for they testify of Jesus.

But we must not forget that it is after all a spirit, and that the spirit in this case indicates a moral elevation and a moral bent. We cannot be in sympathy with that spirit unless we have imbibed its influence, have been raised to its elevation, and been directed by its bent. *If any man have not the spirit of Christ, he is none of His,* and still less can we be His if we have not the true spirit of the *prophets* which testifies of Him. That spirit is the spirit of righteousness, of truth, of justice, of indignation against the oppressor, of unswerving faith, of undying hope, of inextinguishable love. It is undoubtedly far more to be animated by that spirit than it is to hold some dry and barren theory about the predictive endowments of the prophets, and yet be strangers to their spirit. Rather let us be permeated by their spirit, knowing that it is not theirs, but God's, in order that, confessing that they *spake as they were moved by the Holy Ghost*, we may also believe that, being so moved, they were chosen by Him to put on record words that should evermore bear witness to His foreknowledge, and that,

> " As little children lisp and tell of heaven,
> So thoughts beyond their thought to those high bards were given."

If, however, *the testimony of Jesus is the spirit of prophecy*, we may be sure that no acknowledgment even of the witness of Divine foreknowledge which is stamped upon it, no recognition of the truly pre-dictive elements pervading it, will avail as a substi-tute for the possession of that spirit which is not only the spirit of prophecy but also the spirit of Jesus. If we cannot see Jesus in prophecy, it is not because His spirit is not there, but because we have not looked upon Him, nor seen Him as He is, nor imbibed His spirit. It was when He sent back the messengers to John with the story of the mighty works that they had witnessed, works that must steadfastly and for ever refuse to be explained away as other than super-human or supernatural, and works that were crowned with and culminated in the preaching of the Gospel to the poor, that He said, *Blessed is he whosoever shall not be offended in me.* The context there suggests that the offence may come in one of three ways. It can hardly come in any other. It may come in reluctance to bear the discipline of trial which alle-giance to Christ may bring with it, as perhaps in the case of John it was then threatening to do. It may come in repugnance to the terms of that Gospel which is addressed only to the poor, whether they be the poor in spirit or in estate; or it may come in unwillingness to receive the manifold converging evidence that silently but emphatically points us to the conclusion that from time to time in the world's history God has made choice of agencies other than merely human, natural, or ordinary, to convey the message of His will and to authenticate it to man, and that one of those agencies is prophecy, which cannot be calmly and completely surveyed in its moral and spiritual characteristics, its gradual development and growing distinctness, its combining testimony and converging effect, without being acknowledged as a record not of human but of super-human, of Divine foreknowledge and significance.

At all events, as Christ has presented His own message to us, He has not obscurely intimated that such an acknowledgment is part of the historic foundation of His Gospel, and is inseparably mingled with its substance; and that, as we cannot have the spirit without the form, the life without the being it animates, so neither can we have prophecy without prediction, for that *Abraham rejoiced to see His day, that he saw it and was glad,* that Moses wrote of Him, and if we believe not the writings of the Lawgiver we cannot believe the words of the Saviour, † that all things which were written in the law of Moses and in the Prophets and in the Psalms concerning Him could

* John viii. 56.   † John v. 47.

not but be fulfilled,* and that it behoved Him to suffer and to rise from the dead the third day because it was so written in the scriptures of the Prophets, and because their testimony to Him was the very spirit of their prophecies.

At least it is an undeniable fact that as far as we can form any idea of what the teaching of Christ Himself was, He took His stand upon the declarations of the prophets, and taught His disciples that they were fulfilled in Him and were intended to be fulfilled in Him ; and most assuredly this is a fair and legitimate inference from the works of His first disciples. It is in the abstract conceivable that this position is one which may require to be modified, but hardly so unless the position which He claimed for Himself and which they claimed for Him requires modification likewise ; hardly so unless the verdict of the Christian Church must be reversed, and the Church herself be compelled to forego the name of Christian, and to deny to Him who will then cease to be her Lord and Master His right to the name of Christ.

But more than this, it would seem that we cannot do justice to the words and language no less than to the voices of the prophets, not only as Christ and His apostles interpret them, but even as they themselves imperatively demand to be interpreted, without admitting that their prophetic endowment carried prediction with it; that prophecy, as the Old Testa-

* Luke xxiv. 44, 26. Cf. Matt. xvi. 21, xxvi. 54 ; Mark xiv. 49, etc., etc.

ment enshrines it, is a reality and a fact in its two-fold character, as a declaration of the Divine will and its revelation of the unborn future ; and that the prophets have left behind them written records which are for all ages a witness to the Divine foreknowledge, because it is the testimony to *Jesus* that is the *spirit* of Prophecy.

NOTE A.

THE GENUINENESS OF THE BOOK OF DANIEL.

"IT is no longer denied," says Dr. Davidson, ("Introduction to Old Testament," vol. iii., p. 162,) "that the book" of Daniel "was "written by one person." Eichhorn supposed two, Bertholdt and Augusti as many as nine different authors. Their views are now abandoned. "The two leading divisions" of the book "are so related "that the one implies the existence of the other. Both have the same "characteristic of style, spirit, ideas, and manner. Thus i. 17 refers "to ii. 16, etc.; i. 19, 20 and ii. 49 refer to iii. 12, etc.; i. 2 is meant "to prepare the way for v. 2. Comp. iii. 12 with ii. 49, v. 11, and "ii. 48; v. 21 and iv. 22; vi. 1 and v. 30; viii. 1 and vii. 2; ix. 21 "and viii. 16; xii. 7 and vii. 25. Not only do the constituents of "the two parts hang together among themselves, presenting similar "features, but they also refer to one another. Hence ii. 4—vi. and "vii.—xii., with i., ii. 3, cannot be assigned to two authors, the "second prior to the first, and having the latter as an introduction "to it. They have the strongest similarity in language and tenour, "pointing unmistakably to one and the same author."

As this entirely coincides with our own view, we gladly quote it. The Dean of Westminster still seems to think the book may be assigned to different authors. "Jewish Church," iii.: note on the date of the book of Daniel, pp. 69—74. Bleek agrees with Davidson, Eng. ed. by Venables, ii. 200. If, however, the book is one, as, notwithstanding its bilingual character, it bears very strong evidence of being, our path is much simplified for dealing with it. The eleventh chapter has undoubtedly certain features that might dispose us on *à priori* grounds to regard it as a later production, but we are delivered from any such temptation if there are no critical reasons for severing it from the rest, as there manifestly are not. If the book is one, it must be dealt with as a whole.

17

With regard to the external evidence for the genuineness of Daniel, Dr. Westcott has expressed himself thus : " Externally the book is as " well attested as any book of Scripture, and there is nothing to show " that Porphyry urged any historical objections against it ; but it brings " the belief in miracle and prediction, in the Divine power and fore- " knowledge as active among men, to a startling test, and according " to the character of this belief in the individual must be his judgment " upon the book " ("|Dict. of the Bible," *art.* Daniel). This is most true ; indeed, it is almost impossible to keep the exercise of our critical faculty free from the influence which the subject-matter of the book is so liable to exert upon it, and yet nothing can be more needful. We will first notice the points which are assumed to be of force against the genuineness of the book, and endeavour fairly to estimate them.

1. Its position in the Hebrew Canon. " It is not among the " prophets, but in the Hagiographa, and there too as one of the last " books," says Davidson. An insinuation is made here which is hardly fair. The third volume of the Jewish Scriptures comprised those books which did not belong, on the one hand, to the law of Moses, or, on the other, to the works of those who were by calling and office prophets. Thus Joshua, Judges, Samuel, and Kings were called The former Prophets, being supposed to be the works of prophets. The division, however, was somewhat arbitrary, and the ultimate principles which guided the selection are a matter of con- jecture ; for instance, Ruth is probably as much entitled to its place among The former Prophets as Judges or Samuel, certainly as regards the period to which it refers ; but it is relegated to the Hagiographa. Lamentations, acknowledged to be the work of Jeremiah, is never- theless not found with his writings among the later prophets, but among the Hagiographa. On the other hand, David, though acknow- ledged as a prophet, does not find his place among the prophets, but among The Psalms as the first book in the Hagiographa. What may have been the actual reason for placing Daniel where he is, it is impossible for us now to say ; but, at all events, it is a rash inference not borne out by analogy to conclude that the reason was that the second volume of the Canon was closed when Daniel was written, but the third still open for the reception of later and less-esteemed books, and that as such his book was there inserted when it appeared. This is a purely imaginary reason, and by no means the only probable or even imaginable one.

If we are to conclude that because Daniel is in the Hagiographa therefore the book is late, it would be equally fair to conclude that we have no Psalms of or before the time of David, and no Proverbs rightly ascribed to Solomon. It is manifest that considerations of date did not determine the position of the books, because there are certainly Psalms older than any of the Prophets so called.

But what is the place of Daniel in the Kethuvim or Sacred Writings? He is placed *first* after the five *megilloth*, or Rolls—*i.e.*, Canticles, Ruth, Lamentations, Ecclesiastes, and Esther. These five "Rolls" were regarded as a sub-class by themselves of great value, and therefore were placed in juxtaposition immediately after the three great books, Psalms, Proverbs, and Job. But this being so, Daniel takes the lead of all the remaining books, and is placed *before* Ezra and Nehemiah. Now if, as is evident, Nehemiah was placed *after* Ezra because belonging to a period later than Ezra, is it an unwarrantable inference to assume that Ezra was placed after Daniel for a like reason? If we are at liberty to infer anything with regard to the age of a book from its place in the Canon, surely, could we once disabuse our minds of the impression that Daniel if genuine ought to find his place among the prophets, we might infer from the actual position of Daniel that he was placed before Ezra because he was believed to be older than Ezra. On the supposition that the book was written B.C. 165, it surely is a very grave difficulty to account for its present position *before* Chronicles, Nehemiah, and Ezra, which must have been in existence previously.

We do not lay stress on the possible traces that exist of another arrangement in Josephus, who calls Daniel " one of the greatest of " the prophets," and the Septuagint, where Daniel comes after Ezekiel ; because it seems that the above considerations fully explain the existing arrangement so far as it affects the *age* of Daniel.

2. The silence of Jesus the son of Sirach in Ecclesiasticus xlix. This is no doubt remarkable, but it may be questioned whether the rough-and-ready supposition that Daniel was unknown to Jesus the son of Sirach is the true explanation of the fact. We rather are disposed to concur with Dr. Westcott, who says, " If the book of " Daniel was already placed among the Hagiographa at the time " when the Wisdom of Sirach was written, the omission of the name of " Daniel is most natural."—" D. B.," *s.v.* Daniel. After the writer has expended much time on the earlier worthies of the nation, he hastens somewhat rapidly over the later ones, mentioning only Zerubbabel, Joshua the son of Josedech, and Nehemiah, with the exception that

he bestows a long panegyric upon Simon the son of Onias, whom he no doubt regarded with special reverence and affection as nearer to his own times. After the utmost has been made of the significance of this omission, it does not seem to be very important, unless it can be shown that the list was intended to be and ought to have been a complete one, which it clearly is not. Why should Nehemiah be specified rather than Ezra? And if the book of Daniel preceded Ezra and Nehemiah, as it now does in the Canon, why is the mention of Nehemiah, the latest book, any indication that the writer was unacquainted with Daniel, whose deeds were recorded in a previous book? It is too much to assume that Nehemiah was added to the Canon after the time of the son of Sirach; but if he was not, we may naturally assume that his place then was his place now, and therefore the allusion which implies the existence of the book of Nehemiah may be held to imply also that of the book of Daniel, which was placed before it.

3. Davidson says that "the Messianic idea of 'one like to the Son of "man coming in the clouds of heaven' appears to have been unknown "to Zechariah." But we can draw no inference of this kind from the fact that one writer does not seem to be acquainted with the works of another, any more than we can from the fact of his not mentioning him. Where does Zechariah mention Haggai, or show any acquaintance with his great prophecy about *the desire of all nations?* It has, however, been often shown that the influence of the book of Daniel is probably to be discerned in the opening visions of Zechariah. See, for example, Pusey on Daniel, p. 359. It is, at all events, more probable that the influence of Daniel is to be traced in Zechariah than that the visions in Daniel are in any way the expansion of those in Zechariah. If the angelology of Daniel has not influenced Zechariah, still less can it be conceived of as in any degree developed out of his writings, as a late origin of the book might lead us to suppose would be the case.

4. No valid argument can be drawn from the definiteness of the prophecies, as so often is done, because that is to *grant* the assumption that all definite prophecies are late, whereas we have first to prove what is the date of these prophecies, and then to determine how that affects our theories. It was this assumed principle that vitiated the judgment of Dr. Arnold, and caused him to lend the great weight of his influence to the opinion that Daniel was not genuine. He said in reference to his sermons on Prophecy, "The points in particular

" on which I did not wish to enter, if I could help it, but which very
" likely I shall be found to touch on, relate to the latter chapters of
" Daniel, *which, if genuine, would be a clear exception to my canon of*
" *interpretation*, as there can be no reasonable spiritual meaning made
" out of the kings of the North and South"—quoted by Tregelles on
Daniel, p. 261, n. If those works only are genuine out of which we
can make a reasonable spiritual meaning, we sanction a new critical
canon which may give rise to unsuspected and wonderful results.
Our verdict on the books of Scripture must depend *solely* upon the
evidence. If our verdict on Daniel depends on this, there can be no
doubt as to what it will be. Theories of interpretation must follow
facts, and not facts our theories of interpretation. It is asked (Davidson, iii. 173), " If the alleged predictions of remote events" in Daniel
" be really such, why are details discontinued at the death of
" Antiochus ?" If it is admitted, as it must be, that the death of
Antiochus marked a crisis in the history of the Jews, may we not ask
what further events the critic would wish or expect to have specified?
That the end of Antiochus did not correspond with the prophecy of
Daniel xi. is itself one of the strongest proofs that that prophecy
was not intended to refer to him, as it must have been if it was really
written in his time. It is likewise entirely unjustifiable to *assume*
that, as the events in ch. xii. had no intelligible meaning in the times
after Antiochus, so they have no meaning still. This depends entirely
on our faith in the document, which ought to depend entirely on the
evidence. That evidence is nearly as strong as it can be.

5. " The analogy of prophecy would lead us to expect that a seer
" living in the Babylonian captivity and writing about the future of
" his country, would first glance at the deliverance from oppression to
" be soon realised, to which a greater deliverance in the Messianic age
" might be appended. . . . Deliverance from Babylon is not predicted."
(Davidson, iii. 173.) Deliverance from Babylon is not predicted in
the chapter referring, it is said, to Antiochus, because that chapter is
assigned to the *third* year of Cyrus, or two years after his edict. So
far the Return was a fact of the past. Instead, therefore, of expect-
ing, as we are told by Davidson, Bleek, and others that we should
have done, that the prophet would have concerned himself with
directing " his prophetic glance to the liberation of his people from
" the then existing Babylonian slavery," this is precisely that which
he would not and could not do if he really had the revelation, as he
says, in the third year of Cyrus. He was no longer concerned with

that deliverance, but with another of which he says the time appointed was long (x. 1). We are continually told that the prophets' starting-point is in their own time, and this assumption is made a canon of the conditions of prophecy from which the prophets can by no means escape. It is on this ground that the latter chapters of Isaiah are denied to be his, and it is accepted as a universal principle. But a little investigation of the conditions of prophecy will show that it is untenable as a theory of universal application. When God said to Abram, " Know of a surety that thy seed shall be a stranger in a land that is not theirs, and shall serve them, and they shall afflict them four hundred years," and as yet he had no child, where was the starting-point in the immediate present? But if this narrative is *true*, it prepares us for the subsequent phenomena of prophecy. When Jacob said, " The sceptre shall not depart from Judah, nor a lawgiver from beween his feet, until Shiloh come, and unto him shall the gathering of the people be," where was the starting-point in the immediate present, when as yet Judah had no lawgiver? Was this prophecy, or was it not ? At all events, our decision respecting prophecy must be an induction of the existing facts. When the dying Moses said, " A prophet shall the Lord your God raise up unto you of your brethren like unto me," where was there any immediate prospect of fulfilment to start from, seeing that several centuries elapsed before even " Samuel the prophet " ? It is preposterous to refer this promise to the race of prophets, because no one of them all claimed to be, or was regarded as being, like unto Moses, and also because the prophet spoken of is manifestly *one*. " He shall speak unto them all that I shall command him ; and it shall come to pass that whosoever will not hearken unto my words, which he shall speak in my name, I will require it of him." When the promise afterwards expands, as it does, to include the whole race of prophets, it only serves to show that it here contemplates one as pre-eminent among the race who would contrast favourably with the race in speaking all that was commanded him, and in not speaking presumptuously. See John xvii. 8, and 1 Kings xxii. 11—25 ; Jer. xxviii. 1—17, etc.

When Balaam said, " I shall see him, *but not now :* I shall behold him, *but not nigh :* there shall come a star out of Jacob, and a sceptre shall rise out of Israel, and shall smite the corners of Moab, and destroy all the children of Sheth," where was the assumed starting-point in the present ? Is not such a starting-point expressly disclaimed by the terms of the prophecy?   And this fact is independent of our interpretation of the prophecy.

When Hosea said, " They shall be wanderers among the nations," and when Amos said, " For, lo, I will command, and I will sift the house of Israel among all nations, like as corn is sifted in a sieve, yet shall not the least grain fall upon the earth," where was the starting-point in the immediate present that made it more possible for the unassisted human foresight to discover what five-and-twenty centuries have conspired only to show to be more true?

When Micah wrote, probably in the days of Hezekiah, " They shall smite the judge of Israel with a rod upon the cheek; but thou, Bethlehem Ephratah, though thou be little among the thousands of Judah, yet out of thee shall he come forth unto me that is to be ruler in Israel ; whose goings forth have been from of old, from ever-lasting," where was the starting-point in the immediate present that made this promise more intelligible, or intelligible in any degree? And when he ended his prophecies with the words, " Thou wilt perform the truth to Jacob, and the mercy to Abraham, which Thou hast sworn unto our fathers from the days of old," may we not rather say that he took his stand upon the past than upon the present, and looked forward to the indefinite and unlimited future? Lastly, when Malachi wrote, " Behold, I will send my messenger, and he shall prepare the way before me : and the Lord whom ye seek shall suddenly come to his temple, even the messenger of the covenant whom ye delight in : behold, he shall come, saith the Lord of hosts ; " and when he said, " Behold, I will send you Elijah the prophet before the coming of the great and dreadful day of the Lord," where was the starting-point in the immediate present that served to explain his words or to make it even probable what he meant? In short, in framing for ourselves this canon of the operation of the prophetic energy, we invent a precon-ception which is contradicted and falsified by existing facts, and is therefore shown to be a canon which will stand us in no stead for the interpretation of prophecy, but rather mislead us, because at variance with manifest phenomena. The theory is not commensurate with all the conditions of the problem, as these few instances may serve to show.

6. The visionary and apocalyptic character of the book is alleged as a proof of its late origin. But as visions are common to many of the prophets (*e.g.*, Isaiah, Jeremiah, Ezekiel, Amos, and Zechariah), their greater abundance in Daniel, seeing it is a fact, does not seem to be more appropriate to the era of the Maccabees than to that of the

captivity; or indeed so much so, inasmuch as the former was a period of excitement and activity, the latter one of enforced repose. Surely the visions of Ezekiel, who was a captive like Daniel, make it antecedently probable that visions might be found in the genuine writings of Daniel. And further, it must not be forgotten that Daniel's visions are more or less connected with, if they do not spring out of, the unfolding of the future which was revealed to Nebuchadnezzar, and not to Daniel, in a dream. This is an objection which is simply futile. The cases of Ezekiel and Zechariah afford conclusive proof that visions were not otherwise than characteristic of the age of the captivity; whereas prophecy, in any of its manifestations,—and surely that of visions was one of them,—was a thing confessedly unknown in the age of the Maccabees (see 1 Macc. iv. 44—46, ix. 27, xiv. 41). We shall search in vain for any vision like those in Ezekiel, Daniel, or Zechariah, in the apocryphal books of Scripture, if even we need except 2 Esdras, which is confessedly later, and partly also indebted to Daniel; and therefore we have no ground to assume that a work of the period of the Maccabees would be apocalyptic in its character, while we have ample evidence that the writings of the period of the captivity were so characterised.

Those who indulge in conjecture as to the possible authorship of Daniel in the time of Antiochus, are too apt not to consider all that their hypothesis involves. For instance, Bleek thinks it " very natural that " the pious should await with especial longing for the appearance of " the salvation promised to their fathers by the mouth of the prophets; " and it may easily be imagined that they would give way to the hope " that their heavy oppression would soon come to an end, and that then " the Messianic salvation would immediately appear" (ii. 208). But is it not plain that if this book derived any of its authority from the way in which it ministered to this hope, it would at once lose that authority as soon as the experience of fact made it clear that the fall even of Antiochus Epiphanes was not the prelude to the advent of the Messiah ? The failure of the supposed prophecies in this respect would be the strongest possible reason for their not being regarded as authentic, just as the obvious failure of many of Dr. Cumming's interpretations of prophecy in our own times is also entirely fatal to the supposition that they were correct interpretations.

It is even more inconceivable that we should imagine with the same writer (p. 211) that " in the age of Antiochus Epiphanes, when " Jehovah's people again fell into such grievous distress, their attention

" would be directed both to the predictions of other prophets, and also
" to Jeremiah's utterances as to the seventy years; and they would
" inquire whether they would not allow of an interpretation by which a
" correct, speedy, and complete fulfilment of the Divine promises con-
" tained in them might be hoped for. It is such an explanation as this
" which is here placed in the mouth of the angel in the communication
" to Daniel, that the seventy years were at the point of expiring just
" at that very time—viz., the time of Antiochus Epiphanes."   For is it
not open to demonstration that no arrangement or manipulation of the
seventy years can bring their termination anywhere at all near the
time at which it is assumed that this new interpretation of Jeremiah's
prophecy was propounded,—and propounded, moreover, for the purpose
of consoling the persecuted by the near prospect of deliverance at the
time promised?   It is so very much more easy to fabricate and devise
conjectures than it is to make them correspond with all the requirements of the case, even if we give ourselves the trouble of testing
them to see if they will correspond.   Here a moment's consideration
will serve to show that the hypothesis cannot be made to fit into the
exigencies of the problem it is made to solve.   It is proposed as a
rough-and-ready solution, which deludes by the facility and readiness
with which it is proposed; but it is really no solution at all.   It is no
sooner tested by application to the indispensable requirements of the
case in point, than it breaks down, absolutely and irretrievably.

" The arguments for the late composition of the book " of Daniel,
says the Dean of Westminster, " Jewish Church," iii., p. 71, " (*i.e.*,
" B.C. 168—164), are partly external and partly internal.
" 1. The external arguments are as follows :—
" (*a*) It is not arranged in the Hebrew Canon with the ' Prophets,'
" but with the miscellaneous ' Hagiographa ' (the Psalms, Proverbs,
" Job, Ecclesiastes, Canticles, Ezra, Nehemiah, and Chronicles), *i.e.*,
" the part avowedly of later date and lesser authority, and constantly
" receiving fresh additions."
As I have already shown, the contents of the Hagiographa are
(some of them, at all events) older than any of the writings of the
prophets; and they certainly were so in the belief of those who
arranged the Canon, for otherwise the supposed works of David and
Solomon would not have been placed among them.   The inference, therefore, " of later date " falls to the ground.   That of " lesser authority "
also is invalid, because though of *relatively* " lesser authority," their

absolute authority was determined by their place in the Canon. Had the *authority* of Daniel been doubtful, the book would not have been in the Canon. Had it first appeared B.C. 165, no critic will venture to say that its "authority" would not have been doubtful.

"(*b*) Daniel is not mentioned by Ezra, Nehemiah, Zechariah, "Haggai, nor in the catalogue of authors by the son of Sirach (Ecclus. "xlix. 8—10), which is the more remarkable from his mention of all "the other prophets. The only counterpoise to the argument for this "omission is that in Ecclus. xlix. 13 Ezra is left out."

But this is sufficient to show that, strange as the omission is, we cannot base a positive argument upon it, because silence is uncertain, and moreover the actual place of Daniel in the Canon is before both Ezra, and Nehemiah who is mentioned. This objection has already been answered.

"(*c*) The Greek translation of the book is involved in obscurity. In "the place of that of the Seventy was substituted, for some unknown "reason ('hoc cur acciderit nescio,' says Jerome), a translation by "Theodotion; and both are inextricably mixed up with Greek addi- "tions, which, though part of the Canon of the Eastern and of the Latin "Churches, have been rejected by the Protestant Churches, and one of "which (the History of Susannah) is apparently of Greek origin, as may "be inferred from the play on two Greek words (Susanna 55, 59)."

It is certain, however, that the first book of Maccabees contains evidence of an acquaintance with the Greek translation of Daniel, for the striking phrase "abomination of desolation" (Dan. ix. 27, $\beta\delta\epsilon\lambda\nu\gamma\mu\alpha$ $\tau\hat{\omega}\nu\ \epsilon\rho\eta\mu\omega\sigma\epsilon\omega\nu$) appears in 1 Macc. i. 54 as $\beta\delta\epsilon\lambda\nu\gamma\mu\alpha\ \epsilon\rho\eta\mu\omega\sigma\epsilon\omega\varsigma$, and $\pi\epsilon\sigma\sigma\nu\nu\tau\alpha\iota\ \tau\rho\alpha\nu\mu\alpha\tau\iota\alpha\iota\ \pi\sigma\lambda\lambda\sigma\iota$ of Dan. xi. 27 becomes $\epsilon\pi\epsilon\sigma\sigma\nu\ \tau\rho\alpha\nu\mu\alpha\tau\iota\alpha\iota$ $\pi\sigma\lambda\lambda\sigma\iota$ in 1 Macc. ix. 40. Moreover, the phraseology of Dan. xii. 1 is bor- rowed, with a modification, in 1 Macc. ix. 27. As the origin of 1 Macc. must be assigned to within seventy years of the late date assigned to Daniel, the latter book must not only have been in repute, but have become sufficiently famous to have been translated at that time, and known in its translation. And if the first book of Maccabees was written, as some think, in Hebrew, this is not the less remarkable if Daniel was only a recent production. It is certain that the writer of 1 Macc. was acquainted with Daniel (see 1 Macc. ii. 59, 60). No one can for a moment suppose that Daniel was first written in Greek, whatever may have been the "origin" of "Susanna"; but had the book of Daniel first appeared in Hebrew in 165 B.C., is it at all likely that it would soon have been translated into Greek as one of the books of the sacred Canon ?   The displacement of the Septuagint version certainly has the effect of throwing the probable date of Daniel further back. Whatever is the date of 1 Macc., it is to be noted that Ecclesiasticus, which is earlier still, and probably prior to 165 B.C., is hardly to be explained in xvii. 17 without reference to Daniel.   That the Greek translation, therefore, of the book is involved in obscurity is no ground of suspicion for the early existence of the Hebrew and Aramaic original.

"2. The internal arguments are as follows :—

"(*a*) The use of Greek words, κιθάρα and σαμβύκη, συμφωνία and "ψαλτήριον, in the Hebrew of iii. 5, 7, 10.   In the case of κιθάρα the "argument is strengthened by the fact that in Ezek. xxvii. 13 and "Psalm cxxxvi. 2 [cxxxvii. 2 ?] (unquestionably of the epoch of the "Captivity) the word for harp is still *kinnur* [kinnor ?]."

The use of Greek words in Daniel has been well nigh abandoned as a proof of its late origin, and assuredly the use of *kinnor* in Ezekiel and Psalms is no evidence either that the word was not known to Daniel, or that κιθάρα may not have been also known to Ezekiel and the captives in Babylon who hung their harps upon the trees there.   It is moreover highly probable that the specific instruments used by the Jews in captivity would differ from those at Nebuchadnezzar's dedication festival, and the names vary accordingly.

"(*b*) The difficulty of reconciling much of the story as it now "stands with Ezekiel's mention of Daniel as on a level with Noah "and Job, and as an oracle of wisdom (xiv. 14, xxviii. 3), when, "according to Dan. i. 1, he must have been a mere youth."

The date of Ezekiel xiv. is certainly not earlier than the sixth month of the sixth year of Jehoiachin's captivity (see viii. 1 and xx. 1), or about B.C. 594—that is to say, about twelve years after Daniel had come to Babylon.   As Ezekiel himself was an exile in the land of the captivity, it is perfectly obvious that the history of his distinguished and powerful countryman would be well known to him ; while Dr. Pusey has shown the extreme naturalness of the collocation of Daniel with Noah and Job, and also the tacit reference to the deliverance of the wise men of Babylon effected by Daniel, in the words "they shall deliver neither sons nor daughters" ("Daniel the Prophet," p. 108, third ed.)   The other reference to Daniel in Ezekiel (xxviii. 3 ; cf. xxvi. 1) is some five years later, apparently when Daniel's reputation for wisdom must have been fully established (see Dan. i. 4).   As a matter of fact, therefore, the casual allusions in Ezekiel correspond accurately with the narrative in Daniel, but yet in a way thoroughly artless and undesigned. According to Dan. i. 1, he was when Ezekiel made mention of him certainly not a "mere youth," but probably about thirty years old, the age of Joseph when he stood before Pharaoh, and of our Lord when He entered on His ministry.

"(c) The matter-of-fact descriptions of the leagues and conflicts be-
"tween the Græco-Syrian and Græco-Egyptian kings, and of the reign
"of Antiochus IV., in Dan. xi. 1—45, which, if written three hundred
"years before that time, would be without parallel or likeness in
"Hebrew prophecy. These descriptions are minute, with the minute-
"ness of a contemporary chronicler, and many of their details lack any
"particle of moral and spiritual interest such as might account for so
"signal a violation, if so be, of the style of Biblical prophecy. This,
"accordingly, is the chief argument for fixing the date of the book at
"the time when these conflicts occurred—an argument which, in the
"case of any other book (as, for example, the 'Sibylline Oracles' or
"the Book of Enoch) would be conclusive."

Most unquestionably; because neither of these books is attested with a particle of the external evidence which is so strong in the case of Daniel. It will probably be admitted that if Daniel is genuine, it is also authentic; but if the matters of fact related in Daniel were matters of history, there is undeniably nothing more wonderful in these predictions than there is in those events. The question really is, whether there is evidence for the unity of the book of Daniel, and whether there is evidence for the book being genuine. There is no reason to suppose that ch. xi. is not an integral portion of the book, and there is abundant evidence to show that the book is genuine. This being so, therefore, the character of ch. xi. must determine our notions of Biblical prophecy, and not our notions of Biblical prophecy decide, in the face of the evidence, that Daniel xi. is not genuine. There may, however, be much more moral and spiritual interest even in these dry details than we at first suppose, if they really are an indication and evidence of God's tender and presiding care for His people.

"On the side of the earlier date (*i.e.* b.c. 570—536), the external
"arguments are as follows :—

[N.B. The latest date in Daniel is 534, and therefore the book, as a whole, cannot be earlier than that.]

"(a) The assertion of Josephus (*Ant.* xi. 8) that Jaddua showed
"to Alexander the predictions of his conquests in the Book of Daniel.

" But the doubt which rests over the story generally, and the acknow-
" ledged incorrectness of some of its details (see Dr. Westcott in
" Dictionary of the Bible,—' Alexander ', and Lecture xlvii.) deprive
" this allusion of serious weight; and it is difficult not to suspect
" something of an apologetic tone in Josephus, *Ant.* x. 11. 7.
" ' Methinks the historian doth protest too much.' "

It is remarkable that in the article of Westcott here referred to, he
says, " But admitting the incorrectness of the details of the tradition
" as given by Josephus, there are several points which confirm the truth
" of the main fact . . . . above all the privileges which Alexander is
" said to have conferred upon the Jews, including the remission of
" tribute every sabbatical year, existed in later times, and imply some
" such relation between the Jews and the great conqueror as Josephus
" describes.   Internal evidence is decidedly in favour of the story,
" even in its picturesque fulness."

It must not be forgotten, moreover, that Josephus was in no way
concerned to maintain the genuineness of Daniel, seeing that Porphyry
had not yet denied it.   He is therefore, so far, a purely independent
witness ; does not " protest " at all, but only testify without design,
to the undoubted esteem in which the book was held by his own
nation and in his own time.   In this respect there cannot well be
higher testimony of that age ; and it is inconceivable that a book which
first started into existence B.C. 165 should have acquired the renown
which led Josephus to say of it, " We believe that Daniel conversed
" with God ; for he did not only prophesy of future events, as did the
" other prophets, but he also determined the time of their accomplish-
" ment; and while the prophets used to foretell misfortunes, and on that
" account were disagreeable both to kings and to the multitude, Daniel
" was to them a prophet of good things, and this to such a degree that,
" by the agreeable nature of his predictions, he procured the goodwill
" of all men ; and by the accomplishment of them he procured the
" belief of their truth, and the opinion of a sort of divinity for himself
" among the multitude."   Is it likely that the whole nation could have
been so deceived by an unknown writer who palmed off upon them
his previously unknown production under the name of a man otherwise
almost unknown in B.C. 165 ?

" (*b*) The allusion to the furnace and the lions' den in the dying
" speech of Mattathias, A.D. [B.C. ?] 167 (1 Macc. ii. 59, 60).   But this
" (granting the exact accuracy of the report of the speech of Mattathias),
" in a book written as late as B.C. 107—therefore certainly after the

" publication of the book of Daniel on any hypothesis—does not testify
" to more than the previous existence of the traditions of these events,
" of which there need be no question."

Dr. Pusey has thoroughly disposed of the points involved here (see
" Daniel the Prophet," p. 370).   It is of course useless to debate the
question whether the speech of Mattathias is or is not accurate, as we
have and can have no evidence on the matter ; but the point for us to
determine is whether a person writing less than sixty years after the
alleged publication of Daniel would deliberately *represent* a man who
died two years before the publication of that book as alluding to circumstances of which the book itself was the only record.   It is calmly
assumed that all the events of Daniel's life were embodied in floating
traditions before the book was written, whereas, apart from the book
of Daniel and this mention in 1 Macc., there is no vestige of any such
tradition, except those in Ezekiel.   Now, had there been only the
assumed floating traditions in existence B.C. 167, it is, we may say,
certain that they would not have been alluded to, as they are in the
speech of Mattathias by *him*, in the midst of events acknowledged to
have been recorded in writing, and that in canonical scriptures.   The
only question, therefore, that remains is, Would he have been *represented* within sixty years afterwards as thus alluding to them ?   Only
by making assumptions altogether unwarrantable can we answer Yes.
The balance of probability as arising from the evidence is distinctly
the other way.

" (*c*) The reference in the Received Text of two of the Gospels to
" the Book of ' Daniel the Prophet.'   But the force of this reference
" is weakened by the omission of the name in the Syriac version of
" Matt. xxiv. 15, and by its entire absence from the best MSS. of Mark
" xiii. 14, and in all the MSS. of Luke xxi. 24.   And under any cir-
" cumstances it would only prove, what is not doubted, that at the time
" of the Christian era the book had been received into the Canon—in
" Palestine, without the Greek additions; at Alexandria, with them."

The reference to St. Luke is unintelligible, because no text reads it
there.   The phrase *is* found in the Syriac version of Matt. xxiv. 15
in Walton's Polyglot and in Dr. Lee's edition, so that this statement
is unintelligible ;* and if the words were actually spoken by our Lord
they would be significant in a high degree, because technically and
officially Daniel was not a prophet.   If, therefore, our Lord called
him so, it could only have been because He set the stamp of His

* I find it is omitted in the second edition.

approval and recognition to the subject-matter of his prophecies. But whether this was so or not, there is the evidence of St. Mark as well as St. Matthew that our Lord quoted from the *book* of Daniel with the emphatic parenthesis, *Whoso readeth, let him understand.* There is, therefore, and can be, no question but that He set His seal to the prophecies of Daniel and taught men to watch for their fulfilment, as the sure word of prophecy noted in the scripture of truth. Critically we may, perhaps, question the exact amount of additional authority that this would give to a purely critical decision ; but that our Lord appealed to the book as to sacred scripture, and commended it to the study of His disciples, is surely incompatible with the supposed origin of it as a fictitious story, embodying only traditional narratives and imaginary predictions of an unknown writer and a pseudo-prophet.

It is only too obvious that men disparage the genuineness of Daniel because of the startling and stupendous narratives it contains. If the book can be reasonably supposed to be of doubtful authority, then it is a simple matter dealing with the marvels recorded, because then they become doubtful too. Miracle and prophecy are alike relegated to the haze of the impalpable obscure, and we are left in the suspense of indecision and the uncertainty of pious sentiment. Whereas, if Daniel is genuine and authentic, then the whole question of the supernatural in prophecy and miracle is determined once for all in a startling and conclusive manner—a consummation by no means to be desired, or, if probable, to be endured.

" The internal arguments in favour of the earlier date rest on the " exactness of the references to Chaldean usages, and of coincidence " with the monumental inscriptions . . . . Of the coincidences with " the Babylonian monuments, the most striking is the name of Bil-shar- " uzur as an equivalent to Belshazzar, which, before the recent dis- " covery of this word at Babylon, was not known except from Daniel. " On the other hand, Darius the Mede is still an unsolved enigma . . . " The result is, therefore, that the arguments incline largely to the side " of the later date ; and this result is strengthened by the consideration " (1) that though something may be said to attenuate the force of " each argument singly, yet each derives additional weight from the " collective weight of all ; and (2) that the objections raised to some " of them pass over almost or altogether the most conclusive, no " parallel instance having been adduced from the Hebrew Scriptures " to the details of the eleventh chapter, nor any explanation of such " an exception from the general style of Biblical Prophecy."

I cannot but think—indeed, I am convinced—that the impartial reader who takes the trouble to read what has now been said on both sides will come to the conclusion that the arguments, so far as they rest on *evidence*, incline largely to the side of the *earlier* date.

It may be as well to quote the opinions expressed on this matter by one of the highest critical authorities in this country or elsewhere, the Regius Professor of Divinity at Cambridge, Dr. Westcott. He says, in his article on the Book of Daniel, in the " Dictionary of the Bible," " The use of Greek technical terms marks a period when commerce " had already united Persia and Greece ; and the occurrence of pecu- " liar words which admit of an explanation by reference to Aryan and " not to Semitic roots is almost inexplicable on the supposition that " the prophecies are a Palestinian forgery of the Maccabæan age."

With regard to the value of the testimony of Josephus, he says :— " Whatever credit may be given to the details of his narrative, it at " least shows the unquestioning belief in the prophetic worth of the " book which existed among the Jews in his time."

" The testimony of the Synagogue and the Church gave a clear " expression to the judgment implied by the early and authoritative " use of the book, and pronounced it to contain authentic prophecies " of Daniel without contradiction, with one exception (*i.e.* Porphyry), " till modern times."

" It is admitted that the contents of the book are exceptional and " surprising ; but revelation is itself a miracle, however it be given, " and essentially as inconceivable as any miracle."

" Generally it may be said that while the book presents in many " respects a startling and exceptional character, yet it is far more " difficult to explain its composition in the Maccabæan period than to " connect the peculiarities which it exhibits with the exigencies of " the Return."

These opinions were expressed some years ago, but we have no reason to suppose they have been changed.

It cannot be denied that *externally* there is no evidence whatever of a positive kind against the genuineness of Daniel. What indications there are—for they cannot be called evidence—are of a negative and wholly subjective kind. For instance, the omission of the name of Daniel in Ecclesiasticus, though strange, can be otherwise accounted for than by supposing the book not then known ; and if xvii. 17 implies a knowledge of Daniel, as it certainly *may* do, it of course effectually disposes of the argument from, and counterbalances this omission. The book of Baruch, which is probably as old as, if no older than, the late date assigned to Daniel, bears evidence of acquaintance with that book. (See Pusey, p. 361.) On the other hand, the positive evidence of Josephus being of a purely spontaneous character, as it clearly is—for he could have had no motive in saying what he said, since he held no brief for Daniel more than any other book of Scripture—is very strong as evidence of what was and had been the current opinion of the nation. How could he or any one have supposed that the conquests of Alexander the Great had been *predicted* in Daniel if the book was of the time of the Maccabees? and even if his story about Jaddua is fabricated, what would it have had to rest on if not this general belief?—he could not have fabricated *that.*

It will be seen, therefore, that the " arguments " above spoken of, when examined, are virtually insubstantial; and this being so, their " collective weight " cannot be of any consideration in itself, and still less can it lend additional weight to " each argument singly." We can only conclude that the evidence *against* the Maccabæan origin of Daniel is of an objective character, while the presumptions for it are wholly subjective.

With regard to the other point, that no parallel instance of detailed prophecy can be adduced from Scripture, this must depend wholly upon our previous verdict on the date of Scripture. If we adopt revolutionary notions about the books, we shall then be careful to make facts bend accordingly; but it must be allowed without now going into these questions, that, taking them as they appear *primâ facie,* we find the time of sojourn in Egypt was *foretold* to Abraham, and that this fact was known and remembered at the time of the exodus, and was appealed to notwithstanding the patent discrepance on the surface of the narrative ;*. that the destruction of the builder of Jericho was foretold,† and likewise the desolation of Jeroboam's altar with the *name* of the king who should accomplish the overthrow of his unauthorised worship ; ‡ that the name of Cyrus as the king who was to lay the foundation of the temple was twice foretold by Isaiah ; § and that many of the latter prophecies of Zechariah are hardly less definite than those of Daniel. At all events, in these instances we have examples of the *kind* of prophecy that astonishes us in Daniel, although there can be no doubt that in him it reaches its climax. To

* Gen. xv. 13; Ex. xii. 40, 41.   ‡ 1 Kings xiii. 2.
† Josh. vi. 26 ; 1 Kings xvi. 34.   § Isa. xliv. 28; xlv. 2.

me it seems absolutely certain that there are specimens of prophecy in its predictive aspect in Daniel that no special pleading can set aside or explain ; and this being so, it is merely a matter of degree whether we acknowledge more or less.

It is clear, however, when we take into consideration the several instances named above, we must either admit the force of the cumulative evidence for prophecy, or must suppose that the several books in which these predictions occur were so arranged and modified for the express purpose of presenting that appearance of prophecy which as a matter of fact they do present. Is this consistent, we may ask, not with some particular theory of inspiration, but with the acknowledgment of any such authentication of the Scripture record as would show it to be the medium of a veritable revelation given and not invented ? As Dr. Westcott says, " ' Revelation,' however communicated, is itself a miracle, and essentially as inconceivable as any miracle." Is there any evidence that such a revelation has been given and preserved, or is the idea essentially erroneous, and as such to be discarded ? To me it seems that the Bible as a fact is the permanent obstacle to so discarding it. " The general style of Biblical prophecy " is, *per se*, as little to be accounted for, if it means what it says, as any actual prediction would be. Before we can implicitly trust any single declaration of Scripture as an authorised, and therefore reliable assertion.—such, for example, as *God is Love*,—we must admit the possibility of such knowledge being so communicated as to be thereby authorised ; but no sooner is this done than it becomes logically conceivable that the method of communication selected for conveying revelation might embrace the agencies of miracle and prophecy ; and whether or not this has been the case must be determined by evidence ; but if we do not shut our eyes to the evidence for the genuineness of Daniel, which is not fairly to be set aside, we must admit the operation of prophecy in its predictive aspect there.

NOTE B.

PROFESSOR KUENEN ON THE SEVENTY WEEKS OF DANIEL.

The weight of Professor Kuenen's charge against the prophets of Israel depends nearly as much upon what they do not say, and what he would have expected them to say, as upon what they have actually said. His object appears to be to show that the prophets had no more knowledge than other men of the events of the future; that they did not see it mapped out before them as we do in looking back over it after it has become history. But it is no part of the defence of prophecy to traverse this notion with a direct negative. In the circumstances of actual life it would be impossible to obtain the *same* view of the same landscape from two opposite points. A district we have ourselves travelled over assumes a very different appearance on looking back upon it from that which it had before we set out; at all events, it is the same reversed. In prophecy, therefore, it is absurd to expect that the prophet's vision of the future, and still more his view of the vision, should correspond with our view of the past. It is not to be supposed that the prophet knew distinctly what form the events he spoke of would take; and nothing, therefore, is gained when it is shown, as of course it can easily be shown, that he was ignorant of this precise form. Nothing, moreover, is gained when in the same way it is shown that later prophets were not always consistent with earlier ones. If prophecy was a living and growing thing, it was not to be expected that they would be. But this, instead of disproving the reality of prophecy, tends rather to show its reality as well as to modify our misconceptions as to its true nature. Our position is, that there is evidence in the writings of the prophets of a meaning and continuous scheme running through their prophecies, gradually unfolding and expanding itself in a way that the prophets themselves could not have directed, but in such a manner and to such an extent as to warrant us in regarding their writings as a veritable record of divine foreknowledge ; and this conclusion is established and confirmed to us when we see traces, as we plainly may, even of actual prediction from time to time, which cannot be ascribed to natural foresight, and yet which in a remarkable manner was found afterwards fulfilling itself in fact. It is obvious that the maintenance of this position must depend in a great degree on the date assigned to the various books, and therefore involves a very lengthened argument ; but our purpose has been to take a few crucial instances and to show how strong they are ; while in the same manner it may be shown that the antagonistic argument is marked with very serious flaws. If the cases selected can be made out, they are in themselves sufficient to neutralise the effect of the opposite theory, but are after all only select instances of a crucial kind to which others may be added—samples of many more ; and if in like manner one definite flaw can be detected in the antagonistic argument, it may serve to waken in us distrust of the rest. Professor Kuenen's avowed purpose is to overthrow what he calls "supernaturalism." His treatment of his subject is a powerful effort in that direction, but it is only so because he has overlooked or shut his eyes to certain facts, and argued on a particular basis with regard to others. We have no wish to deny many of his statements with regard to prophecy ; but for our purpose it is not necessary that they should be denied : our own position is independent of them, as also it is of his conclusions, because in many cases we are persuaded that they are erroneous.

We examine, for example, his treatment of the book of Daniel in his work on Prophecy, i. 301—320 (English edition, 260—275).

" It now clearly appears," says he, " in a manner which is indispu-
" table, that we were justified in ranging the prophecies regarding the
" future of Israel under ' the unfulfilled predictions.' The reality has
" contradicted the expectation with regard to every particular which
" is advanced in their prophecies. The return of the captives formed
" a sharp contrast to the brilliant anticipations of the prophets ; the
" reunion of Judah and Ephraim never took place at all ; the restora-
" tion of the Davidic monarchy was not once attempted ; neither in the
" material nor spiritual domain did the condition of those who returned
" correspond to the lofty expectation ; and no one can pretend to say
" that the sovereignty of Israel over the nations, or the accession of
" the Gentiles to Jahvism, are events which have ever been realised."

This is a very fair sample of Professor Kuenen's position ; and on his standing-ground his assertion is not wholly untrue. But were we intended to treat prophecy in this bald and matter-of-fact manner? Are we not asking of prophecy that which it never professed to give us? May not the mistake lie in our misconception quite as much as in the anticipation of the prophets? What if " the brilliant anticipations " of the prophets, while they formed a sort of preliminary instalment of completion in events which Kuenen does not deny, were not intended, not by the prophets, but by the Divine Spirit who spoke by them, to exhaust themselves completely in those events? At least, when I read the fortieth chapter of Isaiah, I cannot but feel that it was written for me as well as for Zerubbabel and those who went up from Babylon with him. Nor can a whole college of professors make it clear to me that I am wrong in feeling that it applies to me, any more than I should say that Zerubbabel was wrong in feeling that it applied to him. And it is this manifoldness and profundity of meaning in the prophecy which shows it to be prophecy, just as much as it would be shown by an established case of fulfilled prediction. But he who denies the one is consistent also in denying the the other. It is the object of this writer to show me what I do not need to be shown, that my use of the prophet's words did not enter into the prophet's mind. I never supposed *it* did, any more than I supposed that *I* did; but that is no proof that his words were not intended to have the effect they have, or that he was not a special agent and instrument of God when he was empowered and authorised to write them. It is this that Kuenen labours hard to show, but I do not find that he has shown it, even by assuming and asserting, contrary, as I believe, to all evidence, that they were written by the mysterious and impalpable second Isaiah at the time of the Return.

In like manner " the reunion of Judah and Ephraim " never took place as the prophets may have expected it, though it is certain that after the captivity, under whatever conditions, the nation was never more two, but one ; but that is no evidence either that a spiritual union was not effected when the congregation of Israel was merged in the Christian Church, or that in the counsels of the Most High there may not yet be some further reunion in store. If prophecy is a divine thing, a supernatural thing, it may well be so ; if not, the course of history is thus far what it is, and we are at liberty to bring from prophecy what light we can to bear upon it. The nature of that light will vary with the eye that sees it ; it will be darkness only to the blind. In like manner " the restoration of the Davidic monarchy

" was not once attempted," it is quite true; but the prophecies remained what they were, equally distinct and definite; and ages afterwards we are told of one of whom it was said, " The Lord God shall give unto Him the throne of His father David, and He shall rule over the house of Jacob for ever, and of His kingdom there shall be no end." I believe this was what, not the prophets, possibly, but the Divine Spirit meant, and therefore that the actual fulfilment was better, because more in accordance with His mind, than the anticipated fulfilment; and if the words of the angel Gabriel were in any sense true of Jesus, I am still at liberty to claim His dominion as *the* fulfilment of promises which were undeniably spoken by prophets, and which, in proportion as they were prophetic promises, were not improbably, but most likely, spoken in a sense in which they were not understood. I cannot agree, therefore, with the Professor when he says, " We see " here facts against which all arguments are shattered." Rather to my mind it seems that *the* argument from prophecy remains exactly where it was before Kuenen touched it.

" The oracle," says Kuenen, in the ninth chapter of Daniel, " sub- " stitutes for the seventy *years* seventy *year-weeks* (*i.e.* four hundred " and ninety years). Is the writer, then, of opinion that the pre- " diction of Jeremiah would not be (or had not been) fulfilled after " seventy common years ? Undoubtedly he is. And this judgment " does not surprise us, if it be the case that he knew what happened " at the end of the captivity in and after the year 536 B.C."

This is an instance of the impossibility of keeping our verdict in these matters clear of our previous conceptions. Certainly if Daniel is not genuine, the writer did know all this; but we, on our side, must not forget that the writer does not profess to know this, but on the contrary to be receiving a communication not in the first year of Cyrus, or 536 B.C., but in the first year of Darius the Mede, which must have been at least a year or two before—according to our Bibles 538 B.C. The writer represents himself as being sure that the seventy years must nearly have expired. His doubt arises from the fact that he did not know precisely when they began. It was of a piece with the dealings of God in Providence to leave the prophecy, while definite in the duration of seventy years, uncertain as to the computation of those years, because otherwise there would have been no room for the exercise of human faith or human patience. Had it been possible to determine exactly when the seventy years began, and therefore when they would end, Daniel would have had no occasion

to fast and pray that they might be speedily accomplished.   It was in
this uncertainty that his trial lay, just as in matters of conflicting or
uncertain duty it is that the trial of our faith lies ; but here also was
his sustentation, because he knew that he had a sure word of God to
which to trust.   Precisely in the same spirit it is that Kuenen says,
p. 261, " The time is now past for speaking of a postponed realisation
" of the promises.   Whoever, at the present time, still expects the
" restoration of the Israelitish nation, as the prophets have described
" it, expects *another thing altogether* than that which they announced.
" They predicted the termination, the glorious termination, not of the
" present, but of the former captivity of the Israelites.   The existing
" state of things, of which we all are witnesses, is in irreconcileable
" opposition to their expectations."

To which I reply, let any one read Deut. iv. 27, Amos ix. 9, Lev.
xxvi. 33, Deut. xxviii. 62—64, etc., and say whether there is not a
correspondence between these menaces and the existing state of Israel,
and whether there is any other nation in the world of whom the like
was said and can now be said.   It is of course easy to deny that the
prophets *meant* this ; it is impossible to deny that they *said* it.   It is
impossible to suppose that the words can mean this, unless we believe
in a veritable Divine revelation ; but if we do, it is impossible to deny
that here we may find sufficient ground for the belief.   Kuenen does
not believe in a Divine revelation, and therefore he denies the proof
of it.   There are those who not only believe in it, but will continue
to believe in it *because* they believe in the proof of it that the facts
supply.   It is impossible that the two can ever agree, but the fault
lies not in the alleged insufficiency of the proof, but in the deficiency
of the mental faculty that is not able to grasp, and does not wish to
be held by the conclusion to which the otherwise inexplicable facts
point.

The unique position of Israel in the world's history points to a
cause which is unique—the exceptional dealings of God with them.
The exceptional in God's dealings renders probable an exceptional
element in their literature, renders probable the exceptional operation
of prophecy.   But if the energy was an imparted and Divine energy,
its activity and exercise would be manifested independently of the
human instruments in whom it was manifested, and by whom it was
put forth.   To say, therefore, that to expect the restoration of Israel
is to expect *another thing altogether* than that which the prophets
announced, is to say nothing at all that any one cares to dispute.   Of

course it is another thing; but it by no means follows that it is not *the* thing that the God of Israel intended, and no one can prove that it is not, unless as a previous condition he assumes the non-existence of any faith in the present operation of the living God of Israel. If we grant this, then all the rest follows; but it by no means follows as a necessary and natural inference from the arguments alleged to prove it.

In like manner, to insist on verbal points of difference between the above passages and the existing condition of Israel is beside the mark, because the captivity and dispersion of Israel were conditions that were to be realised under various circumstances and at various epochs of their history, and if the existing phase of it does not fulfil all the conditions of the prophecies, the whole course of history undeniably does in a way that is truly marvellous. Any one who surveys the present political aspect of things in the east of Europe must surely allow that more remarkable and apparently improbable things have happened than even a general return of all the Jews to their own land, though this is by no means the only conceivable way in which the prophecies might be fulfilled, nor, were it to happen, would it be anything else than *another thing altogether* from that which the prophets expected, however strangely it might correspond with that which they *announced*.

" Jeremiah had announced," says Kuenen, p. 264, " the restoration " of Jerusalem after seventy years. It is thus *à priori* probable that, " according to the author of Daniel, the golden age of Israel would " dawn after the lapse of the seventy year-weeks, or 490 years, which " he substitutes for the seventy years. This is actually expressed in " an unambiguous manner in verse 24: in the seventy year-weeks the " unrighteousness (of the enemies of Israel) shall reach its climax. " (Comp. Daniel viii. 23.) At the end of that period, ' eternal right- "cousness' shall be ' brought in,' and the prophecy (of Israel's " felicity) be confirmed (by the issue)."

To us it seems entirely gratuitous to imagine that it is *à priori* probable that in expanding the seventy years of Jeremiah into seventy year-weeks, we are intended to count them both from the same point of departure. That there is such an expansion no one who studies prophecy would wish to deny; but if the same point of departure is intended, why, then, is the actual date given of the interview with the angel? Surely the most *natural* inference *à priori* would be that the years were to be counted from the date given. We, it is granted, do not so count them ; but surely, of the two suppositions, it is more natural to count the weeks from the present time assigned than from the past time of Jeremiah's prophecy.

But then we must bear in mind that on the hypothesis the author is writing in B.C. 165. Granting, therefore, that he did refer to that prophecy of Jeremiah in the fourth year of Jehoiakim, what is the relation of 606 B.C. to 165 B.C. ? and how is that relation affected by the 490 years ? The difference is 441, and not 490. Now it seems very odd that a man writing in 165 B.C. to encourage the co-religionists of his own time should adopt this means of doing it, and tell them that *their* troubles would end in fifty years' time, and that for this singularly accurate and appropriate prediction this writer should have been forthwith recognised, as according to Josephus the was, as one of the greatest of the prophets. We know that sixty years afterwards, when the whole 490 years on this theory had more than run out, his book must have attained to the dignity of canonical Scripture, because of the reference to it and the use made of it by the writer of 1 Macc., B.C. 107. It seems to us, then, that the seventy weeks alone, on any interpretation of them, are sufficient to disprove the theory.

" But what is the point of departure ? When do the seventy year-
" weeks begin ? The writer answers (ver. 25), 'from the going forth
" of a word to restore and to build Jerusalem.' It is not said *from*
" *whom* that word goes forth ; and just because of that it most readily
" occurs to the mind to think of Jahveh (compare in ver. 23, 'at the
" beginning of thy prayer a word [or commandment] went forth,'
" namely, from Jahveh) ; but also specifically of that word of Jahveh
" to which the whole prediction is attached—that is, of the prophecy of
" Jeremiah relating to the rebuilding of Jerusalem. In this way, more-
" over, the beginning of Daniel's seventy year-weeks coincides with the
" commencement of Jeremiah's seventy years—which certainly is most
" natural, not to say absolutely necessary. It may be said to be very
" singular that the defenders of the genuineness of the book understand
" by ' the going forth of a word' the later promulgation of a royal
" decree, either that of Cyrus (536 B.C.), or of Artaxerxes Longimanus
" (457 B.C.) ; because it would thence follow that Daniel had been
" enlightened by God as regards the duration and course of a certain
" interval, but had been left in uncertainty with respect to the begin-
" ning of that period. Was not the whole revelation in that way
" rendered illusory ?" Undoubtedly it was if the purpose and method
of the revelation were to be that which Kuenen assumes they were.

But how was it in the analogous case of Jeremiah himself? The first time he utters his prophecy of seventy years is in ch. xxv. 11, 12, or the fourth year of Jehoiakim, but he repeats the same prophecy in ch. xxix. 10, apparently about seven years afterwards. We are therefore left in doubt when the seventy years are to begin, and consequently when they are to end. And if this difficulty attaches to our study of the prophecy and its accomplishment, as it does, how much more must it have been so in the prophet's own time ! But was then "the whole revelation in that way rendered illusory?" Evidently Daniel did not so regard it, or, if we may not cite him, Zechariah did not so regard it (i. 12, vii. 5), nor did the writers of Ezra and Chronicles so regard it. "Let it not be forgotten," says Bp. Moorhouse, "in connection with this point, that to have made "prophecy so explicit that not even unbelief could mistake it, would "have been to defeat the great ends of our moral probation. If God "had written history before it happened, not only in its great principles, "but also in its minute details, what room had been left for the possible "rebellion of the evil, or for the trust and expectation of the faithful!" —"The Expectation of the Christ," p. 20, *n*. The office of prophecy to stimulate inquiry and expectation, but not to satisfy curiosity or to interfere with the free action and development of human history, is a point entirely overlooked by the critics, who say that, had such and such a prophecy been intended to refer to this or that event, it would have been more explicit and less open to ambiguity. Had Daniel known exactly when the seventy years began, he would have known exactly when they would end, and then we should have had no prayer like that in ch. ix., nor any of the profound lessons with which it is fraught.

With regard to "the going forth of the word" (ver. 25), it is manifestly gratuitous to make it identical with the "word" that "came forth" in the 23rd verse, just as it would be to make the first "word" (commandment) in ver. 23 identical with the second "word" (matter) in the same verse. The meaning of the "word" in ver. 25 is conditioned and determined by the complement of the phrase "to restore and to build Jerusalem ;" and this must surely be something yet to come, and not something then already past. We are thus directed not to the original prophecy of Jeremiah, nor to the date of the present vision, but to one of such words or commandments then still to come, the first of which was in 536 B.C. and the last in 457 B.C. That this "word" can by no manner of means be referred to the original prophecy of Jeremiah, apart from the verbal difficulties of so referring it, I take to be absolutely certain from its failure to satisfy the conditions of the prophecy, supposing it to be written in 105 B.C. I have met with no satisfactory attempt on the part of those who hold this date to explain the meaning of the prophecy no their hypothesis—which stands therefore self-condemned.

"Let us inquire, then," says Kuenen, "whether the facts which are " presented in the oracle afford us the certainty which we seek. The " last year-week seems to be the least doubtful. 'The middle of that " week shall cause sacrifice and oblation to cease' (ver. 27). This " evidently refers to the suspension of the public worship in the temple " of Jerusalem, in the month Chisleu (December) of the year 167 B.C., " which is also mentioned elsewhere in the book of Daniel (vii. 25, " viii. 11, 12; xi. 31), and a thing which especially deserves our " attention; then also the space of three-and-a-half years (=the half of " a year-week) precedes the time of the end (vii. 25; xii. 7), as here " it precedes the close of the seventieth or last year-week. This " combination is confirmed by the further fact that in Dan. ix. 27, as in " other places also, the 'astounding abomination'—*i.e.* the little altar " intended for the offerings to Jupiter Capitolinus, which was placed " on the altar of burnt-offerings by command of Antiochus Epiphanes " —is brought into immediate connection with the suspension of " public worship (compare ch. viii. 13; xi. 31; xii. 11). Further, " everything that is told us in verses 26, 27, of the last year-week " coincides with the supposition that the middle of this last year-week " falls in December 167 B.C., and therefore its beginning in June 170 " B.C. At the beginning of these seven years 'an anointed one is " cut off, and there is none (anointed one) for him:' the high priest " Onias III. is murdered at Antioch in 170 B.C."

Even admitting that the desecration of the Temple was the event referred to by the words " shall cause the sacrifice and the oblation to cease," Kuenen is certainly not right in his computation. For this event happened, according to him, in December 167 B.C., and therefore the beginning of the last year-week in June 170 B.C. But Antiochus Epiphanes came to the throne in 175 B.C.; and it was not less than three years afterwards, according to 2 Macc. iv. 23, that Onias was slain, which would bring it to 172, or possibly 171 B.C.; but there is no authority whatever for saying that Onias was murdered at Antioch in June 170 B.C., and yet unless this can be made out the application of the "oracle" fails. With regard to the other half year-week it is plain that there is no greater correspondence with the history, inasmuch as the desecration of the Temple lasted for three years exactly, and not for three years and a half (*see* 2 Macc. x. 5). To imagine, therefore, that the origin of this prophecy is to be sought in the events of June 170—June 163 B.C., is altogether "illusory," for there is no correspondence. Equally unsatisfactory is Kuenen's method of dealing with the words "He shall confirm the covenant with many for one week," which he interprets of "the covenant between Jahveh and His people;" and adds, "Elsewhere "also the author expresses the conviction that the hostile measures "of Antiochus had, contrary to his intention, the effect of confirming "the worship of Jahveh" (ch. xi. 32, 33), p. 267, for this was not a distinctive characteristic of any *seven* years of his reign. As Dr. Pusey says, "Antiochus did not confirm any covenant for seven "years, nor did he make sacrifice to cease for half of those seven "years, nor was any Messias, or any one alleged to be a Messias, cut "off during those seven years; nor was the Temple destroyed; nor "were there any seven years, in the period selected, of one uniform "marked character" (p. 224). And yet nothing can be more clear than that if this prophecy was written at the time supposed, and was to pass as a prophecy 'given,' as Josephus says, '408 years before to Daniel' (*Ant.* xii. 7. 6), and succeeded in doing so, it could only be because of its minute agreement with the events and incidents of the time. There was no such agreement, therefore this was not the cause of the fame of the prophecy, still less was it the cause of its existence, therefore there is no reason to believe that the prophecy was other than genuine.

Dr. Kuenen, however, is witness to himself that the apparent prophecy which was written, according to him, with reference to the events of Antiochus IV., does not correspond, as we should expect it would, even with these events. "The description," he says (p. 267), "of the seventieth year-week corresponds in all its various "features with the history of the years 170 to 163 B.C. There is "only one point of difference. After the last week has elapsed—not "earlier, but also not later—the author expects the destruction of the "'astounding abomination' (ver. 27*b*), and contemporaneously with "that the dawning of Israel's golden age (ver. 24). In reality, the "temple at Jerusalem was purified not three-and-a-half, but three "years after the suspension of the public worship (compare 1 Macc. "iv. 52 with i. 54, 59); but neither at that time, nor half a year "later, did that great revolution in favour of the Jews, which is

"here announced, take place. This relation of the prediction to the
"reality finds its satisfactory explanation *exclusively* in the suppo-
"sition that it had been written *after* the cessation of the daily
"sacrifice (December 167), and *before* its restoration (December 164).
"Other passages allow us to determine still more exactly the time at
"which the book was composed, and to assign it to the year 165 B.C."

So then, though this is a feigned prophecy having reference to
current events, it yet did not correspond with those events, but was
nevertheless received with so much avidity as a genuine prophecy that
its author was reckoned as one of the greatest of the prophets, though
he is admitted to have been in the dark with regard to the events of
his own time. But then to be sure how could he be expected to know
them before they came to pass!

It is to be observed, moreover, that Kuenen here assumes that the
last of the seventy weeks = 170 to 163 B.C.; but 163 + 490 = 653,
(which would bring us to the reign of Manasseh and not Jehoiakim),
and not 606, the year from which he says the seventy years are to be
counted. Whatever difficulty there may be in this prophecy, and it
certainly is difficult, it is clearly not removed by the suggestions
here made and proposed, as though they were sufficient to explain it.

" The traditional interpretation of Dan. ix. 26, 27," says Kuenen,
" is, on the other hand, irreconcilably opposed on all points to the
" words of the writer. It sees in the ' anointed one,' (ver. 26,) Jesus,
" and finds here the announcement both of His atoning death, and
" of the capture and destruction of Jerusalem by Titus in the year
" 70 A.D. But every one sees that the text does not permit such an
" explanation. In verse 26th the cutting off of an anointed one, and
" the profanation (or destruction) of city and temple are mentioned in
" immediate juxtaposition, and both these events are placed after
" the sixty-two weeks, which come after the first seven, that is, in the
" beginning of the seventieth week, the middle of which is men-
" tioned in verse 27th. According to the Messianic interpretation,
" verse 26th refers to the death of Jesus, which happens in the
" middle of the last year-week ; and to the destruction of Jerusalem,
" which took place *thirty-five years after the last year-week !*"

It is to be borne in mind that verse 24 has fixed the limit of
seventy weeks to accomplish certain results ; these seventy weeks
are afterwards divided into 7 + 62 + 1. It cannot but be, therefore,
that the last three verses of the chapter must recount in detail the
results of verse 24 ; but as it expands them, so also may it add to

them. As therefore nothing is said in verse 24 about the abomination of desolation in verse 27, it is gratuitous and contrary to analysis to assume that because the cutting off of the anointed one and the destruction of city and temple are mentioned in immediate juxtaposition (they are however separated by the Ethnach, and a new clause is begun), therefore they are to follow one another in immediate sequence. That our Lord regarded the sequence as very close is shown by His own words, "This generation shall not pass away till all these things be fulfilled." There is no evidence whatever to show that the destruction of Jerusalem, if that is what is meant, was to occur within the seventy weeks, still less in the seventieth week. The middle of the seventieth week (ver. 27), not the beginning of it, as is arbitrarily asserted, was to witness the cutting off of the anointed one ; after that all is foreshortened, and the time might be, as far as the language allows, thirty-five years, or even more. Of course it is impossible to make this good to any one who sees nothing supernatural in the death of Jesus, or who denies the supernatural in prophecy ; but at least there is nothing in the language of this prophecy to render it impossible that the Divine Spirit chose this method of predicting the death of the only-begotten and the well-beloved, or to prevent those who believe that Jesus was the Christ accepting this as the meaning of it. To say that because the morning and evening sacrifices "were not abolished in the middle "of the seventieth year-week, but were regularly offered until the year "70 A.D.," and that "if the author had meant that those sacrifices "would have had no more virtue, he would undoubtedly have said "so, and not have asserted that the middle of the week ' would make "them cease,'" is only saying that had Professor Kuenen written this prophecy, and meant this, he would have said so ; but surely the Epistle to the Hebrews has done more than anything else to abolish sacrifice and offering, while it has only done so by dwelling on the absolute and permanent value of the great sacrifice which was offered in the middle of the seventieth year-week. A man or a system may receive a death-blow, and yet linger for some time afterwards.

It is not surprising that Kuenen follows the accents in verse 25, which according to Dr. Pusey the Jews altered *dishonestly* (p. 173 : what is his evidence for this assertion ?), and makes the restoration and building up of Jerusalem occupy the whole period of 434 years, which he says "the author characterises as a troublous or straitened "time with a view to the future which, according to his conviction,

" awaits the city. The lot of Jerusalem had in truth been much sub-
" ject to vicissitudes, still years of repose and comparative prosperity
" had not been wanting. But the most flourishing state to which she
" had attained might, when compared with her destination, be left
" out of account; for had not one slavery ceased only to make room
" for another ? "

But if this is allowed, though the interpretation seems highly
improbable, is it not strange to say that " from the oracle of Jeremiah
" till Cyrus, forty-nine years elapse," and that " the seven year-weeks
" which here precede (is it his appearance as king of the Persians ?
" or the promulgation of his edict in favour of the Jews ?) agree very
" well with the actual chronology " ? For Kuenen himself says, " The
" prophecy of Jeremiah dates from the fourth year of Jehoiakim,
" 604 B.C." (p. 272). Now forty-nine years from this date brings us to
555 B.C., but the victory of Cyrus over Astyages was 559 B.C., which
overthrows the chronology; and his edict in favour of the Jews was
twenty-three years later, which is yet more fatal to it. Besides,
though the latter event might have caused the Jews to regard him
as a Messiah, it is very improbable that the writer of Daniel would
choose a point in his history more than twenty years before, and an
incident in no way affecting the Jews, from which to count the
oracle of Jeremiah. Certainly the amended interpretation offers us
no improvement. The present punctuation of verse 25 is undoubtedly
a difficulty in the way of the Messianic interpretation of it; but there
is very strong reason, from the evidence of the entire context, to
doubt whether that punctuation can be right, contrary as it is also
to the Greek (see note to Lecture XII., p. 236). Is it probable, on
the face of it, that in two consecutive verses the writer should use a
phrase not elsewhere found in this peculiar way, in two different
senses, as referring to two different persons ? And though the absence
of the article, on which Kuenen insists, is so far in favour of his view,
it is surely altogether accounted for if the term is used, as it appears
to be, as an appellative. And even admitting that by the first
Messiah Cyrus may be meant, as in Isaiah xlv. 1, yet then what consolation could the men of the Maccabæan age receive from a prophecy
which held out to them the promise of troublous times still to run till
the 434 years were fulfilled ? If the Messianic interpretation of this
mysterious prophecy is rejected, it is absolutely certain that no satisfactory meaning can be offered by the theory which would imagine
it to have been a mere invention of the year B.C. 165. Any one

writing what was to pass for a prophecy of his own times would surely be more careful to make it correspond with them. In short, just as the seventy weeks of verse 24 cannot by any possibility be made to square with the times of Antiochus Epiphanes, so is the subsequent analysis of them absolutely inappropriate and unmeaning when applied to that era. So that the reasons for the genuineness of Daniel are substantially and materially strengthened by the inapplicability of this prophecy to the Maccabæan times, when it is gratuitously supposed to have arisen. To be sure, the other interpretation involves the conclusion that it is not only prophetic but predictive, and that involves belief in the supernatural, which is not to be endured; but as far as mere evidence goes, the preponderance of proof is all in favour of it.

On the other hand, no real difficulty is presented even if we allow the force of Kuenen's remark: "It is self-evident that the restoration "of Jerusalem in the troublous times must extend over the 7 + 62 "weeks, and not merely over the seven weeks," only there arises this fatal objection—that the words are not more explicable by reference to the history, if we suppose them written in 165 B.C., than they would be on the traditional hypothesis. On the whole, therefore, it seems more in accordance with the history to refer the first seven year-weeks to the troubled times of Ezra and Nehemiah, which are known to have been nearly, and *may* have been exactly, forty-nine years (*see* Pusey, p. 175).

There is no force whatever in Kuenen's remark, "It is asserted, "indeed, that 'anointed' (*mashiach*, Messiah) was the universally "received appellation of the approaching king of David's family; but "this assertion is untrue: no one trace of any such use of this word "can be pointed out anywhere in the Old Testament" (p. 270). Clearly not: that is the very point. It is undeniable that in the time of Christ the term had received its well-known application. Whence had it received it? Does any one suppose that the use was *invented* by the writers of the New Testament? But, if not, they had received it from their fathers; and if this was not the principal passage which suggested it, then was it in 165 B.C. a standing memorial of the prevalent use of the phrase at that time; for to suppose that then for the first time this application of the phrase was invented and forthwith adopted is on the face of it manifestly impossible, and contrary to all reason. The mere occurrence of the word in the New Testament is the witness to a hope, the hope is the witness to a belief, the belief requires to be accounted for : it is accounted for, if the literature that enshrined and fostered it is divinely authenticated ; it is not otherwise to be accounted for, therefore we must either leave it unexplained, or accept what the explanation of it involves.

Kuenen asks, " What man ever expresses himself thus : 'Till A. B. " are $7+62$ weeks,' and immediately thereafter, 'After $7+62$ weeks " A. B. is cut off' ? why is it not said at once that A. B. will be cut off " after $7+62$ weeks ?" (p. 271.) To which it may be replied that, for some reason or other, the seven weeks and the sixty-and-two weeks are separated the one from the other, either by the coming of a Messiah or by the rebuilding of the city and wall, and that there is a difference between the coming of a Messiah and the cutting off of a Messiah, and that there seems to be nothing unreasonable in saying that a certain period shall elapse before such an one arises, or is acknowledged, or what not, but that after that period he shall be cut off. It shall be so long till so-and-so, but after that period is come he shall be cut off. If the end of his coming was that he might be cut off, if he was born in order that he might die, there is surely nothing unreasonable in such language. Deny the validity of the cause, and the effect is unexplained ; not, however, because there is no explanation, but only because this explanation is rejected. But the other interpretation is certainly not more intelligible, nor more in accordance with any known facts of history.

The construction of this prophecy is well worth observing. In ver. 24 the seventy weeks are surveyed as a whole. In ver. 25 the seven weeks and sixty-two weeks are particularly characterised. In ver. 26 an undefined period subsequent to the sixty-and-nine weeks is described, and in ver. 27 the seventieth week as the commencement of that undefined period is specially dealt with, and special attention is directed to the middle of the week. Thus the prophecy seems to go on circling with a narrower and yet more narrow circle, till it is concentrated upon the particular event of the last week, which is the most prominent and important of all. How this seventieth week, which upon Kuenen's supposition must have fallen 121—114 B.C., can be made to answer to any events in or about the time of Antiochus Epiphanes, seems perfectly unintelligible. Well may he say, (p. 272,) " We on our side readily grant that our interpretation of Dan. ix. " 24—27 does not agree fully with the chronology any more than it " rests upon it. But this signifies, in other words, that the writer of " the book of Daniel had formed another conception of the duration

" of the different periods than we hold at the present day. The pro-
" phecy of Jeremiah dates from the fourth year of Jehoiakim, 604 B.C.
" The writer places Cyrus seven year-weeks after that,—*i.e.* in 555 B.C.
" This is tolerably accurate. [! ! !] If it be assumed that he was thinking
" of a later oracle of Jeremiah (ch. xxix., xxx., or xxxi.), then the seven
" year-weeks bring us to the year 544 or 537 B.C., that is, still nearer
" to the issuing of the edict in favour of the Jews, 536 B.C. Up to this
" point therefore there is no difficulty. [?] But now the interval between
" Cyrus and the death of Onias III., comprising in fact 385 years (that
" is, if we reckon from 555 to 170 B.C. : if we count from 544 or 537
" B.C., the interval is 374 or 367 years), is estimated by the writer as
" being sixty-two year-weeks, that is, 434 years. *We cannot reconcile*
" *this difference.*   [The italics here are ours.]   It is true, indeed, that
" the difficulty is at once removed, and the chronology brought into
" perfect order, by the supposition that the seven year-weeks do not
" precede the sixty-two, but run parallel with them ; (from 604 to 170
" B.C. there are 434 years [not 490]—that is, sixty-two year-weeks ;
" while between 586 and 527 B.C. there intervene precisely forty-nine
" years—that is, seven year-weeks) ; but that supposition, although
" approved of by eminent expositors, seems to be irreconcilable with
" the words of the author, and cannot therefore be admitted."

These, it will be allowed, are considerable admissions for any one
to make who professes to interpret Daniel, and to show from his
interpretation that he is no prophet. The reader will be able to
judge for himself whether the proposed interpretation has such conspicuous advantages over the Messianic application as to involve the
rejection of the latter, and with it the genuineness of Daniel which
is established by the patent superiority of the former. As far as we
are able to arrive at an impartial critical decision, this is certainly not
the case ; but, on the contrary, the manifest fitness of all the more
prominent features of the prophecy of the seventy weeks to the advent
of Christ, to His three years and a half ministry, to the approximate
interval between His death and the opening of the door of faith to
the Gentiles, is so remarkable, and undeniably so much greater and
more accurate than any that has been proposed, that we are after all
constrained to accept it as the true one, and to find in that an additional indication that the prophet spoke by a power not his own, and
that, as he tells us, this wonderful announcement was made to him
distinctly in answer to earnest prayer by a messenger sent from God.
This may seem very childish, and very old-fashioned, and very impro-

bable, but we nevertheless believe it to be after all the conclusion that is most reasonable and most in accordance with fact; at all events not less reasonable than Professor Kuenen's, while on his own showing it certainly is not less in accordance with the history.

But let us examine his account of the genesis of this oracle. He tells us that the writer having determined that by Jeremiah's seventy years were meant year-weeks, " all the rest followed now as a matter " of course. The interval between the death of Onias III. and the " desecration of the temple at Jerusalem comprises three-and-a-half " years: thus the beginning and the middle of the last year-week were " both pointed out, and at the same time it was certain that the joyful " future of Israel would begin three-and-a-half years after the profa- " nation of the temple. But then also in the year that Onias died " (170 B.C.) sixty-nine year-weeks *must* have elapsed since the prediction " of Jeremiah, and these were again divided into seven, and sixty-two " year-weeks, in the way already known to us. How natural is it that " this chronology should not fully correspond to the reality!" (p. 273.)

This is manifestly a loose way of dealing with an " oracle" which was on the hypothesis written with reference to contemporary events, and which, because of the wonderful manner in which it reflected those events, was forthwith supposed to have been the work of Daniel three centuries and a half before. This is the *crux* of the modern hypothesis—that it fails to supply us with any idea of the actual circumstances under which it can be conceived as at all credible or possible that the " oracle" arose, and, having arisen, attained the celebrity it undeniably did for the reasons proposed. This would assuredly be a phenomenon unparalleled in the annals of literature.

But let us look a little closer at Kuenen's dates. He says that Onias died 170 B.C. (The margin in the A. V. of 2 Macc. iv. 32—38 gives the date as 171, which is adopted by Dr. Westcott in the Bible Dict., *s. v.* Onias. Dr. Pusey, p. 223, gives it as 172, but the date commonly accepted is 171.) Accepting this date of 170, how can Kuenen say that there were three years and a half from that time till the desecration of the temple, which was in 168 ? Moreover sixty-nine year-weeks (=483 years) from 170 B.C. will bring us to 653 B.C., or nearly fifty years before the " oracle" of Jeremiah. It is, indeed, " natural that this chronology should not fully correspond to the " reality." But is not this also a very inadequate " *genesis*" for the whole " oracle " ?

NOTE C.

THE FUNCTION OF PROPHECY IN THE DIVINE RECORDS.

SUPPOSING the existence of prophecy to be established as a fact, what purpose does it serve in the œconomy of Divine revelation? Has it any special function peculiar to itself? What do we gain by its presence, and should we lose anything by its absence? Can we willingly consent to the disparagement of prophecy without impoverishing our inheritance in the riches of the Divine grace bestowed upon us in Revelation? These are questions which seem to deserve an answer. Let us try to find one.

The literature of the Old Testament is not more remarkable in its poetical books than it is in its purely historical portions. Most of the historical books have records or fragments of prophecies embodied in them, even if we may not rightly question whether much of the history itself is not prophetic. We cannot turn the first pages of Genesis without meeting with what professes to be a Divine promise, and is therefore of the nature of a prophecy; and as we proceed, we find a promise made to Cain, to Noah, to Abraham, to Isaac, and to Jacob, while the last chapter but one appears to shadow forth the destiny of the sons of Israel for many generations.

But then it may be questioned whether the history of Abraham and of Joseph, for example, are not themselves prophetic, and do not themselves indicate the fortunes of the chosen people in the present and the future, as well as in the past. Abraham, wandering among the cities of Canaan, but having no possession there, is not unlike his descendants even now. Joseph, going down into Egypt and becoming its saviour, is an historical prophecy or a prophetic history of the mission of Israel in the world. And many other significant parallels might be pointed out, which are so striking and instructive

as to make it something more than probable that their significance
was designed. But if this is the case, we see at once that prophecy
is but a higher manifestation of an energy which is latent in Scripture
as a whole. No other book can be named in which the like features
can be discovered of the individuals of a nation, or of the nation
itself, foreshadowing in their history the fortunes and destiny of the
nation for many ages to come. This is conspicuously the case with
that nation whose history is contained in the Bible. The oppression
and bondage of Israel in Egypt and its deliverance therefrom may be
said to have foreshadowed the captivity in Babylon and the return, as
the captivity foreshadowed a yet greater exile after the destruction of
Jerusalem, to be followed it may be by a yet greater return. The
forty years' wandering in the wilderness also foreshadowed a much
longer wandering in the wilderness of the nations, which may likewise
not improbably be the prelude to a literal or typical entry into the
promised land.

And, yet further, the fortunes of Israel from the very first have
been singularly illustrative and anticipatory of the fortunes of the
Christian Church from the beginning until now, when many features
of the parallel still hold good. And as this is a matter of fact, and
not merely of the interpretation of facts, it serves to show that there
is in the *history* even of Scripture such a prophetic element as may
suffice to prepare us for the possible existence of other manifestations
of prophecy. If the book seems to show as in a glass the character
of a large and important chapter of human history for many ages to
come, it would seem to be antecedently not improbable that these
documents may contain even more marked instances of the exercise
of the prophetic activity. At all events, professed examples of it
would be in keeping with the documents, and the documents with
them ; and even if we were to abolish every professed prophecy from
the book, we should still not get rid of the prophetic aspect of the
history which it has preserved.

And it is manifest that this character of the history is not one
which has been artificially and by design communicated to it. The
history of Abraham was not written because subsequent events in
a long course of ages had illustrated it ; because on any theory of the
composition of Genesis it must have been prior to those events. The
history of the captivity was not invented because of its supposed
analogy to any other subsequent events ; and yet during the captivity
itself it had been declared by the prophet Ezekiel, *I will bring you*

*into the wilderness of the people,**—whatever that expression may mean.

If then this is the framework in which prophecy is set, what is the function of the prophecies? This can only be ascertained by an investigation or analysis of their chief features. There can be no question but that the prophets claimed to be the enunciators of the will of God. Their phraseology, *The word of the Lord came unto me; Thus saith the Lord,* not only has not been adopted by any one else, but were it to be adopted by any one it would at once be felt to be incongruous, unbecoming, and blasphemous. However, therefore, we may account for the verbal phenomena, there can be no doubt that the prophets claimed to be the spokesmen of the Divine Spirit, and that not seldom in opposition to their own will and to their personal interest.

It is moreover sufficiently clear that the prophets did lay claim at times to the prediction of events yet future. Not only do their writings contain instances of their so doing, but the latter chapters of Isaiah expressly challenge to any one but the Lord this power of foretelling the unknown events of the future. We have only to open the prophets anywhere casually to see at once that they do profess to declare things that shall happen or ever they come to pass. It is useless, therefore, to deny to them the claim, even if it is impossible to make it good. But is this after all so difficult as some would have us believe? Take for instance Amos, one of the earliest of the prophets, who is acknowledged to have written nearly 800 years B.C., in the contemporary reigns of Uzziah and Jeroboam II. What do we read in his last chapter? *Behold, the eyes of the Lord God are upon the sinful kingdom, and I will destroy it from off the face of the earth : saving that I will not utterly destroy the house of Jacob, saith the Lord. For, lo, I will command, and I will sift the house of Israel among all nations, like as corn is sifted in a sieve, yet shall not the least grain fall upon the earth.* Now, this claims to be spoken as a Divine message, and in the name of the Lord. It was spoken at a time when the kingdom of Israel was in its highest prosperity, before the first incursions of Assyria, while a long line of distinguished monarchs had still to reign in Judah, and with reference to secular history probably several years before the first Olympiad. At this time, then, Amos declared that the sinful kingdom, apparently Israel, should be destroyed, but that the house of Jacob should not utterly be destroyed, that *the*

* Ezekiel xx. 35.

house of Israel should be sifted among all nations, but that the least grain should not fall upon the earth. We look back now upon the words of the prophet from a distance of five-and-twenty centuries. Have these four statements been ratified by history, or have they not? Was any endowment of human foresight and intelligence, any amount of human wisdom, able at the time when Amos wrote to promise or to foresee that it would be as he said after that lapse of time? There can be but one answer. Which of us would venture to say how it shall be with any national or public institution five-and-twenty years to come? It is not necessary to maintain that Amos saw mentally when he wrote the present condition of Israel; it is not possible to deny that . what he wrote has been verified. Is that any evidence of the truth of his claim to be a messenger of God, or is it not? Again, where is there any instance in the history of any other nation of its destinies in the far future being thus foretold? Can Greece point to it? Can Rome point to it? Can we ourselves point to it? But if not, may we not say with Kuenen, "The Israelitish prophet is a unique "phenomenon in history"? (p. 591.) But may we not also say, as he does not say, that there are tokens here of a wisdom that is not merely natural, of a knowledge that is more than human? Are not the prophet's words the human index of a will that five-and-twenty centuries ago intended to fulfil itself in history, and has done so?

Take another instance of about the same time from another prophet —Hosea. *The children of Israel shall abide many days without a king, and without a prince, and without a sacrifice, and without an image, and without an ephod, and without teraphim: afterward shall the children of Israel return, and seek the Lord their God and David their king; and shall fear the Lord and His goodness in the latter days.* Here again we ourselves are witnesses to the graphic accuracy of the former statement; whereas none can say that the foreknowledge of the prophet's words may not embrace an area of time as far distant from the present as we ourselves are from him. Can this be explained naturally, or can it not? If it cannot, why should we hesitate to ascribe to his words, if not to him, the evidence of a foreknowledge which is more than human, and which therefore is in favour of the mission to which he laid claim being a real one?

To take one more instance, from a prophecy to which we can assign the actual date of 520 B.C. At the close of what we may call the first great act of the drama of Israel's national life, after the monarchy had passed away, and the prophets' calling was about to cease, Haggai declared of the newly built temple—*The latter glory of this house shall be greater than the former, saith the Lord of hosts: and in this place will I give peace, saith the Lord of hosts.*   Here was a distinct promise uttered in the most solemn way in the name of the Lord.   There was at the time no apparent prospect of its fulfilment, for the promise itself was given because of the manifest inferiority of the restored temple.   Nor is it at all likely that the temple of Zerubbabel ever equalled in splendour the temple of Solomon; and even if the temple of Herod approached it in magnificence, yet then the lapse of five centuries was required before the prophet's words could be made good; but it is evident that he was not speaking of its comparative material splendour, but of another and a greater glory altogether, for he added, *In this place I will give peace, saith the Lord of hosts.*   But if his words were true at all, there is only one way in which they were proved true, and that was by the advent of the Prince of Peace.   In no other single point could the restored temple venture to compare with Solomon's temple, but in this respect it was utterly incomparable to it.   We dare not say that this was the fulfilment of the prophet's words, and we cannot point, as in the former cases, to something of which we ourselves are witnesses; but we can say, as before, that the course of history has brought an unexpected flood of light to bear upon his words, and if we admit the possibility of his being an agent of the Divine Being, it is hard to deny that in the greater glory that visited the temple in the latter days the seal of God was set to his audacious and repeated claim to have spoken in the name of the Lord of hosts.

We might multiply instances without number, but these are sufficient as illustrations that the prophets did make themselves responsible for statements which no discretion or foresight would have enabled them to make, which the circumstances of their times could not explain, as in the instances just given, and which the lapse of many centuries has only shown to be more and more true.   And while the attempt is made to account for prophecy as a merely natural phenomenon, it seems to be well to direct attention to a few crucial passages, and to challenge the verdict upon them as to whether or not they can be adequately explained but as the deliberate utterances of men who were authorised to make them in virtue of the commission which they held as the prophets of the Most High.   Can their words be justly regarded but as a record of the Divine foreknowledge ?

While, however, the supernatural element in prophecy is denied, an unwonted function is attributed to the prophets. They are advanced as the authors, directly or indirectly, of the Mosaic law. Whereas in the New Testament the phrase is consistently * the Law and the Prophets, we are told to substitute for it the Prophets and the Law, for the astounding reason that " the final redaction of the present Pentateuch was " preceded chronologically by the entire series of the canonical Pro- " phets." † It may be very much easier to make an assertion like this than it is to disprove it; and yet not because it is *true* for all that. It is an old slander that all religion is the invention of priests, but it is a new discovery that the Mosaic Law was the invention of the prophets. In that case one hardly understands how the priests allowed themselves to be superseded in their legitimate function of deceiving mankind. The prophet and the priest did not always act in harmony, but, as so often happens, their mutual jealousy was productive of some beneficial results. It would naturally act as a mutual check. The priests would hardly venture to fabricate a law with the prophets looking on, and the prophets, who were comparatively a late order of men, would have some natural difficulty in gaining the assent of a class who boasted their descent from Aaron to an ethical and ritual code of their own invention. We are not told how the *natural* obstacles in this arrangement were surmounted; we are only told of the supernatural difficulties of the law and prophecy. But it is scarcely open to question that Malachi, the last of the prophets, was acquainted with the law as we have it, and with no other form of it. He refers to it in its present form, including Deuteronomy, as entrusted to Moses by God in Horeb. Whether he was right or wrong, that was the belief of his day. He clearly was unconscious of any change in the law which he had from what it had been in the time of Moses. If he had been, he would not have spoken as he did. He also recognised the function of the priest as a teacher of the law,—evidently this same law, for he says, *The priest's lips should keep knowledge, and they should seek the law at his mouth, for he is the messenger of the Lord of hosts.*‡ There is no evidence of the existence of any other law; there is no reason to believe that this was not the law he was to teach; there is every reason to believe it was. About contemporary with Malachi we have the testimony of Nehemiah, whose ninth

* This is commonly so : the reverse order, however, is found in Matt. xi. 13 ; but see Luke xv. 16, 29, 31, and compare Matt. v. 17, vii. 12, xxii. 40; Acts xiii. 15, xxviii. 23 ; Rom. iii. 21 ; John viii. 52. 53.

† Kuenen, *Prophets and Prophecy in Israel,* p. 561.

‡ ii. 7.

chapter is studded with the phraseology of the Pentateuch, and with references to the national records. It is clear that Nehemiah knew the law, which apparently was then so old that to some present its language had become obsolete and needed an interpreter ;[*] it was then believed to be the Law of Moses which the Lord God of Israel had given him, and in which Ezra was a ready scribe. He had evidently brought it with him from Babylon. Had he found it there ? If so, is it possible that he could have believed it to be the work of Moses, or that the nation generally could have done so ? At all events, in the previous century, two generations before Ezra, we find Haggai making reference to this same law, of which he regards the priests as the natural guardians. His references can be verified in our existing law. He then must have known it in Babylon, and reverenced and prized it there ; not, however, because it originated in Babylon, but because it belonged to the beloved fatherland, and had been brought with his fathers into captivity from their ancestral home. It is evident that the law was regarded as a common standard both by priest and prophet, by which both were alike bound. Had the priests tampered with the law, the prophets would have been the first to charge them with it. Had the prophets forged the law, they would not have made the priests the keepers of it, nor would they have been willing to keep it. Moreover, as the priesthood was hereditary, and could be traced up to Aaron, and as they were the recognised teachers of the law, its origin would naturally be coeval and co-ordinate with their own, for the function spoken of by Malachi was that prescribed by the law itself: *That ye may teach the children of Israel all the statutes which the Lord hath spoken unto them by the hand of Moses :*[†] and consequently before the priests could teach the law, there must have been a law for them to teach. It is admitted that this is not demonstrative evidence, for that we can seldom obtain : it is, however, evidence with an *a priori* probability. Nor does it avail to insist upon the recorded breaches of the law, as in the case of Josiah's passover or Nehemiah's feast of tabernacles ; for if that were a legitimate inference from the statement of the historian, and he had been interested in conveying an opposite impression, what would have been easier than for him to be silent on the matter ? Had the law been observed either in letter or in spirit, where would have been the function of the prophet ? The non-observance of the law is no proof of its nonexistence. A law may be in abeyance or in desuetude, or its violation

* Neh. viii. 8.　　　　† Lev. x. 11.

may be connived at. It is absurd, moreover, to expect detailed reference to the law in the writings of the prophets. That there is much verbal reference is undeniable. It is enough to remember that, as far as it is possible to trace the history, the law was ever regarded by the Jews as a sacred whole. It was manifestly so in the time of the Maccabees and in the time of Malachi. We have no reason to believe it ever was otherwise regarded ; we have every reason to believe it was always regarded as a sacred whole. As far, therefore, as this is the case, one clear reference to a part is a reference to the whole.

Now, there is one part of the law referred to and insisted upon alike by Ezekiel, Jeremiah, and Isaiah, not to mention other prophets; and this is the law of the Sabbath. The institution of the Sabbath, like the institution of the passover, was derived from the law, and known only from the law. The observance of every Sabbath and of every passover, whether perfect or incomplete, was a standing witness to the deliverance from Egypt and to the thunders of Sinai, no less than every breaking of bread and pouring out of wine in the Christian Church is a standing witness to the events of the last supper in the upper chamber. You cannot account for the one but on the supposition of the other, It is certain, therefore, that Isaiah, Jeremiah, and Ezekiel knew so much of the law as is implied by their knowledge of the Sabbath, but this brings us back to a time when the kingdom was divided. And Amos likewise, in prophesying to the northern kingdom, charges them with their profanation of the Sabbath. So much, therefore, of the law as this implies was known to and recognised by the northern kingdom. But it is morally impossible that a law that was recognised in the divided kingdom even to this extent could have originated after the division of the kingdom. It must have been older than the national schism. This brings us to the time of Solomon—a period long before the era of the canonical prophets. Where, then, is the probability or the possibility that the canonical prophets invented the law ? It is a theory, we need not hesitate to say, in flat contradiction of all the evidence. The New Testament phrase, " the law and the prophets," is strictly accurate, is amply supported by the fullest evidence, and cannot be with any semblance of justice impeached. The prophets virtually, if not formally, took their stand upon the law, could have had no existence but for the law, and to a man would have echoed the words of Isaiah, *To the law and to the testimony, if they speak not according to this word it is because there is* *no light in them.**   It would be easy to show that the writings of the oldest prophets, Hosea, Joel, and Amos, were full of traces which betoken a knowledge of the law, so that if they were not the natural product of such knowledge, then a yet more wonderful alternative must be taken, and we must suppose that the law was fabricated by a number of unknown men in such a way as to exhibit all these minute points of contact with the prophets, and *that* for the sake and with the intent of leading us off upon the false issue that the law was older than the prophets, when in reality it was compiled out of their writings.   But no one in his right mind could for a moment suppose *that.*   It follows, therefore, that we may confidently accept the writings of the prophets as bearing tacit and unintentional evidence to a knowledge of the law which was substantially the same as we have it now, for aught that appears to the contrary, and *that* a knowledge also which was shared by those to whom they ministered.   One function, therefore, of prophecy in the sacred Scriptures which it does fulfil, whether or not it was intended to do so, is that of a witness to an older revelation.   The prophets stand midway between the two branches of the Israelitish literature, which are the law and the other writings represented by the Psalms.   This is their technical position, and it is one that is based on their natural characteristics, and is in strict accordance with their acknowledged mission.   Nor can it for a moment be doubted that in the case of any other literature— whether Greek, Roman, Hindoo, or what not—if any book were attested as the law is attested by the prophets, it would at once be held to be conclusive evidence of its priority.   When Thucydides or Plato quotes Homer, we accept it as undeniable evidence that Homer was known to them and in their day, not that the Homeric poems were written in order to substantiate or illustrate their quotations. But if this is a legitimate inference in their case, how should it be otherwise in the case of a prophet like Hosea, for example, whose brief writings and sententious and abrupt style make the occurrence of passages having clear reference to the law to be all the more remarkable?   When, for example, Hosea manifests, as he does, intimate knowledge of the history of Jacob, is it more reasonable to assume that in the eighth century before Christ the unwritten traditions of a thousand years before were so numerous that prophet and people were alike familiar with them, or that since a writing does exist which has singular correspondence with the prophet's language,

* Isaiah viii. 20.

and is the only one ever known to have existed, this writing was known also to the prophet and familiar to the people, seeing that it is preposterous to suppose that the history of Jacob in Genesis was compiled from the suggestions in Hosea rather than that these suggestions were borrowed from the history. There *may* have been other poems besides Homer's, containing the quotations of Plato and Thucydides, but at all events we have Homer's, and as they do contain them, the only reasonable inference is that it was these poems to which they referred, and not any others which may have existed, but in all probability did not; least of all is it likely that these passages were subsequently inserted in the poems of Homer because these writers had made use of them. But the analogy is not one whit less applicable to the writings of the prophets, but even more so; nor would it be possible to resist the force of it, were it not for the unlimited reserve of conjecture upon which rash speculators think it right to draw. The only consolation is that the common sense of the multitude is oftentimes wiser than the far-fetched wisdom of critics and savants.

This function of the prophets, however, though very important, is nevertheless subordinate to a higher one. The era of canonical prophecy extended over about four centuries. There is no dispute as to this period, which is about equivalent to that from Chaucer to Wordsworth, or a little less. Like other things mundane, it was marked by epochs of growth, maturity, and decay. But all the prophets,—fifteen in number (not including Daniel),—were alike in their claim to a Divine mission, and in the integrity and sublimity with which they discharged it. Now it is not alleged that there is any similar phenomenon in all literature. The canonical prophets stand alone in the whole cycle of the world's written monuments. Is their consistent position and character, then, in confirmation of their claim, or is it not? Does that claim become more or less significant when viewed in relation to their personal greatness? Is the sublimity and magnificence of Isaiah an additional reason for regarding him as the subject of "pious illusions"? or is it altogether in favour of his calling being as far higher than that of any other bard as his poetry transcends theirs? What are the highest flights of Homer compared with the forty-ninth or the sixtieth of Isaiah? Read the two in any translation, and let the hearer judge. If one is the voice of man, the other is most assuredly the voice of God. But this is what it claims to be, and therefore its accents are worthy of the claim. And we may take these two chapters as fair samples of the rest, and as representations so far of the function of the prophet. Nor is there any question as to their meaning; it is clear and obvious, so that he who runs may read it, and he who reads may understand it. A vast increase is promised to the ideal Israel, as the chosen worshippers of the Lord. We are asked to believe that this was written at the time of the return;—then be it so. But turn from these sublime flights to the undoubted works of that and the subsequent period,—namely, those of Haggai, Ezra, Nehemiah. Does the history of the latter, and the hints suggested by it, supply in any degree the basis for the prophet's anticipations? Does it not rather present the most deplorable and futile contrast that can be conceived? Can the feeble realities of the time have been the actual source of the prophet's inspiration? It is impossible. Nor is any other historical feature in the next four hundred years in the least degree more hopeful. The notion, therefore, that the prophet winged his flight from the historic circumstances of the return is altogether incongruous and absurd. There was nothing in what *we know* of those times to lend him inspiration. To be sure, there *may* have been, but that is merely conjectural. As far as we know from the indubitable records that remain to us, there was an absolute dearth of everything of the kind. As, therefore, probability is entirely against the idea of these prophecies being produced then, so is there nothing in the history of Israel, from Hezekiah to our Lord, which can at all account for them. And yet then the prophet's language is as a witness to all time: *Kings shall be thy nursing fathers, and their queens thy nursing mothers . . . . and all flesh shall know that I the Lord am thy Saviour and thy Redeemer, the mighty one of Jacob.** That, however, which the prophet whenever he wrote was never destined to see with his own eyes has been witnessed often in the past, and we ourselves can witness it to-day. Is it, or is it not, a fulfilment of that language? Does it confirm or falsify the prophet's claim? Most unquestionably we cannot suppose that Isaiah had the same clear mental intelligence of what we behold as we have who witness it. But what of that? All the more evident is it that his language surpassed his own conceptions, and therefore all the more evident is it that his claim to be a prophet of the Lord was valid. And it is this remarkable fact that prophecy did distinctly foreshadow the rejection of Israel and the ingathering of the Gentiles that stamps it as a more than human

* Isaiah xlix. 23, 26.

agency ; for what human foresight could have discerned this in the future ? And yet the present condition of Israel and of the world corresponds therewith.

A remarkable parallel has been drawn by those who take delight in the comparison of religions,* between the fortunes of Brahminism and Buddhism, and those of Judaism and Christianity. Brahminism gave birth to Buddhism, as Judaism gave birth to Christianity ; but Buddhism took root chiefly in non-Aryan races, just as Christianity took root chiefly in non-Semitic races. It is very interesting and very remarkable, but here the parallel ceases ; and those who dwell on the comparison should carry it still further, then not the comparison but the contrast will be striking,—for nowhere in the Vedas is there anything that can be regarded as an anticipation of this fact. The development, if such it was, pursued its course naturally, and was not predicted ; but with Judaism it was altogether different. There we meet in the prophetic writings with the most distinct anticipations of the event, and the history of five-and-twenty centuries is sketched in outline so far as it relates to the rejection of Israel and the admission of the Gentiles. And, before we determine that there is nothing which is not natural in prophecy, we must decide how these very remarkable features are to be explained. I do not hesitate to say that they baffle explanation on any merely natural basis. *The Gentiles shall come to thy light, and kings to the brightness of thy rising . . . The sons also of them that afflicted thee shall come bending unto thee, and all they that despised thee shall bow themselves down at the soles of thy feet, and they shall call thee the city of the Lord, the Zion of the Holy One of Israel.*†

Of course it is possible to say that this is nothing more than a highly poetical expression of the prophet's hopes for his nation, but the significant fact is that the poetry became verified by history, and so verified that the hand of man could have had no part in it. As therefore we point to the finger of God in the history, so also do we lay claim to hear the voice of God in the poetry. It is because God and not man has authenticated this poetry, as He has authenticated no other, that we accept the poetry as not merely man's, but God's. And we affirm that it was one function of the prophets to give utterance to such poetry, to become the spokesmen to the nation of hopes, aspirations and prophecies, which were as far above the general level of their age as their language was beyond any circum-

* See Max Müller's " Science of Religion," p. 103, sq.   † Isaiah lx. 3, 14.

stances of the time which could have suggested it.   There is reason, then, to believe that there is evidence in prophecy of a Divine spirit breathing through its records, which was the endowment and not the product of those who wrote them.   So far as this is true,—and I believe the more we consider it the truer we shall find it,—there is to be discovered here the basis and framework of truly supernatural features which may very possibly confront us.   The supernatural is not to be expected except where it can be seen to be consistent and congruous with the environment.   It is demonstrable that in the Hebrew literature there is a combination of circumstances that renders it conceivable that we might find the presence of the supernatural. There, if anywhere, it would fit in with consistency and congruity. Given a history more remarkable in its undoubted features than any other—a literature in character and most essential features absolutely unparalleled, and in style unsurpassed by any—and where, if at all, is the presence of the supernatural to be appropriately met with, if not here ?   And if there is intrinsic evidence of it here, do not these circumstances make it *à priori* probable ?   Prophecy is exactly that development which, antecedently, we might expect.   Given an earlier revelation by the hand of Moses, and that revelation a veritable and real one, and the subsequent development of prophecy becomes naturally conceivable.   The law becomes the basis of prophecy, and prophecy the confirmation of the law.   But to suppose that prophecy was the natural offshoot of Canaanitish soothsaying, and that from such an environment Isaiah was produced, with all the goodly fellow-ship of the prophets, and that by them or from their writings the law was compiled and fabricated, is to build a pyramid upon its apex, and ascribe an effect to a cause incapable of producing it.

The remaining function of prophecy, which is that of prediction, must be briefly touched upon.   Of course those who regard prophecy as a merely natural endowment deny that it possesses any elements of prediction.   Strictly speaking, it is impossible to prove or disprove this.   But the question really is whether the statements of the pro-phets are literally susceptible of a meaning which can be limited to their own terms.   And if this is so, how is it that they are still endowed with an imperishable vitality which is continually adjusting itself to new conditions and circumstances ?   How is it that the character of Christ more nearly answers to the delineations of pro-phecy than any other ?   How is it that the broad history of the Christian Church corresponds with the declarations of prophecy so nearly as it does?   And how is it that the present condition of the Jewish nation is that which Moses and the prophets declared it should be?   We may deny that these are instances of prediction, but it may be replied, What would be so if these are not? while, on the other hand, we have but to postulate the possible existence of prediction to find that the writings of the prophets are thickly strewn with the tokens of it.   Supposing that it does exist, the evidences of it meet us on every hand.   What, then, is the function of predictive prophecy?   It is apparently designed to confer that amount of permanent and abiding testimony to the prophet's mission and language which nothing else could give.   Here it is that they are seen to be the bearers of a Divine message, not merely by the strength of their convictions, the elevation of their moral sentiment, the exaltation of their character, but by the evidence which they bring with them of having spoken words which could not be their own, of having made promises that it was not possible for man to make or to fulfil, and of having laid the foundations of a character and a constitution, of an ideal kingdom of righteousness, and of a world-wide polity which the experience of eighteen centuries has only combined to show to be still ideal, although ever approximating more and more nearly to the real, the actual, and the possible.   The prophets were so conspicuously before their age, are still so conspicuously before our age, that that fact alone is sufficient to establish for them the claim to be the special messengers of God, and to show not that they were so much the conscious utterers of predictions, as that by their ministry and in their language God gave to His people predictive prophecy which the perpetual lapse of ages will only show to be more and more Divine because more and more true.

NOTE D.

THE CREDENTIALS OF REVELATION.

IN the present state of religious thought it is important that we should endeavour to understand what are the credentials of revelation. If it is possible for us to have a revelation—that is to say, a body of Divine truth—committed to us, which has not been discovered and could not be discovered, what are the conditions under which such a body of truth could be received, and how would those conditions affect the mass of mankind in relation to it? A clear apprehension on these points would be of essential service in many of the religious discussions of our time.

In the first place, then, we must take for granted the possibility of a revelation being given by God and received by man. It would be waste of time to prove this, and it is unlikely that any one who denied it would be influenced by anything that could be said. It may not, however, be superfluous to point out the absolute need there is for such a revelation as we have mentioned, under the circumstances in which we are placed.

It may be admitted, perhaps, that the being of a supreme God, though amounting as it does to a very high degree of probability, is not a matter of demonstration. No one has ever succeeded in *showing* God to the intellectual eye, any more than he has discovered Him to the bodily organ. But yet, in a very large number of cases, the being of God is as much a fact to the spiritual apprehension as a mathematical demonstration would be to the intellectual faculty. How, then, are we to regard the consciousness of this apprehension? It is admitted to be not a demonstration, but yet it is declared to be a moral conviction or certainty of no less force. The intellect, however, properly speaking, is not, at all events, directly concerned in it; not that the intellect is altogether otiose in the matter, for it acquiesces or co-operates, but is subordinate. It is another faculty that is immediately concerned, whether we call this faculty the spirit or the soul, or faith ; but with regard to the being of God, this faculty is what the eye is to the body, what perception is to the mind. Nor is there any reason to believe that this faculty does not vary in its nature and quality in different persons, even as the mental perception varies, and the faculty of natural sight varies.

If this is so, and it were commonly recognised as a fact, there would be an obvious method of escape from many of the perplexities of religion. We should at all events give up the task of seeking to make all men see alike spiritually, as we do not try to make them all appreciate the same mental operations, or see alike with their bodily eyes. But here those who are *endowed* with the faculty would be acknowledged as the standards to test it, just as the acute and educated are recognised as the standards in matters involving the exercise of the mind, and as the seeing and not the blind can alone measure the accuracy with which objects of sense are apprehended.

And, certainly, as the negative testimony of those who lacked either of these faculties would not be accepted in opposition to the positive testimony of the others in their several spheres, so neither should the negative testimony of those who are unable to discover God avail to set aside the positive testimony of those who know Him.

We thus arrive at the position that since the being of God is undemonstrable it is nevertheless capable of apprehension spiritually, but is to be regarded as being so in varying degrees according to the endowments of various persons. In some the power of apprehension is undoubtedly quicker than it is in others. All we have to insist upon at present is the *fact* that there is this difference, and that it is to be recognised as a fact, and not to be set aside as the result of a freak or idiosyncracy unworthy of the attention of enlightened men.

But now we come to another point. Given the fact that there is a God, and given the fact that some men have the power of apprehending Him, which others have not, how are we to regard the operation of this conceded faculty ? On the hypothesis, it is not to be affirmed for a moment that these men *create* the God whom they apprehend, for His possible existence is admitted. But what about the operation of that faculty whereby they apprehend Him ? Is it more justly to be regarded as a discovery on their part, or as a revelation on His ? Of course to them it will have all the characteristics of a discovery. There will be the suddenness of it, the unexpectedness of it, and the joy resulting from it. They will feel as at the discovery of hidden treasure. But there will be this difference: that whereas in the case of hidden treasure there could be nothing but a dull and dead discovery, however joyous, in the other case, seeing it was the *life* that was discovered, there would be the element of life in the discovery which would make it a revelation. Everything would turn, therefore, upon the life of the object discovered. The hidden treasure was there before the eye fell upon it and discovered it; the God was there before—the eye was opened, and it beheld Him.

Now it seems that, admitting the accuracy of this statement, the question would be one of living personality. In the case of the lifeless treasure there could be no operation of will; in the case of the discovery of God there could not be anything else. If God had been willing that He should *not* be discovered, He would have remained hidden. That He did not remain hidden was because He was willing to reveal Himself. And certainly the degree of personal and spontaneous activity that we attribute to this operation will depend entirely upon the degree and nature of the vitality and conscious activity that we ascribe to God. If personal, active, conscious life is not the attribute of God, then, so far as we acknowledge the facts of this discovery at all, it will be nothing more than a discovery the credit of which we may take entirely to ourselves. And then, admitting these facts, we shall have to adjust them as we best may to the conditions and requirements of the particular system that we espouse.

But so far as we accept the idea of a *living* God, so far we shall be prepared to admit that every discovery of Divine truth on the part of man is a true indication of an actual revelation on the part of God. Strictly speaking, therefore, there may be much revelation within the limits of natural, or at all events of ordinary operation. There may be no suspension of or interference with any natural laws, and yet a true revelation may be imparted.

And yet all the time it is to be borne in mind that this revelation under these circumstances is itself not natural. It is not a revelation of the powers of nature, it is not a revelation of anything that nature—understanding by that term the physical and material universe—has to reveal. The physical and material universe has no moral virtues to reveal, has no righteousness to reveal, has no purity to reveal, has no moral truth to reveal, has no love to reveal. I do not say that the physical universe belies these things; I only say that it is silent about

them, or stops short of them, or only speaks of them *after* they have
from other sources been spoken about. The revelation of *God*, even
when within the limits of the natural, is a revelation independent of,
external to, and apart from nature ; it is a revelation about *other
things*. The apprehension by the individual heart of the Father in
heaven is a revelation within the limits of the natural ; but it is not
a revelation that nature can bestow, for it is not a revelation that
many of her students and votaries acknowledge, or at all events there
are many who do not acknowledge it. In this sense, therefore, even
the most ordinary revelation of the Father to the individual heart is
a *supernatural* revelation—a revelation which, with nature alone for
our guide, we should never have had, a revelation of which there is
no evidence in all the literature of Greece and Rome, a revelation
which is dimly and obscurely intimated in the Old Testament, a
revelation which is confined to the New in its fulness and reality.
But forasmuch as even this revelation to the individual heart is in its
very nature a *supersensuous* and *supernatural* revelation, though within
the limits of the natural, the possibility seems to be thereby suggested
that under special circumstances this revelation might carry in its
train, or be associated with, incidents and accidents that should be
beyond the limits of the natural.

And here, of course, we should enter the world of history, and our
decision would be nothing more than a matter of evidence and a
matter of testimony. But since the doctrine of the Fatherhood of
God is one of the special revelations of the New Testament, and there
is no reason to believe that we should ever have known any more
about it than the ancients knew had it not been for the New Testament,
let us see how the doctrine is there inculcated. The Person who first
taught it was Jesus Christ, and He claimed to be the Son of God.
Was it therefore a discovery on His part, or was it a revelation in
Him ? It is useless to ask whether it was a revelation *to* Him, for
that carries us no farther than we have arrived already ; but was it
a revelation *in* Him ? That is to say, was the doctrine based upon
a fact and the result of a fact ? Was He Himself the proof and
evidence of the doctrine which He taught ? Was He the demonstration
of the Fatherhood of God by being Himself the Son of God ? If so, it
is undeniable that so far the doctrine would be made a matter of
demonstration. To accept the Son would be to accept the Father ;
to acknowledge the Son would be to acknowledge the Father also.
But then to do this would be to travel quite beyond the limits of the

natural for the demonstration, for Christ could not be the Son of God in any sense that would make our position more certain than before without being so in a sense in which no one else ever was, or can be, the Son of God. Now the whole of the New Testament is the proof or evidence that Jesus is the Son of God. We cannot investigate that evidence here, for it would lead us too far afield; but it is needful to show that if the witness of the New Testament is accepted, then the doctrine of the Fatherhood of God rests on a basis of supernatural fact, for it rests on the personal claims of the historic man Christ Jesus. We, of course, have to decide upon these claims; but if we admit the claims, then we have unquestionably a basis of supernatural fact on which the Fatherhood of God rests. And then the ultimate revelation becomes a matter of history and a matter of fact. The truth of God's Fatherhood can never be borne in upon any individual mind without a revelation, as we saw, but that is a revelation within the limits of the natural. No law of nature is displaced or set aside; but the fact on which the truth of that revelation itself depends is the reality of certain facts which, so far as they are really facts, do most undoubtedly interfere with the course of nature, and displace natural law.

For no one can for a moment maintain that the incarnation of the Lord of life can, under any view of it, be regarded as a *natural* fact. If we accept that fact, we accept the supernatural pure and simple, and the after operation of it is a matter only of evidence and degree, for it unquestionably is in operation here to the highest possible extent. If, therefore, we want to know the value of the doctrine or conception of God's Fatherhood, we cannot find it in nature or within the limits of the natural, but must travel beyond those limits to the person of Christ. If, however, Christ was only a natural man, we can have no evidence that God is our Father, for He becomes our Father only in such sense as that nature is our mother. And we know the kind of comfort we derive from the fact of nature being our mother. What we want to know is how the *living* God feels towards us who live in His natural world, and this we cannot know unless He has revealed it to us as we believe He has revealed it to us in Christ. If, however, He has revealed it to us in Him, He has only revealed it to us by stepping out of the area of what is physically and materially possible, and giving us a sign which we may know to be from Him because it can only come from one who is Lord *over* nature.

We have seen, then, that for such a doctrine as the Fatherhood of

God it is absolutely necessary, if it is to be anything more than an uncertain idea or vague notion, that it should have its root in a supernatural fact. The authority of Christ is no higher than the authority of Plato if He does not stand on a higher basis than Plato. We may personally concede to Him any amount of deference or reverence, but that will not alter the state of the case if He is not equal to His claims. It is not what we are pleased to give to Him, but what He demands of us. He has no right to demand this of us if He is not what He said He was; but if He has no right to demand it of us, then we can no longer be sure that God is our Father; nay, we may be sure that He is not, or at least that He has not, as a *living* God, given us any token that He is. Yea, we may go further, and say that on the *natural* theory it is not possible either for God to give or for us to receive any such token of His regard, for in doing so He would cease to be what He is—the God of nature, or the *natural* God.

And we are led to the same conclusion when we push our inquiries in any other direction. Let us suppose that we want to know whether mercy and righteousness are attributes of God or not. We may say that the question is an absurd one. But this will depend simply upon our concept of God. If we choose to *assume* that God is merciful and righteous, then we may legitimately be called upon to make good our assumption, which will be no light task. But we want to know whether God is in His own nature merciful and righteous, and whether He *prefers* mercy and righteousness in men and wishes men to be merciful and righteous. Now I maintain that we cannot *know* this unless He tells us so. We may surmise it, we may determine it upon mature consideration as upon the whole most probable, but we cannot *know* it unless He reveals it to us in such a way as that *after* the revelation doubt becomes impossible. Now if He speaks to us to that effect then we do so *know* it. Only it has to be observed that He cannot so speak within the limits of the natural. He must draw aside the curtain of nature and show us that which nature cannot show us: He must *reveal* to us His truth. If His personal will moves in the direction of preference for mercy and righteousness and we are to *know* that it does, then He must tell us so, and He must tell us so in such a way as that the memorial of it may become authoritative. We cannot expect that we are to be the persons whom He is thus to tell, but we have a right to expect, seeing the obvious necessity for this knowledge, that He will give it to some persons with whom it may abide so that the record of it may be authoritative. Now the theory of Divine revelation implies that this has been the case. It is clear that the obvious necessity or desirableness of this knowledge is no evidence that it has been imparted, but if it had been imparted then the need would have been anticipated and the desire granted. And Divine revelation comes to us with this claim that it has considered our obvious need and met our wishes by anticipation. What then is the evidence that this has been so ?

In the first place we have the *bonâ-fide* statement that the desired revelation has been given, and secondly we have the revelation itself in substance in the record of it. God has declared Himself a merciful and righteous God. Is this a statement that is credible in itself ? Certainly those who would say that the unaided religious instincts of man could and would infallibly have attained unto it have no right to say that it is otherwise, seeing that they would probably assent to it. But at all events there is that in our own inmost nature that seems to acknowledge its truth. We have no temptation, therefore, it may be presumed, to reject the revelation on its own merits. It is consonant with that which antecedently we might have expected the revelation would have been, whether or not we ourselves could independently have arrived at it. The only question, therefore, that we need consider is the statement that it was revealed.

But then we have before seen that whenever an abstract truth like this, which the mind at once recognises as a truth, is apprehended for the first time, it has all the characteristics of a revelation, and may be more properly regarded as a revelation than as a discovery, even though it be made within the limits of the natural. If, however, it be made beyond those limits, it is hardly likely that it can be otherwise regarded.

We seem to have got, therefore, in the knowledge of this truth, supposing it to be a truth, to all intents and purposes an intrinsic revelation. What then about the way in which it was communicated ? This is a matter of historic evidence, and to be so treated. What then are the facts ? The possession of this knowledge at a very early period of the world's history—at a time when mankind generally had no perception of any truth of the kind.

There is evidence reaching back, on the very lowest computation, to a thousand years before Christ—for example, in the Psalms of David—of the knowledge of this truth, at a time when Greek literature was as yet unborn, and centuries had to elapse before the foundations of Rome were laid.   And even if it be alleged that some passages in the Veda seem to show that the ancient inhabitants of India were not altogether strangers to such thoughts, yet surely no one but an enthusiast or a specialist would for a moment place the revelation of the Vaidik hymns on a level with the revelation of the Psalmists of Israel.   To do so would be to manifest a singular want of aptitude for the comparison which has thus to be made.   One is like the action of a man groping timidly in the dark, the other like that of one in the confidence and security of noontide light.   We gladly hail the efforts of the Hindoo bard in his search after truth ; but we are constrained to admit, in spite of ourselves, that the Hebrew Psalmist has found it.   *And now, Lord, what is my hope? truly my hope is even in Thee.**   *In God is my salvation and my glory; the rock of my strength and my refuge is in God.   Trust in Him at all times, ye people; pour out your heart before Him; God is a refuge for us."†*

Now this difference is a difference of fact, and not simply a matter of opinion.   How then is it to be accounted for ?   The Hebrew poet or prophet believed that God Himself had awakened this sense of truth in him, had created and sent forth the light that shone in his heart.   The Hindoo poet had no thought of the kind.   Was the Hebrew Psalmist right or wrong ?   As there is and can be no question about the comparative value of his light, was it light from the fountain of Light, or was it self-created ?   Was he wrong when he said, *With Thee is the well of life, and in Thy light shall we see light ?‡*   Surely, if at a thousand years before Christ so insignificant a person as a Hebrew shepherd rejoiced in this light alone among the inhabitants of the earth, is not the very fact of his possession of the light an indication that he was not wrong as to the source from which it was derived, since, as we have seen, a truth of this kind, when borne in upon the mind, is more justly to be regarded as a revelation than as a discovery ?   There is everything in the historic circumstances of David, and his position in the world and the world's history, to confirm the supposition that in his case it was a true revelation.

We arrive, then, at an axiom before enunciated, that the thing revealed is itself the ultimate proof of revelation.   If that proof is rejected, no other will suffice to convince.   But there arises the further question, Supposing it in the abstract possible to confirm the reality of such a revelation as indeed coming from God, how is this to be done ?   It does not seem to be in any way conceivable except

* Ps. xxxix. 7.   † Ps. lxii. 7, 8.   ‡ Ps. xxxvi. 9.

the living God were to give some evidence of His life and personal interest in the truth revealed, and were to speak in such a way as to make it no longer possible for those to whom He spoke to doubt that He had spoken. According to our records this is exactly what He did.

But then it must never be forgotten that, supposing this to have been actually done, the area within which the revelation so given would be conclusive and indubitable would be necessarily limited to those to whom it was vouchsafed, and *to all others only who were willing to accept their testimony.* Revelation, therefore, at second hand is from the very nature of the case dependent upon faith. Even supposing the testimony never so valid and trustworthy, it could only be conclusive where it was believed.

It is absolutely certain, therefore, that revelation in the abstract must be dependent, at all events at second hand, upon faith, and that the faith of testimony. If *A* has a revelation, unless *B* believes *A* it will not be a revelation to him. But is it not also certain that, supposing a revelation given, it must also at first hand be dependent upon faith? Unless *A* believes he has a revelation, he does not receive one, even though a true revelation should be granted. Revelation, therefore, even in the very first instance, presupposes faith in the recipient. The point, therefore, that we have most jealously to guard is this,—that the revelation creates and calls forth the faith, and that the faith does not create, invent, imagine or exaggerate the revelation. It is impossible to overestimate the importance of the latter precaution, just as it is impossible to over-look the necessity of the former provision and the truth that it enunciates. The position of the anti-supernaturalists is that it is subjective faith alone that gives birth to supposed revelation—that the idea of supernatural divine revelation is nothing more than fancy-bred.

This, however, is a position that is essentially more fatal to faith than it is subversive of revelation; for it is evident from what has been said that the very idea of revelation, supposing it conceivable, implies the existence of faith: the absence of faith would frustrate a revelation even if given, would render it nugatory and impotent. To say, therefore, that there can be no revelation deprives faith of any object on which to rest, and *baulks* it. This, however, is something very different from proving the non-existence of revelation, which is con-ceivable as a fact independently of our proofs and disproofs, and which as a fact would be unaffected by them except as regards its effect upon ourselves. From the very nature of the case, revelation can reach only those who *believe*. To represent revelation, therefore, as the product or effect of faith is an inversion of the process, just as if we were to say that light is a creation of the eye that receives it. The eye, it is true, may become disordered and see distortedly; but that is no reason why we should discredit or distrust the function of sight generally. *If thine eye is single thy whole body is full of light; if thine eye is evil thy whole body is full of darkness. Take heed that the light that is in thee be not darkness.**

As, therefore, revelation is conceivable as a fact without our recognition of it; as also it can only be received where there is faith to receive it; as moreover it quickens and elicits faith, but is not created by it, what are the credentials which mark it when given? There can be but two : the substantive nature of the revelation itself, the appreciation of which must necessarily vary as the receptive power of the recipient varies; and confirming signs within or without the sphere of natural law, which tend to bear witness to the living operation of a living God, who takes interest in the progress and success of His word, which He has declared shall not return unto Him void. These signs, of whatever kind they are, must be dependent upon sensible experience in the first case, and upon accurate testimony in the second. Those who tasted the water that was made wine at Cana of Galilee, or who witnessed the feeding of many thousands with a few loaves and fishes, had sensible experience of the power of the Presence that was with them; and if these acts were really done, there could be no difference of opinion as to their meaning. Being once done, moreover, they were done for ever; nor would their effect, which depended solely upon their being *facts*, ever pass away through lapse of time. They had no need to be repeated, were that possible, for this obvious reason.

But then the question of their being facts must depend, secondly, upon the accuracy and trustworthiness of the testimony by which they were recorded. Here, again, it is conceivable that the testimony might be in its character unimpeachable, and yet it is clear that that testimony would be dependent for its effect upon the *faith* of the person receiving it. We may reject that testimony, and it will cease to influence us, and yet all the time the testimony may be valid, and that which it records a fact. Here then, again, the connection between revelation and faith is at once apparent. The revelation, *if*

* Luke xi. 34, 35.

made, elicits faith and acts accordingly, or it fails to do so ; but the faith in no sense creates the revelation. And in this particular case it could not do so without impeaching the testimony of alleged eye-witnesses and the sensible experience of vast multitudes of men who could not possibly be deceived.

These instances are drawn from the New Testament, but the remarks apply equally to the Old. The multitudes who saw the waters of the Red Sea divide as they came forth out of Egypt could have no doubt of the mission of their leader or of the power of Him in whose name he led them ; and the memory of this stupendous event was stamped upon the whole of the nation's subsequent literature and history, while the perpetual memorial of the Passover was the standing witness to the event recorded. No historic incident is better authenticated ; but the revelation with which it was fraught was only for those who witnessed it in the first place, and afterwards for those only who accepted the record of their experience. But this acceptance is impossible without *faith*. The history may be never so certain, the revelation implied in it never so clear, but both will be ineffectual where there is not faith. The revelation may fail to elicit faith, but most assuredly the faith will not create the revelation ; and that it did not do so in the first instance is, as far as we can tell, a matter of simple fact, dependent on the ordinary laws of human evidence, which are unquestionably satisfied here.

It may be said, however, that the Exodus is a far-off event, the date even of which is not certain, and that we have no more to do with this event than we have with the battle of Marathon. But let us pause awhile. The proof of the battle of Marathon is in the check that it gave to the tide of Persian conquest, and the effects of that check which yet remain. We are perhaps not wholly independent of or unin-fluenced by even these. But what is the net result of the Exodus which survives also to the present day ? It is simply this : *I am the Lord thy God, which brought thee out of the land of Egypt.* That which records the fact vouches also for the statement ; the two are inseparably bound up together : shall we say that they stand or fall together ? The fact is declared to have been wrought in attestation of the truth. The fact was intended as the revelation of a person who claimed to have wrought the fact. It is possible that those who were witnesses to the fact were impervious to the revelation. *They could not enter in because of unbelief.* Certainly in this case faith did not create the revelation ; but certainly also, now as then, the revelation cannot be independent of our faith.   Nor is it likely that we shall in any true sense receive the revelation and yet withhold our faith from the fact with which it is associated.   Indeed, the very words, *I am the Lord thy God*, as the personal statement of a very sublime truth, involve the operation of the supernatural no less than the facts of the Exodus itself; for they involve a recognition of the momentous fact that God has spoken, and therefore has revealed Himself.

But what are the credentials of this revelation?   Are they not the Exodus itself, and a long series of marvellous providences and interpositions in behalf of a selected people?   Are they not a unique literature among the monuments of human genius?   Are they not the mission and *name* of Jesus Christ Himself, and the history of the Christian Church from the day of Pentecost until now?   But are these credentials independent of our faith in any single instance?   Or can we receive the truth—*I am the Lord thy God*—without receiving them?   Or, on the other hand, is it even apparently probable that our faith, or the faith of others, has invented these credentials, or created the revelation that they attest?   It is no more probable that our faith has done this, than it is that when we open our hearts to the revelation—*I am the Lord thy God*—our faith creates the God who is so revealed, or creates the revelation by which He so reveals Himself.   But as we cannot have even this inward and personal revelation without the operation of the supernatural within the limits of nature, so neither can we have the original and historic revelation which it but repeats without the operation of the supernatural in history, beyond the limits of nature, in the inscrutable voice with which God first spoke, and in the great historic events with which he confirmed the words spoken, and established the revelation of Himself.

What has been said applies of course equally to that subject which we have been more especially considering—namely, prophecy.   The question of questions for us to determine in this matter is, Did the faith of the prophets create the revelation which they heralded, or was there a real and veritable revelation of the Divine will, which their faith indeed enabled them to receive, but which it did not create?   Upon the answer which we give to this question it will depend whether or not they were self-deceived, the victims and self-deluded dupes of their own " moral earnestness."   They spoke, forsooth, in the name of God, but God did not speak by them; they came as the messengers of God, but it was not God who sent them with any message.   This is verily a most tremendous issue, and it is one which we must decide ; the age demands it of us ; the thought and condition of our time imperatively urge it upon us. According to modern teachers,* that in the prophets which is self-evidently true is a word of God to us. But what is there beyond the field of mathematical science that is thus self-evidently or demonstrably true ? What is there in morals that is self-evidently true ? Is the law of property self-evidently true ? Are not the ancient landmarks even here being visibly threatened now ? Is the law that respects human life self-evidently true ? Who is to determine upon what conditions it may be set aside ? Is the iniquity or the justice of certain recent wars self-evidently clear ? Is it impossible, as a matter of fact, for two opinions to be held about them ? Is the law involved in the seventh commandment self-evidently true ? This is a question which those who reject Christianity will find it very hard to answer. If, therefore, only that in prophecy which finds an echo in our own heart is a word of God, there may be very little, or there may be nothing, that will stand the test. But if the mission of the prophets was the actual result of a valid commission, then is it one which, as it could not have been discharged without faith, so is it one which we also cannot appreciate or rightly gauge without corresponding faith. But God leaves Himself not without witness. He spoke by the prophets, and the witness He gave of Himself by them was sufficient for their own day. And ages afterwards, when the echo of their words had long died away, He revived His witness of Himself by the marvellous application of which their words were found to be capable, and by the confirmation with which they were established in the life and death and resurrection of His Son. And now to us, if our hearts are opened by Him to receive their words, He will again renew His witness of Himself by working in them the conviction that the scriptures of the prophets are an abiding record of the Divine foreknowledge.

* " Each of their words that finds an echo in your heart and your conscience —and their number is great—is to you a word of God."—Kuenen, p. 593.

9 783337 221881